The Finest Blend

Issues in Distance Education
Series editor: George Veletsianos

Selected Titles in the Series

The Theory and Practice of Online Learning, Second Edition
Edited by Terry Anderson

Emerging Technologies in Distance Education
Edited by George Veletsianos

Flexible Pedagogy, Flexible Practice: Notes from the Trenches of Distance
Education
Edited by Elizabeth Burge, Chère Campbell Gibson, and Terry Gibson

Teaching in Blended Learning Environments: Creating and Sustaining
Communities of Inquiry
Norman D. Vaughan, Martha Cleveland-Innes, and D. Randy Garrison

Online Distance Education: Towards a Research Agenda
Edited by Olaf Zawacki-Richter and Terry Anderson

Teaching Crowds: Learning and Social Media
Jon Dron and Terry Anderson

Learning in Virtual Worlds: Research and Applications
Edited by Sue Gregory, Mark J. W. Lee, Barney Dalgarno, and Belinda Tynan

Emergence and Innovation in Digital Learning: Foundations and Applications
Edited by George Veletsianos

An Online Doctorate for Researching Professionals
Swapna Kumar and Kara Dawson

Assessment Strategies for Online Learning: Engagement and Authenticity
Dianne Conrad and Jason Openo

25 Years of Ed Tech
Martin Weller

The Finest Blend: Graduate Education in Canada
Edited by Gale Parchoma, Michael Power, and Jennifer Lock

The
Finest
Blend

Graduate Education
in Canada

Edited by Gale Parchoma, Michael Power,
and Jennifer Lock

AU PRESS

Copyright © 2020 Gale Parchoma, Michael Power, and Jennifer Lock
Published by AU Press, Athabasca University
1200, 10011 – 109 Street, Edmonton, AB T5J 3S8

Cover and interior design by Sergiy Kozakov
Printed and bound in Canada

ISBN 978-1-77199-277-0 (pbk.)   ISBN 978-1-77199-278-7 (PDF)
ISBN 978-7-7199-279-4 (epub)   doi: 10.15215/aupress/9781771992770.01

Library and Archives Canada Cataloguing in Publication

The finest blend : graduate education in Canada / edited by Gale Parchoma,
    Michael Power, and Jennifer Lock.
Other titles: Finest blend (2020)
Parchoma, Gale, 1958- editor. | Power, Michael (Thomas Michael), 1953-
    editor. | Lock, Jennifer, 1962- editor.
Issues in distance education series.
Includes bibliographical references.
Canadiana (print) 20200300571 | Canadiana (ebook) 2020030058X |
    ISBN 9781771992770 (softcover) | ISBN 9781771992787 (PDF) |
    ISBN 9781771992800 (Kindle) | ISBN 9781771992794 (HTML)
LCSH: Universities and colleges—Canada—Graduate work. | LCSH: Blended
    learning—Canada. | LCSH: Educational technology—Canada.
LCC LB2371.6.C2 F56 2020 | DDC 378.1/550971—dc23

We acknowledge the financial support of the Government of Canada through
the Canada Book Fund (CBF) for our publishing activities and the assistance
provided by the Government of Alberta through the Alberta Media Fund.

Canadä   Alberta
                Government

To Gale Parchoma for her commitment and dedication to the advancement of online and blended learning in Canada. Thank you, Gale, for your leadership in the conceptualization and stewardship of the publication of this book.

Contents

Foreword

When Jennifer Lock and Michael Power asked me to write this foreword, the invitation gave me the opportunity to pause and reflect on my career in teaching and researching blended and online learning and how my own journey intersects with themes covered in *The Finest Blend*. It prompted me to examine the evolution of online and blended learning as reported by 22 researchers working in nine French- and English-language Canadian universities in the chapters of this book.

In 1996, I was assigned to teach a graduate course on digital technology for teachers. We were scheduled to meet Monday through Friday for two hours daily for the month of July. I proposed that, instead of meeting on Fridays, we could have online discussions during the week. I polled the class, and to my surprise all but two teachers had access to a computer and modem at home. The two teachers who did not have a modem said that they could make arrangements with friends to go online. So history was made. I began teaching York University's first partially online graduate course!

After having taught the course this way, what struck me was how successful this mode of teaching really was. I found that teachers were able to gain deeper insights into the topics that we were covering by having a chance to reflect on them and then discuss them with peers. What is more, this mode offered them a measure of flexibility in their personal schedules and made learning more convenient because they did not have to commute to campus on Fridays. Ever since that summer, with few exceptions,

I have been teaching the coursé every year in the mode that later became known as blended learning.

While teaching the course that summer, I witnessed the rapid development of the World Wide Web. My first experience with the web was viewing photos of the 1994 Winter Olympics in Lillehammer, Norway. Prior to that, I had been using email, telnet, gopher, and file transfer protocol (FTP) and had heard only a bit of talk about a new protocol called the World Wide Web. I thought that the web had the potential to revolutionize education by moving away from the strictures of linear text and toward the use of hypertext and graphics to make learning more compelling, while offering students more learning options through online courses. I wrote "The World Wide Web: A Technology to Enhance Teaching and Learning?" (Owston, 1997). This was the first publication in an American Educational Research Association journal that dealt with teaching and learning with the web. In the article, I posited three criteria that needed to be met in order to make the web a viable tool for teaching and learning: the web (1) had to facilitate improved learning, (2) make learning more accessible, and (3) reduce or at least contain the costs of courses.

In 1999, Stan Shapson, associate vice-president of strategic academic initiatives at York University, and I met at the University of Guelph with Virginia Gray, director of Guelph's Office of Open Learning, and Tom Carey, who directed Waterloo University's Learning and Teaching with Technology Centre. We discussed the idea of forming a consortium of pan-Canadian research-intensive universities to study online teaching and learning. We chose to name the consortium COHERE—Collaboration for Online Higher Education Research. For it to be truly pan-Canadian, we had to bring in other national partners. The University of Alberta, Simon Fraser University, the University of Saskatchewan, York University, and Dalhousie University joined, and COHERE was formed. Over the 20 years, the membership of COHERE has changed, but its mission of advancing blended and online teaching and learning in Canada has not. This book emerged as part of a collaboration among a number of Canadian scholars who presented at the COHERE 2015 and 2016 conferences examining voice and text in online graduate programs. This book is the latest example of how the organization has accomplished its mission, in this case by linking 22 researchers from across Canada to examine in depth issues related to blended and online teaching and learning.

What impresses me about this book is the wide range of research on blended and online learning occurring in Canadian higher education. The authors provide overviews of current priority areas in terms of support of technology-enabled learning within graduate university contexts. They share research and practice as they examine instructional design in course development processes, open educational resources, institutional and programmatic supports for learners and teachers, program evaluation, and engagement in the scholarship of teaching and learning. The methodologies shared in the book also vary greatly, including historical, ethnographical, auto-ethnographical, and survey research. It is evident from the chapters that we no longer need research to understand how blended and online learning compares to traditional face-to-face instruction, because blended learning has now become the "new normal" in higher education (Dziuban, Graham, Moskal, Norberg, & Socilia, 2018, p. 1). Our research now needs to examine how we can best use the affordances of technology-enabled learning.

In reading the chapters of this book, I believe that, together with the research of other leading Canadian scholars, a significant body of work on blended and online learning has now emerged in our country. I concur with Lock and Power in their conclusion to this book that blended and online technology has truly fostered a sense of *academic pan-Canadianism.*

Now that Canadian researchers have come together with the publication of this book, we must not lose the momentum. We know that technology is constantly evolving, and our research agendas must evolve as well. Three new areas likely to emerge in the next few years that will command our attention are open educational resources (OERs), learning analytics, and artificial intelligence (AI). The challenge is to continue expanding the research agendas in these new areas within the Canadian university context. I look forward to the time when Canadian researchers come together again to produce a similar volume addressing these new challenges.

Ron Owston, York University

References

Dziuban, C., Graham, C. R., Moskal, P. D., Norberg, A., & Sicilia, N. (2018). Blended learning: The new normal and emerging technologies. *International Journal of Educational Technology in Higher Education, 15*(1), 1–16.

Owston, R. D. (1997). The World Wide Web: A technology to enhance teaching and learning? *Educational Researcher, 26*(2), 27–33.

The
Finest
Blend

Introduction

A Pan-Canadian Perspective on Blended and Online Learning

Michael Power, Gale Parchoma, and
Jennifer Lock

Universities are unique as one of the few millennial institutions known to human societies. These institutions have grown from humble beginnings to encompass a worldwide system of knowledge building and knowledge sharing. Nowhere is this better exemplified than in the development and implementation of technology-enhanced learning, today a universal phenomenon. Key examples are online learning and blended learning, undisputedly major trends in virtually every university in Canada in 2020. *The Finest Blend* deals with research on blended and online learning across the country with contributions from 22 researchers from eight Canadian universities. Both French- and English-language institutions are represented.

The genesis of this edited volume was a series of panels initiated by eastern and western Canadian researchers who attended three national conferences over two years. All panel members were involved in research on various aspects of design, development, and implementation of educational technology at "dual mode" universities, those offering courses both on campus and online. An initial conversation arose in the preparation of separate but jointly planned eastern and western Canadian panel discussions on the roles of voice and text in online graduate programs for the Collaboration for Online Higher Education and Research (COHERE) 2015 conference. Several panel members, along with delegates with shared interests in the topic, worked to prepare a second joint eastern-western panel on voice and text in online graduate programs for the conference stream of the Canadian Society for the Study of Higher Education at Congress in May 2016 at the University of Calgary. There panel members and interested delegates discussed future directions for collaborative work and decided to prepare a proposal for a third panel at COHERE 2016. Additional requests for new contributors were distributed, and panel membership was again renewed. The result is a pan-Canadian collection of current perspectives on the roles of text and voice in theory, design, delivery, facilitation, administration, and evaluation of blended and online graduate education programs.

The opening chapter of this volume provides a critical overview of technology-enhanced strategies implemented by universities to increase access to their programs. Subsequent chapters examine varied conceptualizations of research-based practices in online and blended learning in Canadian graduate education. Across chapters, authors focus on the role of instructional design in course development processes, current issues associated with open educational resources, varied institutional and programmatic supports for learners, departmental supports for faculty development of blended approaches to teaching and learning for adults, program evaluation, and institutional supports for engagement in the scholarship of teaching and learning.

Where on-campus, graduate-level programs have a long history of privileging voice–as in the spoken word–in the learning process through a seminar approach to course design (Jaques, 2000), over the past three decades distance graduate programs have relied heavily on technologically mediated text-based discussions (Garrison, 2011; Moore & Kearsley, 2011). The contrasting foci on differing modes of communication have led to debates on the efficacies of voice and text in the process of supporting graduate students in the development of critical, reflective, and reflexive thinking capabilities (Bell, 2015; Garrison, Anderson & Archer, 2001; Rourke & Kanuka, 2007; Simmons, Parchoma, Jacobsen, Nelson, & Bhola, 2016). Although practical considerations, such as the evolution of the capacities of digital technologies to support inclusively and reliably text- and voice-based communications over time and across diverse contexts have played a central and necessary role in this debate, a lingering concern about the learner's experience has remained. Nearly two decades ago, Sgouropoulou, Koutoumanos, Goodyear, and Skordalakis (2000) argued that, when graduate learners are also practitioners developing research expertise to address practice-based problems, a reliance on text-based communications alone can be insufficient for both students and faculty-based teachers. Similarly, Strijbos, Martens, and Jochems (2004) posited that verbal interaction can be an important dimension of collaborative processes that lead to the attainment of shared learning goals.

The contributing authors in this volume revisit literature-based propositions and current practices in the ongoing debate on how to balance use of voice and text in various blends to support diverse graduate learners. The chapters contribute to contemporary understandings of blended and online learning through research-based analyses of current practices across Canadian dual-mode universities. Across the chapters, historical, socio-economic, cultural, and theoretical perspectives contribute to initiating an inclusive and critical discourse on current praxis in graduate programs in French- and English-language institutions.

In Chapter 1, Michael Power begins the conversation with a global historical overview of how voice and text have alternated and crisscrossed as the main means of communication in place-based, distance, online, and blended approaches to the media- and technologically assisted delivery of graduate programs. Traditional, campus-delivered, graduate-level education has a long history during which voice was prioritized as a medium of communication through the seminar method, whereas distance education, evolving through several generations, mainly targeted undergraduate studies and was largely text based. When online learning became viable in mainstream higher education in the mid-1990s, asynchronous, text-based communications remained the primary means of communication between learners and teachers. The primacy of text in online learning was a logical continuation of the distance education tradition as established by the open university movement. As Internet applications mature and broadband is fully extended across Canada, synchronous-based technologies are being implemented by mainstream universities as a compensatory mechanism for both a lack of instantaneous interaction and feedback among students and faculty members (prevalent in asynchronous, text-based, online learning) and a lack of institutional capacity to design and deliver quality, graduate-level, asynchronous-based courses (often called *online courses, e-learning*, or even *forum courses*). Responsive to students' needs, universities have made a variety of outreach attempts, over the past two decades, to find workable solutions that allow graduate students to enroll in online courses in order to develop high-end competencies. These attempts are portrayed metaphorically by Power as swings of a pendulum that is gradually defining best practices in graduate-level online and blended learning amid technological breakthroughs as well as shortfalls.

In Chapter 2, Jay Wilson discusses the outcomes of an auto-ethnographical study of department chair mentorship and evaluation practices for supporting faculty members who teach in an online graduate education program. In sharing and reflecting on his personal experience, Wilson identifies recommendations for mentoring faculty members. He argues that, rather than simply directing professors to put courses online or "use more technology," there needs to be a systematic means of supporting them in the process of course development. Furthermore, Wilson insists, it is not sufficient just to make the frameworks or taxonomies available; equally important, faculty members need to be shown how to apply them. Therefore, as a mentor, it is important to learn from deep reflection on design practice. There is an underlying appreciation that various strategies and approaches will be used in responding to the individual needs of faculty members.

In Chapter 3, Jennifer Lock and her collaborators report the results of an inquiry into an institutional orientation for new students on textual and audio practices in the online components of a blended graduate program. Students entering online higher education programs might not have the explicit technological knowledge and skills to be successful online learners. A short-term, online orientation program might help students to gain needed online learning skills. Using design-based research, these collaborators explored the instructional design of a new student online orientation and its impact on students' preparation for learning online. They share implications for practice and address micro-, meso-, and macro-levels of inquiry: they identify the importance of instructors' ability to incorporate differentiated instruction, the need for orientation programs to reflect the academic online environment, and administrative support for including online orientation programs for their new students.

Jane Costello and her collaborators provide, in Chapter 4, complementary institutional perspectives on the roles that instructional designers can play in supporting the teaching practices of faculty members in online and blended learning environments. In this self-study, four senior instructional designers share their experiences and reflections in terms of instructional design approaches and considerations for the integration of text, visuals, and audio in graduate online learning. This chapter highlights the critical role of instructional designers and their relationship with content authors who work together in designing rich learning environments that purposefully and effectively integrate media and technologies.

In Chapter 5, Wendy Kraglund-Gauthier reports on her participatory action research that involved instructional designers and faculty practice in support of pedagogical processes in the online environment. The study, conducted in a Faculty of Education, was designed to increase understanding of the changes in teaching practices and pedagogical thinking of faculty members as they transitioned from face-to-face classrooms to an online environment integrating synchronous and asynchronous communication tools. From this research, three institutional factors were identified in support of such a transition: the need for champions of online teaching and learning, changes in organizational culture, and an environment for a community of practice.

Sawsen Lakhal, in Chapter 6, reports on the outcomes of a scholarship of teaching inquiry into one university's blended synchronous design for learning across graduate programs in the Faculty of Education. Transferring from a face-to-face mode to a blended synchronous delivery mode (BSDM) presents universities with many advantages yet also serious challenges (Bower, Dalgarno, Kennedy, Lee, & Kenney, 2015; Lakhal, Bateman, & Bédard, 2017). BSDM has been used in their graduate programs since 2006 because of the particularities of the context in which face-to-face students mix with online students. The programs are designed for teachers currently deployed in anglophone community colleges in Québec. Students who live in the Montréal area are required to attend face-to-face classes, whereas students who live outside the Montréal region attend classes using a web conferencing app. This chapter reports on a scholarship of teaching inquiry into current practices using this mixed course delivery mode as well as the benefits and challenges experienced by faculty members and students while focusing on the use of video/voice and text.

In Chapter 7, Kathy Snow surveys socio-economic influences on incrementally including voice- and text-based open educational resources in the design and delivery of contemporary blended online graduate programs ahead of reporting the results of three case studies of one university's use of open learning resources. Snow argues that in public postsecondary institutions, where the rationale for "opening" focuses on an intent to increase access to education and still maintain quality learning resources and experiences, rather than focusing solely on increasing profitability, the funding model for "opening" can be daunting because associated costs can be prohibitive. These costs affect both faculty members and designers in that garnering institutional support for open access is especially challenging in a fiscal environment in which public funding for universities is decreasing and dependence on student tuition is increasing (OECD, 2012; Tilak, 2015). Snow examines the concept of "open" in the context of one eastern Canadian, publicly funded university's initiatives that situate learning as a social process and in the context of supporting the development of an ecology of learning that extends beyond the confines of time and space of traditional university instruction.

Maurice Taylor and his collaborators explore, in Chapter 8, the current practices of students and professors in one Faculty of Education graduate program that adopted blended learning. Using a qualitative case study research design and the constant comparative technique on three data sources, they identified several themes. Key practices for graduate students included acquiring critical thinking skills, establishing a community of practice, developing trust with colleagues, and realizing the challenges of blended learning. Key practices for professors included discerning factors to motivate change, observing the impacts of blended learning, understanding the meaning of a blended learning pedagogy, and developing a supportive faculty culture. In addition, these themes were analyzed for types and variations of voice and text used by the key informants. One of the main arguments highlighted in the discussion proposes a pair of self-evaluation tools for professors to use for quality improvement of blended learning course design.

In Chapter 9, Gale Parchoma and her collaborators report the results of a two-year virtual ethnographic inquiry into links among designed voice- and text-based tasks in an online graduate research course, traces of students' aspirations for embodiment, and evidence of engagement. The research team used van Manen's (1997) four-dimensional framework (corporeality, spatiality, temporality, and relationality) to examine evidence of aspirations for embodiment in an online learning context. Across these dimensions, student-participants reported desires to be perceived as competent members of a learning community. Stolz's (2015) tri-dimensional (cognitive, emotional, and practical) perspective on engagement informed the data analysis. The findings indicated that, where the course designers had intended purposes for sequenced cycles of formal asynchronous text-based interactions, learner-participants had varied levels of awareness of differences among those purposes. Individual preferences for and ways of engaging in communications via voice and/ or text strongly influenced when, where, and how learner-participants engaged in the course. Although awareness of how the course design was intended to support engagement varied, it did not appear to detract from student engagement.

Jennifer Lock and Michael Power's concluding chapter provides an overview of the major ideas, concerns, and issues arising from the previous chapters. Lock and Power highlight the implications for practice and set out pathways for future research.

This volume of perspectives on blended and online teaching and learning practices in both French- and English-language Canadian dual-mode universities provides openings for future national and international conversations, critiques, and collaborations among researchers, students, and administrators who will forge tomorrow's technology-enhanced learning environments.

References

Bell, A. (2015). *The place of "voice" in collaborative online learning: Postgraduate educator practitioners' experiences*. Unpublished manuscript, Lancaster University, Lancaster, UK.

Bower, M., Dalgarno, B., Kennedy, G. E., Lee, M. J., & Kenney, J. (2015). Design and implementation factors in blended synchronous learning environments: Outcomes from a cross-case analysis. *Computers & Education, 86*, 1–17.

Garrison, D. R. (2011). *E-learning in the 21st century: A framework for research and practice* (2nd ed.). New York, NY: Routledge.

Garrison, D. R., Anderson, T., & Archer, W. (2001). Critical thinking in a community of inquiry. *Internet in Higher Education, 2*(2), 1–24.

Jaques, D. (2000). *Learning in groups: A handbook for improving group learning*. London, UK: Kogan Page.

Lakhal, S., Bateman, D. & Bédard, J. (2017). Blended synchronous delivery modes in graduate programs. *Collected Essays on Learning and Teaching, 10* (2017), 47–60.

Moore, M. G., & Kearsley, G. (2011). *Distance education: A systems view of online learning* (3rd ed.). Belmont, CA: Wadsworth Publishing.

Organization for Economic Cooperation and Development (OECD). (2019). *Education at a glance*. Retrieved from https://www.oecd.org/education/education-at-a-glance/

Rourke, L., & Kanuka, H. (2007). Learning in communities of inquiry: A review of the literature. *International Journal of E-Learning & Distance Education, 23*(1), 19–48.

Sgouropoulou, C., Koutoumanos, A., Goodyear, P., & Skordalakis, E. (2000). Acquiring working knowledge through asynchronous multimedia conferencing. *Educational Technology & Society, 3*(3), 105–111.

Simmons, M., Parchoma, G., Jacobsen, M., Nelson, D., & Bhola, S. (2016). Designing for engagement in an online doctoral research methods course. In M. Takeuchi, A. P. Preciado Babb, & J. Lock (Eds.), IDEAS 2016: Designing for Innovation, Selected Proceedings: *Designing for Innovation* (pp. 81–91), Werklund School of Education, University of Calgary. http://dx.doi.org/10.11575/PRISM/5324

Stolz, S. A. (2015). Embodied learning. *Educational Philosophy and Theory, 47*(5), 474–487. https://doi.org/10.1080/00131857.2013.879694

Strijbos, J. W., Martens, R. L., & Jochems, W. M. G. (2004). Designing for interaction: Six steps to designing computer-supported group-based learning. *Computers & Education, 42*(4), 402–424. doi:10.1016/j.compedu.2003.10.004

Takeuchi, W.A., Babb, A.P Preciado, & Lock, J. (Eds.). (2016, May). IDEAS 2016: Designing for Innovation, Selected Proceedings. Calgary, Canada: Werklund School of Education, University of Calgary. http://dx.doi.org/10.11575/PRISM/5260

Tilak, J. B. G. (2015). Global trends in funding higher education. *International Higher Education, 42*. Retrieved from https://ejournals.bc.edu/ojs/index.php/ihe/article/view/7882/7033

van Manen, M. (1997). *Researching lived experience: Human science for an action sensitive pedagogy* (2nd ed.). London, ON: Althouse Press.

A Critique of Course-Delivery Strategies Implemented by Canadian Universities

Michael Power

Traditional campus-delivered graduate-level education has a long history during which voice was prioritized as a medium of communication through the seminar method (Jaques, 2000), whereas distance education, evolving through several generations, mainly targeted undergraduate studies and was largely text-based (Rowntree, 1994). As the 21st century advances, questions arise as to the role of text (e.g., asynchronous discussion forums) and voice (e.g., synchronous audio discussion) in graduate online learning (OL) and blended learning (BL): Are both text and voice necessary in OL/BL courses? How do faculty and students currently use both? How have Canadian universities been reaching out to off-campus graduate students, and what technologies have they been implementing in course delivery? These are just a few of the questions guiding the writing of this chapter. As Zawacki-Richter and Anderson (2014) state, there is a "strong imbalance" in the distance education and online learning literature: "The micro-perspective (teaching and learning in distance education) is highly over-represented," whereas "other important areas (e.g., costs and benefits, innovation and change management, or intercultural aspects of distance learning) are dreadfully neglected" (p. 5).

The goal of this chapter is thus to lift the veil on the mechanics of OL/BL specifically with regard to the complementary roles of text and voice as implemented by universities in graduate programs across Canada (Bates, 2016). This represents a major challenge, as data on such is often hidden within internal reports, white papers, and memos, even in online course guides designed by administrators and support staff for internal use, aimed at their faculty transitioning online. As a result, information is generally not widely available, especially to outsiders. Some learning management system sites also contain instructions and guidelines, but much remains unshared and thus unknown. Yet the stakes could not be higher as OL and BL are quickly becoming the main means of course delivery for university programs, especially those aimed at professional development. Indeed, according to Kelly (2019), "nearly nine in 10 faculty members (87 percent) at colleges and universities across the country [the United States] said they are using either fully online or a mix of online and face-to-face instruction in their courses" (para. 1). In Canada, the numbers are virtually the same according to Donovan, Seaman, and Bates (2019, p. 6): "85% of responding institutions offering at least some online learning for credit in 2016." Bad choices or those unenlightened by research can result in universities investing large amounts of funding in implementing an OL/BL strategy that does not leverage institutional strengths while ignoring weaknesses. A huge burden can be imposed on administrators and especially on faculty should an inappropriate strategy be implemented. For instance, courses designed to be front-end heavy may not be the best choice since they usually require institutions to incur high-level design, development, and delivery costs (Reiser & Dempsey, 2018). Such courses generally do not leverage existing institutional strengths, such as a great wealth of knowledge expertise among faculty, but rather require a cadre of design staff, which is a known institutional weakness in dual-mode universities (DMUs) (Power, 2008). In addition, given that, at the graduate level, *content volatility* in academic fields (i.e. content that is subject to sudden change, review, and/or revision) is quite high, institutions must think carefully before devoting resources in attempt to set the contents of these fields in stone (Dijkstra, 2000).

With regard to BL, requiring students to come on campus, even for part of their course, may not be a pedagogically valid and strategically viable choice (Boelens, De Wever, & Voet, 2017). Some questions that should be raised are as follows: To what extent does BL obviate the need and subsequent cost of OL? What is the impact of BL on access to higher education? Such considerations may be especially important for decision makers in higher education at a time when Canadian universities are struggling financially amid government cutbacks and claw backs (Usher, 2018). Therefore, it is no exaggeration to say that a lot is riding on how universities design, develop, and deliver OL/BL in general and, within the scope of this book, specifically with regard to graduate studies.

A Paucity of Research

I begin this discussion with a global overview of how universities have, over time, implemented courses and programs through the application of educational technology in order to increase access to their graduate programs while attempting to maintain quality and cost-effectiveness. This particular aspect of higher education is, sadly, sorely lacking in documented studies specifically on DMUs, yet this is not the case for distance education offered at single-mode universities (Daniel, Kanwar, & Uvalić-Trumbić, 2009; Rumble, 2014). Indeed, such initiatives at DMUs have often been the result of individual university administrations, acting singly rather than as a province-wide system, and often falling below the radar of scientific inquiry.

   I position this chapter at the nexus of two fields and two respective subfields of inquiry in higher education (HE). There are a large number and a variety of subfields of research in HE, and many of them overlap. In Figure 1.1, the identified subfields of inquiry *continuing education* (and related terms) and *educational technology* are seen as being independent yet overlapping and intersecting when it comes to *graduate studies* and *online learning*, which also overlap and intersect. It is the nexus of these subfields that is of particular interest and concern to me (e.g., research dealing with OL from an educational technology perspective and graduate studies from a continuing education perspective). I have yet to find one publication that deals squarely with this nexus of inquiry within the context of Canadian DMUs—that is, universities that deliver courses both on campus and online.

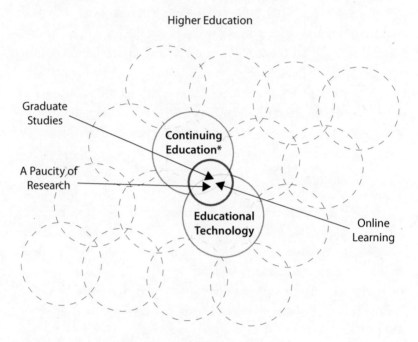

*Adult education, extension (services), lifelong learning

Figure 1.1 A paucity of research at the nexus of sub-fields in higher education.

Outreach

Universities offering traditional, on-campus HE have a long history of technologically enhanced, decentralization strategies—or *outreach strategies*, as I term them—especially at the undergraduate level, whereas graduate-level courses pose particular challenges, which I will explore later. In Figure 1.2, I present a view of the term *outreach* within the context of HE and its attendant pressures.

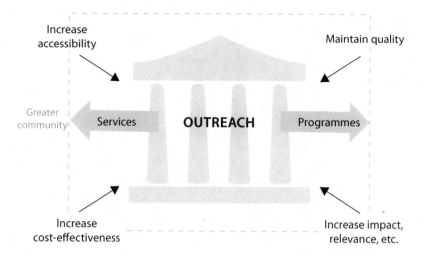

Figure 1.2 A definition of university outreach.

Outreach occurs in the form of programs and services offered by universities to their respective communities and, increasingly, to an international academic community via OL. Given projections for growth in HE worldwide (Sarrico, McQueen, & Samuelson, 2017), institutions are under pressure to not only increase access to their programs and services but also to maintain quality, improve cost-effectiveness, and even demonstrate impact and relevance. This, of course, places them in a bind, captives of the "iron triangle" (Daniel, Kanwar, & Uvalić-Trumbić, 2009).

Sir John Daniel has held many important positions in distance education, from vice-chancellor of the British Open University (BOU) to UNESCO's assistant director-general, and he has been a vocal proponent for lifelong learning by increasing access to HE worldwide, especially among underprivileged and underserved populations. Daniel et al. (2009) have very precisely analyzed the crisis of access that has befallen institutions of HE, especially in developed nations. In short, they focus on three variables that are in dynamic interplay: access, quality, and cost. To break out of what he termed an *iron triangle*, Daniel et al. (2009) state that they see no other way than for governments and national departments of HE to change profoundly the way institutions are currently functioning, from the ground up, ushering in reforms that would make distance education the *modus operandi* of all institutions (see Figure 1.3).

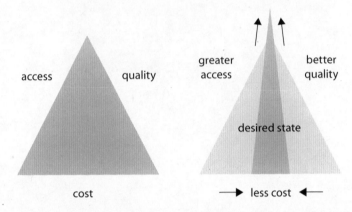

Figure 1.3 Daniel's *Iron Triangle*, demonstrating the current state of higher education and the desired state. Source: Power & Morven-Gould (2011).

In Daniel's analysis, attempts to break out of this iron triangle unavoidably result in one or more of the variables, all necessary, being reduced, diminished, neglected, or, in the case of cost, increased.

Guri-Rosenblit (2014) has characterized the current period as one that involves a large variety of OL providers all seeking "the golden triangle between wide access to higher education, high-quality learning, and economies of scale" (p. 123). In an earlier article (Power & Morven-Gould, 2011), my co-author and I proposed linking these variables to specific stakeholders and their priorities in an attempt to better understand this crisis and find an alternative solution to Daniel's dilemma. I will now examine how universities have attempted to break out of the iron triangle via various outreach strategies, some being more successful than others, yet all falling short of what is required to achieve a complete breakout, especially in terms of scale.

Breakout Attempts

Correspondence Courses (First-Generation DE)

The first alternative to campus-based teaching had rather humble beginnings at the University of London, starting in 1858. This first attempt was undergraduate correspondence education, a limited, text-based option for off-campus students who were usually enrolled in what has been termed *independent studies* (Scott, 1999). In the late 1800s, this form of outreach spread across the Atlantic to take root in the United States at universities such as the University of Chicago (Moore & Kearsley, 2011). However, actual enrolment numbers were low, and, as a result, few courses were ever offered, due in part to resistance from faculty and administration in mainstream universities. In short, the impact of correspondence courses on HE as a whole was fringe at best in terms of numbers, yet such courses can be seen as the seed that would, a century later, sprout and grow into the first open universities, but not before universities tried out other pioneering uses of mass media.

Distance Education via Educational Radio and Television (Second-Generation DE)

As these non-print mass medias first became available in the 1920s and 1930s, universities, namely in North America, tried adopting them for outreach purposes, squarely aimed at adult education (see Keast, 2005). A departure from correspondence courses, these courses brought voice back into the classroom—albeit one-way, not two-way, voice—first in the form of broadcasts and, decades later, in the form of recordings, leveraging a major faculty strength: oral exposition (Buck, 2006).

According to Rosenberg (2001), such unidirectional voice-based courses lacked a key ingredient, which has remained missing right up until computer-based training: interaction with and among students. Without it, courses operated more as vehicles of information than vessels of knowledge development. Moreover, because such initiatives were often seen by university administrators as peripheral to their core target population—and thus to their core activities—funding was always an issue.

As a result, these courses became associated with university extension services that worked—and, in many cases, still work—on a cost recovery basis. Similar to correspondence education, courses offered "over the air" remained few in number and immune from input by traditional academia (Keegan, 1996, 2008). Yet, once again, the lessons learned from such endeavours were not lost on the politicians behind the creation of the BOU.

It is important to mention the role of film and the film projector in training during this period; the prodigious inventor Thomas Edison was quoted as saying that "books will soon be obsolete in the schools. Scholars will soon be instructed through the eye. It is possible to teach every branch of human knowledge with the motion picture" (as cited in Saettler, 1990, p. 141). This, of course, has not happened. Moreover, I cannot include film among the main technologies used in HE; its use has been more prevalent in the military, government, and corporate America (see Williams, 1944). University outreach attempts, modest at best, were always made with the undergraduate student in mind. This is understandable as graduate education was still in its infancy (Jones, 2014) and generally restricted to society's elite, although the effects of Lyndon Johnson's "Great Society" would, in the 1960s, begin to reverberate across all of North America.

The British Open University (Third-Generation DE)

The BOU, opened in 1969, was, to put it frankly, a game changer, at least in the United Kingdom, where systemic barriers to HE were legendary. The BOU was, from its beginning, a political animal, what many saw as a made-to-measure, left-wing ideological dagger aimed at the heart of right-wing elitist HE (Anderson, 1995; Perry, 1976; see also Haines, 1998; The Open University, n.d.). As such, it aroused deep resentment, even ridicule, in more conservative circles. Yet it managed to survive—even prosper—on its own, despite severe and prolonged resistance from traditional academia (Perry, 1976). The BOU incarnated the application of industrial principles, such as the division and specialization of labour, to a yet-untried sector: the university system (Peters, 1967). An example of this is seen in its unique learner support system composed of tutors, initially in touch with learners over the phone, then at "study centers" and, more recently, via online communications (Sewart, 1995). The BOU, with its singular character, that of an upstart institution within a staid academic community, was a cheeky response to an iron-clad system, steeped in a tradition of social injustice, and its success was a testimony to the tenacity of its founders, the intelligence of its faculty, and the determination of its students. Technologically, the BOU combined all earlier forms of distance education—that is, text-heavy correspondence courses plus voice-based radio and television (Wrigley, 2017) —yet it innovated by introducing course packages including instructionally designed, conversational-style written materials. Teaming up with the BBC, its radio and television broadcasts became legendary, even cultural, icons. Later, audio and then videotape recordings were added to courses, although most of the material produced was, and remains, text-based.

A major impediment to adopting such an industrial-based system by mainstream universities was the considerable amount of front-end design—and hence front-end capital—required to produce market-ready courses; indeed, a rather extensive, specialized "course team" (a BOU innovation) was needed to do so—a capital investment well beyond the means of most universities. If one enquires into the instructional designer-to-professor ratio at any mainstream university, even nowadays, it will be found to be woefully far from the norm established by the open university system needed to allow course teams to design and develop quality online courses (Riter, 2016).

Initially dubbed *second-chance universities* by their critics, open universities nonetheless often performed—and continue to perform—on par with mainstream universities (Powell & Keen, 2006). This model of university was based on a truly foreign infrastructure in HE—that of an industrial production line—and the open university faculty workload is quite different from that of mainstream university faculty in that the DE teaching component is completely unbundled, separating course design from course delivery. To wit, as a rule, open university faculty never come in contact with students; their tutors do, despite some recent "blurring of boundaries" (Guri-Rosenblit, 2014, p. 114). In brief, mainstream universities were simply incapable of such dramatic change in a millennial milieu where tradition and collegial management was the norm. Therefore, despite Daniel et al.'s (2009) predictions, even exhortations, it can be stated unequivocally that, for numerous reasons, distance education never did go mainstream in HE (Moore & Kearlsey, 2011), and it likely never shall, per se.

Video Conferencing (Technology Enhanced Learning)

As open university–generated, text-dominated distance education was stymied by doubts about quality among faculty (Perry, 1976) and seen as prohibitively costly by administrators (Bates, 1995; Reiser, 2001), pressure nevertheless continued to mount for increased access to HE, and economic forces pushed universities to offer more accessible graduate programs. In the late 1970s and early 1980s, new initiatives implementing newly available ISDN (high capacity) telephone lines began to pop up throughout North America as many universities created satellite campuses.

Voice-based video conferencing (VC) technology extended the traditional classroom to these remote campuses, especially as the need for increased graduate education occurred, thereby offering students greater access to courses and programs. These initiatives attempted to leverage known faculty strengths such as oral exposition and direct interaction with students while avoiding costly design and development of upfront course materials. Despite promising beginnings, VC's high initial cost of purchase and ongoing costs were impediments to adoption. The nail in VC's coffin, for faculty on the ground—and instructional designers such as myself working in support of them—was the frequent technical glitches that made teaching (and supporting faculty) a more than usual harrowing experience (Berge & Muilenberg, 2001; Power, Dallaire, Dion, & Théberge, 1994). Ultimately, VC became quickly redundant, an ephemeral technology; once the Internet hit the mainstream in the mid-1990s, video conferencing became web conferencing.

Two other technologically enhanced instructional systems were implemented by universities to a limited degree during the 1980s as part of their outreach strategy and deserve a mention: computer-based training (CBT, sometimes known as computer-based instruction) and audiographics, sometimes called "audiographic teleconference" or even "telematics" at the time. (Since the 1980s, the term *telematics* [from the French *télématique*] has taken on a more encompassing meaning, going beyond its original meaning of transferring information through telecommunications.) There were two main differences between these technologies: the former was an offline technology, mainly implemented by business, and the was latter an online technology—though limited, a precursor to the web—more implemented by universities. CBT seemed to hold great promise: the floppy disks contained content, drills, and exercises; yet, in fact, they were often "deadly dull" (Rosenberg, 2001, p. 22).

Audiographics/telematics arrived just prior to the World Wide Web, especially represented by France's Minitel (Mailland & Driscoll, 2017); it combined audioconferencing and computer-sharing capabilities, ideal for DE. But, by the 1990s, the powerful web tsunami swept away everything before it, rendering the most advanced technologies of the day immediately obsolete and levelling the playing field, technologically speaking. The Web thus brings us to the next major outreach strategy: online learning.

Online Learning

Thus far, we have seen a clear oscillation between the dominance of text-based resources as opposed to that of voice-based interaction in outreach strategies adopted by universities; clearly both are needed, yet none of the above-mentioned strategies have allowed for an equal amount of either to distance learners. As depicted in Figure 1.4, in traditional, on-campus teaching, the general tendency was, and continues to be, largely and primarily voice-based instruction. First-generation DE is seen here as a swing of the HE pendulum completely to the other side, represented as a polarization from set-time and set-place instruction to anytime, anywhere instruction. Furthermore, I posit that second-generation DE is characterized by a swing back towards traditional instruction (TRAD), in that voice-based educational radio and television became the main means of course delivery. The advent of the open university, "industrial" tradition in 1969 (third-generation DE) brought about yet another swing of the pendulum, this time back towards the dominance of text as a medium of instruction; yet it was not exclusively so, in that, as mentioned above, second-generation DE technologies, newly invigorated with recording capacity, continued to figure prominently in open university course materials.

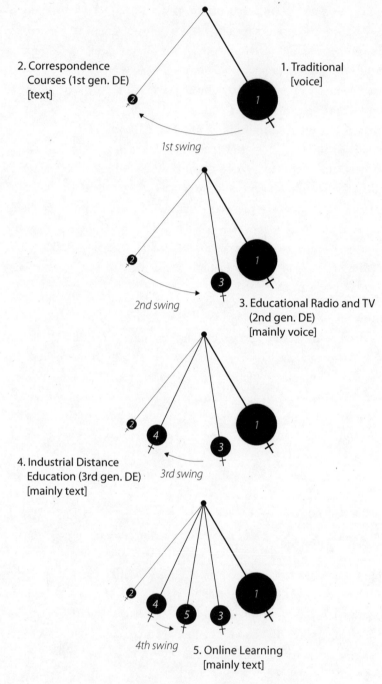

2. Correspondence
Courses (1st gen. DE)
[text]

1. Traditional
[voice]

1st swing

2nd swing

3. Educational Radio and TV
(2nd gen. DE)
[mainly voice]

4. Industrial Distance
Education (3rd gen. DE)
[mainly text]

3rd swing

4th swing

5. Online Learning
[mainly text]

Figure 1.4 An ongoing swing from voice to text and from text to voice.

OL (Figure 1.4) represents, in my view, a swing back towards TRAD, in that DMUs generally implement it in a way that reflects their existing cohort model, as opposed to the "open" (as in ongoing) enrolment policy implemented by open universities. As OL developed within DMU, it included, much like campus-based courses, group work and teamwork, as opposed to the usual individual-based instruction of the open university model. Hence, we can see an ongoing oscillation in course design and delivery strategies as universities search for the "right" outreach strategy. It should be noted that the introduction of OL mainly targets undergraduate education, because enrolment levels provide the budget for upfront course design and development, whereas lower graduate education enrolment numbers often prevent OL's adoption, unless upfront design and development are kept to a minimum.

It appears reasonable to say that OL once again brought text to the forefront at the expense of voice, a form of automation technology designed to replace human interaction. Viable in mainstream HE by the mid-1990s, OL was characterized by asynchronous, text-based communications, the primary means of communication between students and faculty, but more often between students and teaching assistants. On the one hand, HE outreach took a great leap forward when general access to the Internet allowed for large-scale OL deployment (Harasim, 1993), but, on the other hand, it can equally be advanced that it took a great leap backwards in terms of spontaneous and instantaneous interaction between regular faculty and students (Maerof, 2015).

In the case of OL, the primacy of text was a logical continuation of the distance education tradition, as established by the industrially organized open university movement (Keegan, 1996). As Harasim (2011) has stated, "Most commonly, the discourse is text-based and asynchronous" (p. 87). Indeed, it was undisputedly the best means for dispensing the greatest number of courses outside campus; yet it had its limits, namely, exceedingly high costs to achieve quality. In the same way that first-, second-, and even third-generation distance education students felt isolated and experienced various difficulties both socially and academically (Kember, 1995; Tinto, 1975), OL brought with it a new generation of learners experiencing far too high a level of isolation for it to succeed completely (Abrami

& Bures, 1996).[1] Described as a solitary path to learning, especially in light of Generation Y's need for peer contact (Price, 2009), OL was often seen as a cookie-cutter approach to course development (see Kelly, n.d.). As Anderson (2008) has stated in promoting a new, more interactive form of DE, "teachers are no longer confined to the construction of monolithic packages that are not easily modified in response to student need" (p. 296). Yet it is hard to get sound data on these movements, as research dealing with the use of technology in education has not always been completely objective. Indeed, Burge, Hara, and Kling (1999) stated that "most of the literature on CMC (computer-mediated communication) in higher education is 'cautious optimism to hyperbole'" (p. 16), as witnessed by the rise of the "digital learning evangelist" (Kim, 2018).

When you ask instructional designers why faculty become engaged in OL, you may receive a variety of answers (Potvin, Power, & Ronchi, 2014). On the one hand, maybe faculty are committed, philosophically, to extending access to HE and are thus "believers" in OL. On the other hand, they might simply be trying to find a way to escape the drudgery of the classroom by creating a mega-course, the responsibility for which can subsequently be delegated to teaching assistants and that requires but little supervision on his or her part (Power & Vaughan, 2010). The latter reason would naturally allow the faculty member to better pursue their research interests—a rather tempting scenario for most researchers. This is, of course, somewhat speculative on my part, as hard empirical data is difficult to come by, yet 30 years of observation into faculty practices in HE does fill one's mind with hypotheses.

Despite some early successes, institutions quickly realized that regular faculty were resistant to rapid online deployment (Shea, Pickett, & Li, 2005) and often had to have recourse to adjunct faculty in order to get courses online (Sammons, Ruth, & Poulin (2007). Indeed, many

1 Anderson and Garrison had a productive debate going in 2009–2010 about whether OL is a further generation of DE or a unique and distinct phenomenon (Anderson, 2009; Garrison, 2009). It would appear that the "jury is still out" on this, but I concur with Garrison in seeing it as having enough distinct characteristics to be regarded as a separate phenomenon rather than simply a new generation of DE.

faculty felt that OL was incompatible with their teaching styles and were often overwhelmed by student expectations of rapid feedback (Shea et al., 2005). Faculty expressed concerns that the quality of their didactic relationships was impaired by stand-alone, asynchronous (i.e., text) communications (McBrien & Jones, 2009). Moreover, OL, despite its increased flexibility as compared with campus-based courses, was also accompanied by a higher faculty workload, with much higher levels of labour-intensive written communications (Goldman, 2011).

In 1981, Fuller coined the term *knowledge doubling curve*, the idea being that knowledge has been doubling at an increasingly rapid pace (Fuller, 1981, p. 347)—some even say every 12 hours (Schilling, 2013). What this means for educators is that *content volatility* (a concept strangely absent from current academic inquiry into OL) will have a huge impact on which courses get developed for text-based online delivery and which will not. Indeed, *content stability* was once (when DE was the main alternative means of delivery in HE) considered by distance educators to be the ultimate litmus test of whether or not a course would, or could, be deemed a worthy object for course teams (Keegan, 1996). The greater the content stability in a course, the more likely it became a worthy object for DE development. Yet graduate education, as compared with undergraduate education, has, ipso facto, the more volatile of contents, being necessarily more state-of-the-art research informed than more stable undergraduate linked content is. As a result, I would argue that heavily text-based, time-consuming, front-end designed OL appears to not be a viable option for graduate-level online courses, despite the fact that many Canadian universities do design, develop, and deliver such.[2] To address this dilemma, in the early 2000s, universities began taking a step back from OL and experimenting with *blended learning* (BL), thus prompting yet another swing of the pendulum (Bonk & Graham, 2006; Garrison & Vaughan, 2008).

---

2 It should be noted that single-mode universities (such as Athabasca University and Université TÉLUQ) tend to offer asynchronous-based graduate programs, whereas DMUs (such as Memorial University and Université Laval) tend, increasingly, to offer graduate programs that blend synchronous and asynchronous delivery modes.

Before moving on to BL, I give a nod to massive open online courses (MOOCs), what I would term a "flash-in-the-pan" phenomenon, nonetheless notoriously affecting OL. When MOOCs hit mainstream academia in the early 2000s, they did so as a tsunami strikes a rocky shore: there were equal amounts of surprise, dismay, and disbelief, and many people naturally lost their footing. The techno-pedagogical community started asking, are these even "courses" (Zemsky, 2014)? Is a course simply an inventory of resources, such as texts, clips, slides, and so on? Does a course not entail some form of institutionally responsible learner support, beyond mere sporadic and ill-adapted peer-to-peer interaction?

Is a course a course when learner support is reduced to, at best, occasional tutorial support or, at worst, unfettered and unsupervised peer support, with peers usually emanating from all corners of the planet, being highly diversified in terms of background and knowledge? The literature has been replete with statistics on non-completion rates (Jordan, 2014), and MOOCs, in becoming a synonym for OL, did more to discredit OL in the few short years they dominated the headlines than a half century of critique levelled at the single-mode distance education universities. Their appearance has likely set OL back a decade in terms of acceptance and expansion, despite OL's limitations as identified above.

Blended Learning

As the limitations of text-dominant OL began to become apparent and its non-adoption by regular faculty a common stance (Chapman, 2011; Mitchell, Parlamis, & Claiborne, 2014; Wallace, 2007), *blended learning* (BL) entered the lexicon of theorists (Bonk & Graham, 2006; Garrison & Vaughan, 2008) and subsequently the arena of HE.

In Figure 1.5, BL is portrayed as a compromise strategy of sorts, a politically correct swing in the direction of regular faculty who remained adamantly pro-campus and a politically progressive nod in the direction of online innovators intent on changing the status quo through the introduction of disruptive technologies (Christensen, 1997)—hence something for everyone. It was, in my view, a swing back to voice dominance in course delivery.

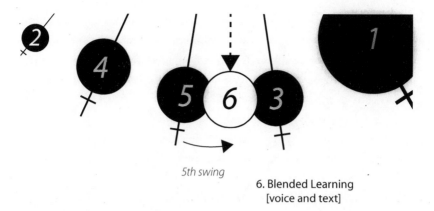

5th swing

6. Blended Learning
[voice and text]

Figure 1.5 A swing back towards a voice-dominant, campus-based delivery strategy.

In hindsight, the emergence of BL appears to be linked to two con-comitant movements, one the result of pushback from faculty with regard to OL, especially with regard to MOOCs. BL appeared in HE about the same time that MOOCs were gathering strength; these text-dominated "massive courses" were seen by many faculty as the ultimate "massi-fication" (see IGI Global, n.d.) of HE, the emergence of the universal mega-professor (Zemsky, 2014). What better to send chills up the spine of an academic (see Kolowich , 2013)? In this light, BL likely seemed more appealing to faculty as a more sustainable form of teaching. The other movement was a sudden realization among university administrators that BL could allow them to decongest their campuses (Owston, York, & Murtha, 2013). DMUs thus started envisaging a compromise between voice-dominant campus-based courses and text-dominant online courses, the result being, as seen in Figure 1.5, some form of BL (Taylor, Vaughan, Ghani, Atas, & Fairbrother, 2018).

The advantage of such an approach was purportedly that faculty could add a new dimension of flexibility to their teaching without taking on too much additional workload by implementing a limited form of OL (Gregory & Lodge, 2015). BL would also allow them to continue their usual practice of meeting students on campus, at least part of the time (Owston et al., 2013). Yet there was a caveat: Students not living close enough to a campus—actual distant learners—were simply left out of the equation, since at least some amount of on-campus seat time was required from them. In short, BL may have addressed the overly text-dominant approach characterized by OL, but it cancelled out previous advances made by DE through successive generations by requiring students to, once again, come to campus. A hundred and fifty years later, BL drew us back to the outreach drawing board.

Despite what I purport—that BL is incapable of meeting off-campus student needs because it reverts back to geographically based universities at a time when OL is making rapid inroads into academia—such is not always the case in the minds of administrators in major institutions. They have made, and continue to make, BL their university's distinguishing characteristic, the axis around which most future developments will take place (Porter, Graham, Spring, & Welch, 2014). Even within the Canadian OL research community, BL is far from being relegated to the ash heap of history, likely given the scale of its implementation. It has always appeared strange to me that researchers have not highlighted this major limitation of BL. Have institutions already invested too much in BL initiatives to allow researchers to freely make inquiries into the actual day-to-day workings of this strategy and its impact on distant learners? I am left with only questions and speculation.

Blended Online Learning Design

As the Internet matured and broadband increased, almost exponentially, making Canada one of the most connected countries in the world, new synchronous-based technologies were being implemented by DMUs (Bower, Dalgarno, Kennedy, Lee, & Kenney, 2015; Power, 2008). Once again, a voice-based attempt was made to increase outreach beyond what other course delivery strategies could offer. As a result, the pendulum swung once more (Figure 1.6) as a new emphasis on voice began to emerge in online courses in order to provide yet more options to administrators, faculty, and graduate students (Power & Vaughan, 2010). Since these new combinations of synchronous voice-based technologies and asynchronous text-based technologies represented a departure from text-only OL, as well as partly campus-based, partly online BL, a new term was required in the literature, one that would adequately describe a new form of online teaching and learning. In 2008, I proposed *blended online learning* (BOL) to describe this new delivery strategy (Power, 2008). It was new in that it was a combination of web-based, text-dominant OL and voice-dominant BL. On the one hand, BOL allows students to complete part of their work online, anytime, anywhere. On the other, it provides students with an opportunity to exchange with peers and faculty in real time. However, rather than on campus, these exchanges take place via synchronous virtual classroom technology.

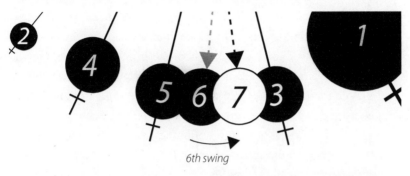

6th swing

7. Blended Online Learning Design
[voice and text]

Figure 1.6 A swing towards a new balance in voice and text in complete online course delivery.

In that 2008 article, entitled "The Emergence of Blended Online Learning," I describe the differences between DE, OL, BL, and BOL and argue in favour of the latter, specifically for graduate-level courses (Power, 2008). In "Head of Gold, Feet of Clay"(Power & Morven-Gould, 2011), my colleague and I argue that BOL offers a better balance between access, quality, and cost-effectiveness, also balancing faculty workload, student feedback expectations, and administrator limitations—something OL could not achieve. As opposed to BL, it was a complete 100% online solution. In hindsight, I now realize that, compared with the other course delivery strategies, BOL also created the best balance possible between text and voice with the least number of hindrances. Later publications saw this term evolve into *blended online learning design*, or BOLD (Morven-Gould & Power, 2015; Power & Morven-Gould, 2011; Power & St. Jacques, 2014; Power & Vaughan, 2010), as I began evolving towards a more constructivist learning design posture within the context of HE, as opposed to the more front-end posture of instructional design, which is more prevalent in the military and corporate sectors than in HE.

The asynchronous text-based component in BOLD is similar to, yet more limited than, a fully asynchronous online course. Thus, a BOLD course does not require substantial front-end design because it leverages existing faculty *resources*: a course syllabus, student activity planning, assigned readings, exams, and so on. As a result, the "asynchronous" part of a course is not stand-alone; it is one part of a given course, the synchronous component being just as important as the asynchronous. As for the synchronous voice-based component implemented via the virtual classroom, it leverages existing faculty skills, such as oral exposition, the Socratic method, group dynamics, and general interaction abilities learned from previous classroom management experience.

As graduate learners are often both practitioners and returning students, text-based communications alone are often insufficient in both scope and depth for satisfactory learner support (Rovai & Jordan, 2010). Moreover, as developments occur rapidly in the literature, faculty designing and delivering graduate courses simply do not have enough time to document everything in text form. Imagine having to transcribe everything that is said during a regular seminar! As a result, voice is an effective and complimentary tool to text (McBrien & Jones, 2009).

A BOLD course is characterized by a webinar design and delivery strategy emphasizing a balance between text and voice—that is, preparatory work in the form of text-based individual activities, followed by voice- and text-based interactive team assignments, which are subsequently followed up by real-time, voice-based exchanges in a virtual classroom space, focused on text-based course content (Power & St. Jacques, 2014). After 12 years of direct experience as a faculty member delivering BOLD courses, I have realized that, although scheduling real-time sessions can be challenging for a graduate-level student population (given that many are practising professionals), students do enrol in such courses, gladly. They say they are content with the newly found spatial freedom these courses allow (no longer having to come to campus as they would for BL-delivered courses) and quite willing to sacrifice temporal freedom in order to experience quality exchanges with peers and their professor and obtain instantaneous and spontaneous feedback (which is sorely lacking in OL). This has been my personal experience as well as the experience of numerous colleagues at my university who have adopted the BOLD strategy (Power & Lapointe, 2018). I have seen programs that were precariously close to being closed actually expand, their cohorts doubling within years. My colleagues and I have also heard what students tell us: BOLD-based courses are day, and asynchronous, text-based OL courses are night, so inhibiting is the degree of the latter's isolation in terms of learning quality. It should be noted that BOLD-delivered courses are optimally delivered by universities to students living within a common time zone (such as in the province of Québec) or one time zone away.

Conclusion

In this chapter, I have identified and candidly critiqued the various technologically enhanced outreach strategies implemented by universities over the past 150 years. This has been based on the existing literature as well as on my own professional teaching experience in HE, specifically in the field of educational technology and distance education/online learning. I have analyzed how each strategy prioritizes either voice or text, rarely both, and I have examined the strengths and weaknesses of each strategy, illustrating how the failures of one strategy have inexorably led to the emergence of another strategy, one deemed more satisfactory in meeting the needs not only of students but also of faculty and administrations. The last strategy I described, BOLD, should be seen as a strategy of compromise: In order to increase access, it implements complete online delivery, and in order to maintain quality, it leverages faculty's greatest strength, voice, in the same way voice has been leveraged in the campus-based classroom for a millennium.

After over 20 years of applying BOLD as an outreach strategy, I have realized that it is a workable solution for busy academics who are often torn between devoting time to improving the quality of their teaching and working on their research program. It has also proven to be a solution for distant learners who have been isolated by OL or excluded by

BL. Moreover, it solves the institutional problem raised by OL of funding costly front-end design by not requiring much more front-end design from faculty than they already provide in their on-campus courses. Given these advantages, and especially the avoidance of the disadvantages of the other outreach strategies, I would enjoin my fellow DE/OL/BL researchers to begin pilots in their institutions, applying BOLD at the graduate course level, in order to either further prove its relevance or disprove it, as per Zawacki-Richter and Anderson's (2014) exhortation for more research on meso-level management, organization, and technology issues.

References

Abrami, P. C., & Bures, E. M. (1996). Computer-supported collaborative learning and distance education. *American Journal of Distance Education, 10*(1), 37–42. https://doi.org/10.1080/08923649609526920

Anderson, R. D. (1995). *Universities and elites in Britain since 1800*. Cambridge, UK: Cambridge University Press.

Anderson, T. (Ed.). (2008). *The theory and practice of online learning* (2nd ed.). Athabasca, AB: Athabasca University Press. Retrieved from http://www. aupress.ca/books/120146/ebook/99Z_Anderson_2008-Theory_and_Practice_ of_Online_Learning.pdf

Anderson, T. (2009). A rose by any other name: Still distance education—A response to D.R. Garrison: Implications of online and blended learning for the conceptual development and practice of distance education. *International Journal of E-Learning & Distance Education 23* (3), 111–116. Retrieved from http://www.ijede.ca/index.php/jde/article/view/653/981

Bates, A. W. (1995). *Technology, open learning and distance education*. New York, NY: Routledge.

Bates, A. W. (2016). *Teaching in a digital age: Guidelines for designing teaching and learning*. Tony Bates Associates Ltd. Retrieved from https://opentextbc.ca/ teachinginadigitalage/

Berge, Z. L., & Muilenburg, L. Y. (2001). Obstacles faced at various stages of capability regarding distance education in institutions of higher learning. *Tech Trends, 46*(4), 40–45. https://doi.org/10.1007/BF02784824

Boelens, R., De Wever, B., & Voet, M. (2017). Four key challenges to the design of blended learning: A systematic literature review. *Educational Research Review, 22*, 1–18. https://doi.org/10.1016/j.edurev.2017.06.001

Bonk, C. J., & Graham, C. R. (Eds.). (2006). *Handbook of blended learning: Global perspectives, local designs*. San Francisco, CA: Pfeiffer Publishing.

Bower, M., Dalgarno, B., Kennedy, G. E., Lee, M. J. W., & Kenney, J. (2015). Design and implementation factors in blended synchronous learning environments: Outcomes from a cross-case analysis. *Computers & Education, 86*, 1–17. https://doi.org/10.1016/j.compedu.2015.03.006

Buck, G. H. (2006). The first wave: The beginnings of radio in Canadian distance education. *Journal of Distance Education/Revue de l'éducation à distance, 21*(1), 75–88. Retrieved from http://www.ijede.ca/index.php/jde/article/viewFile/67/48

Chapman, D. D. (2011). Contingent and tenured/tenure-track faculty: Motivations and incentives to teach distance education courses. *Online Journal of Distance Learning Administration, 14*(3), 1–11. Retrieved from https://www.westga.edu/~distance/ojdla/fall143/chapman143.html

Christensen, C. M. (1997). *The innovator's dilemma*. Boston, MA: Harvard Business School Press.

Dijkstra, S. (2000) Epistemology, psychology of learning and instructional design. In J. M. Spector & T. M. Anderson (Eds.), *Integrated and holistic perspectives on learning, instruction and technology* (pp. 212–232). Dordrecht, Netherlands: Springer. https://doi.org/10.1007/0-306-47584-7_12

Donovan, T., Seaman, J., & Bates, T. (2019). Tracking online and distance education in Canadian universities and colleges: 2018. Canadian National Survey of Online and Distance Education. Retrieved from https://onlinelearningsurveycanada.ca/publications-2018/

Dreyfus, H. (2001). *On the Internet: Thinking in action*. London, UK: Routledge.

Fuller, B. (1981). *Critical path*. New York, NY: St. Martin's Press.

Garrison, D. R. (2009). Implications of online and blended learning for the conceptual development and practice of distance education. *The Journal of Distance Education, 23*(2), 93–104. Retrieved from http://www.jofde.ca/index.php/jde/article/view/471/889

Garrison, D. R., & Vaughan, N. (2008). *Blended learning in higher education: Framework, principles, and guidelines*. San Francisco, CA: Jossey-Bass.

Goldman, Z. (2011). Balancing quality and workload in asynchronous online discussions: A win-win approach for students and instructors. *MERLOT Journal of Online Learning and Teaching, 7*(2), 313–323. Retrieved from http://jolt.merlot.org/vol7no2/goldman_0611.pdf

Gregory, M. S-J., & Lodge, J. M. (2015). Academic workload: The silent barrier to the implementation of technology-enhanced learning strategies in higher education. *Distance Education, 36*(2), 210–230. https://doi.org/10.1080/01587919.2015.1055056

Guri-Rosenblit, S. (2014). Distance education systems and institutions in the online era: An identity crisis. In O. Zawacki-Richter & T. Anderson (Eds.), *Online distance education: Towards a research agenda* (pp. 109–129). Athabasca, AB: Athabasca University Press. https://doi.org/10.15215/aupress/9781927356623.01

Haines, J. (1998, October 1). Open eye: How Harold's pet project became his monument. *The Independent.* Retrieved from https://www.independent.co.uk/news/education/education-news/open-eye-how-harolds-pet-project-became-his-monument-1175330.html

Hara, N., & Kling, R. (1999). Students' frustrations with a web-based distance education course. *First Monday, (4)*12. Retrieved from http://firstmonday.org/article/view/710/620

Harasim, L. (1993). *Global networks: Computers and communication.* Cambridge, MA: MIT Press.

Harasim, L. (2011). *Learning theory and online technologies.* New York, NY: Routledge.

IGI Global. (n.d.). What is massification. Retrieved from https://www.igi-global.com/dictionary/massification/17965

Jaques, D. (2000). *Learning in groups.* London, UK: Kogan Page.

Jones, G. A. (2014). An introduction to higher education in Canada. In K. M. Joshi & S. Paivandi (Eds.), *Higher education across nations* (Vol. 1, pp. 1–38). Delhi, India: B. R. Publishing.

Jordan, K. (2014). Initial trends in enrolment and completion of massive open online courses. *International Review of Research in Open and Distance Learning, (15)*1. https://doi.org/10.19173/irrodl.v15i1.1651

Keast, R. (2005). A brief history of educational broadcasting in Canada. *Canadian Communications Foundation.* Retrieved from http://www.broadcasting-history.ca/in-depth/brief-history-educational-broadcasting-canada

Keegan, D. (1996). *Foundations of distance education* (3rd ed.). London, UK: Routledge.

Keegan, D. (2008). A journey to legitimacy: The historical development of distance education through technology. *TechTrends, 52*, 45. https://doi.org/10.1007/s11528-008-0135-z

Kelly, R. (n.d.). *Online course design: 13 strategies for teaching in a web-based distance learning environment* (Special Report). Madison, WI: Magna Publications, Inc. Retrieved from https://teachingcommons.lakeheadu.ca/sites/default/files/inline-files/Online%20Course%20Design%2013%20Strategies%20for%20teaching%20in%20a%20Web-BAsed%20DLE_0.pdf

Kelly, R. (2019, January 16). Teaching with technology survey: Online, blended dominate today's learning environments. *Campus Technology.* Retrieved from https://campustechnology.com/articles/2019/01/16/survey-online-blended-dominate-todays-learning-environments.aspx

Kember, D. (1995). *Open learning courses for adults*. Englewood Cliffs, NJ: Educational Technology Publications.

Kim, J. (2018, April 23). Irrational optimism and the digital learning evangelist. *Inside Higher Education*. Retrieved from https://www.insidehighered.com/blogs/technology-and-learning/irrational-optimism-and-digital-learning-evangelist

Kolowich, S. (2013, May 2). Why professors at San Jose State won't use a Harvard professor's MOOC. *The Chronicle of Higher Education*. Retrieved from https://www.chronicle.com/article/Why-Professors-at-San-Jose/138941/

Maerof, G. I. (2015). *A classroom of one: How online learning is changing our schools and colleges*. New York, NY: St. Martin's Press.

Mailland, J., & Driscoll, K. (2017). *Minitel: Welcome to the Internet*. Cambridge, MA: The MIT Press.

McBrien, J. L., & Jones, P. (2009). Virtual spaces: Employing a synchronous online classroom to facilitate student engagement in online learning. *International Review of Research in Open and Distance Learning, (10)*3. https://doi.org/10.19173/irrodl.v10i3.605

Mitchell, L. D., Parlamis, J. D., & Claiborne, S. A. (2014). Overcoming faculty avoidance of online education: From resistance to support to active participation. *Journal of Management Education, 39*(3), 350–371. https://doi.org/10.1177/1052562914547964

Moore, M. G., & Kearsley, G. (2011). *Distance education: A systems view of online learning* (3rd ed.). Belmont, CA: Wadsworth Publishing.

Morven-Gould, A., & Power, M. (2015). Leaving the cocoon: University course design and delivery vis-a-vis competitive strategy. *On the Horizon, 23*(1), 58–68. https://doi.org/10.1108/OTH-10-2014-0034

Niemtus, Z. (2017, April 4). The automated university: Bots and drones amid the dreaming spires. *The Guardian*. Retrieved from https://www.theguardian.com/higher-education-network/2017/apr/04/the-automated-university-bots-and-drones-amid-the-dreaming-spires

The Open University. (n.d.). Strategies and policies. Retrieved from http://www.open.ac.uk/about/main/strategy-and-policies

Open University of Israel. (n.d.). University and publisher. Retrieved from https://www-e.openu.ac.il/geninfor/university-publisher.html

Owston, R., York, D., & Murtha, S. (2013). Student perceptions and achievement in a university blended learning strategic initiative. *The Internet and Higher Education, 18*, 38–46. https://doi.org/10.1016/j.iheduc.2012.12.003

Perry, W. (1976). *Open University: A personal account by the first vice-chancellor.* Milton Keynes, UK: The Open University Press.

Peters, O. (1967). Distance education and industrial production: A comparative interpretation in outline. In D. Sewart, D. Keegan, & B. Holmberg (Eds.), *Distance education: International perspectives* (pp. 68–94). London, UK: Croom Helm, 1983.

Porter, W. W., Graham, C. R., Spring, K. A., & Welch, K. R. (2014). Blended learning in higher education: Institutional adoption and implementation. *Computers & Education, 75,* 185–195. https://doi.org/10.1016/j. compedu.2014.02.011

Potvin, C., Power, M., & Ronchi, A. (2014). *Formation en ligne et conseillers et ingénieurs pédagogiques : 20 études de cas.* Québec: Presses de l'Université Laval. https://www.pulaval.com/produit/la-formation-en-ligne-et-les-conseillers-et-ingenieurs-pedagogiques-20-etudes-de-cas

Powell, R. J., & Keen, C. (2006). The axiomatic trap: Stultifying myths in distance education. *Higher Education, 52*(2), 283–301. https://doi.org/10.1007/s10734-004-4501-2

Power, M. (2008). The emergence of blended online learning. *Journal of Online Learning & Teaching, 4*(4). Retrieved from http://jolt.merlot.org/vol4no4/power_1208.htm

Power, M., Dallaire, S., Dionne, M., & Théberge, C. (1994). *L'encadrement des étudiantes et des étudiants en situation d'apprentissage à distance à l'Université du Québec à Rimouski.* Monographie no. 42. GREME conference, Zagreb.

Power, M., & Lapointe, C. (2018, May). Networking educational administrators through e-teaching. 11th International Conference on Networked Learning, Zagreb, Croatia. Retrieved from https://www.networkedlearningconference. org.uk/abstracts/power.html

Power, M., & Morven-Gould, A. (2011). Head of gold, feet of clay: The paradox of online learning. *International Review of Research in Open and Distance Learning, 12*(2), 19–39. https://doi.org/10.19173/irrodl.v12i2.916

Power, M., & St. Jacques, A. (2014). The graduate virtual classroom webinar: A collaborative and constructivist online teaching method. *MERLOT Journal of Online Learning and Teaching, 10*(4), 681–696. Retrieved from http://jolt. merlot.org/vol10no4/Power_1214.pdf

Power, M., & Vaughan, N. (2010). Redesigning online learning for international graduate seminar delivery. *Journal of Distance Education, 42*(2), 19–38. Retrieved from http://www.ijede.ca/index.php/jde/article/view/649/1103

Price, C. (2009). Why don't my students think I'm groovy? The new "R"s for engaging millennial learners. *The Teaching Professor, 23,* 1–6. Retrieved from http://hdl.handle.net/1951/62601

Reiser, R. A., & Dempsey, J. V. (2018). *Trends and issues in instructional design and technology* (4th ed.). Boston: Pearson.

Riter, P. (2016, June 7). The quest for great instructional designers. *Inside Higher Education*. Retrieved from https://www.insidehighered.com/advice/2016/06/07/troublesome-shortage-instructional-designers-essay

Rosenberg, M. (2001). *E-learning: Strategies for delivering knowledge in the digital age*. New York, NY: McGraw-Hill.

Rovai, A. P., & Jordon, H. M. (2010). Blended learning and sense of community: A comparative analysis with traditional and fully online graduate courses. *International Review of Research in Open and Distance Learning, 5*(2). https://doi.org/10.19173/irrodl.v5i2.192

Rowntree, D. (1994). *Preparing materials for open, distance and flexible learning*. London, UK: Kogan Page.

Rumble, G. (2014). The costs and economics of online distance education. In O. Zawacki-Richter & T. Anderson (Eds.), *Online distance education: Towards a research agenda* (pp. 197–216). Athabasca, AB: Athabasca University Press. https://doi.org/10.15215/aupress/9781927356623.01

Saettler, P. (1990). *The evolution of American educational technology*. Englewood, CO: Libraries Unlimited.

Sammons, S. R., Ruth, M., & Poulin, L. (2007). E-learning at a crossroads—What price quality? *EDUCAUSE Quarterly, 2*. Retrieved from https://educause.edu/ir/library/pdf/eqm0724.pdf

Sarrico, C., McQueen, A., & Samuelson, S. (Eds.). (2017). *State of higher education 2015–16*. OECD Higher Education Programme (IMHE). Paris, France: Organisation for Economic Co-operation and Development (OECD). Retrieved from https://www.oecd.org/edu/imhe/The%20State%20of%20Higher%20Education%202015-16.pdf

Schilling, D. R. (2013, April 19). Knowledge doubling every 12 months, soon to be every 12 hours. *Industry Tap*. Retrieved from http://www.industrytap.com/knowledge-doubling-every-12-months-soon-to-be-every-12-hours/3950

Scott, J. C. (1999). The Chautauqua movement: Revolution in popular higher education. *The Journal of Higher Education, 70*(4), 389–412. https://doi.org/10.1080/00221546.1999.11780769

Sewart, D. (1995). *One world, many voices: Quality in open and distance learning*. Milton Keynes, UK: International Council for Distance Education & The Open University.

Shea, P., Pickett, A., & Li, C. S. (2005). Increasing access to higher education: A study of the diffusion of online teaching among 913 college faculty. *International Review of Research in Open and Distance Learning, 6*(2). https://doi.org/10.19173/irrodl.v6i2.238

Taylor, M., Vaughan, N., Ghani, S. K., Atas, S., & Fairbrother, M. (2018). Looking back and looking forward: A glimpse of blended learning in higher education from 2007–2017. *International Journal of Adult Vocational Education and Technology, 9*(1), 1–14. https://doi.org/10.4018/IJAVET.2018010101

Tinto, V. (1975). Dropout from higher education: a theoretical synthesis of recent research. Review of Educational Research, 45(1), 89 – 125.

Usher, A. (2018). *The state of post-secondary education in Canada, 2018.* Toronto, ON: Higher Education Strategy Associates. Retrieved from http://higheredstrategy.com/wp-content/uploads/2018/08/HESA_SPEC_2018_final.pdf

Wallace, L. (2007). Online teaching and university policy: Investigating the disconnect. *International Journal of E-Learning & Distance Education, 22*(1), 87–100. Retrieved from http://www.ijede.ca/index.php/jde/article/view/58/494

Williams, D. R. (1944, November). The film behind the fight. Educational Leadership, 51–54. Retrieved from http://www.ascd.org/ASCD/pdf/journals/ed_lead/el_194411_williams.pdf

Wrigley, A. (2017). Higher education and public engagement: Open University and BBC drama co-productions on BBC2 in the 1970s. *Journal of British Cinema and Television, 14*(3), 377–393. https://doi.org/10.3366/jbctv.2017.0379

Zawacki-Richter, O., & Anderson, T. (2014). *Online distance education: Towards a research agenda.* Athabasca, AB: Athabasca University Press. https://doi.org/10.15215/aupress/9781927356623.01

Zemsky, R. (2014). With a MOOC here and a MOOC there, here a MOOC, there a MOOC, everywhere a MOOC. *The Journal of General Education, 63*(4), 237–243. https://doi.org/10.5325/jgeneeduc.63.4.0237

The Role of the Department Chair in Supporting Online Graduate Programs in Education
An Auto-Ethnographical Study of Mentorship and Evaluation

Jay Wilson

In this chapter, I examine my administrative experiences while working to support faculty members in their uses of a wide range of approaches and technologies in course design and development at the graduate level. The chapter is a response to the issues identified by Zawacki-Richter and Anderson (2014) for further research on blended and online learning and by Hicks (2014) in regard to the need for institutional support for instructor professional development in delivering on online learning. This chapter will be useful to administrators and faculty members alike as they attempt to understand online and technology-supported programming.

The department chair's role in supporting and evaluating the delivery of well-designed and effective online programs in graduate education is an under-researched area. I report the findings of an auto-ethnographical study (Ellis & Bochner, 2000) of my department chair experiences while supporting a range of early, mid-, and late-career professors' work in online learning course development and delivery. I critically examine opportunities and challenges that I encountered in using an academic

mentorship approach, which involves face-to-face contact with instructors, as recommended in the work of Savage, Karp, and Logue (2004),
in combination with Puentedura's (2006, 2011) substitution, augmentation, modification, and redefinition (SAMR) model, for supporting and
evaluating the application of technology in the design and delivery of
online programs in graduate education. Puentedura's model provides
an accessible (Roth, 2015), peer-reviewed (Romrell, Kidder, & Wood,
2014) structure for conversations about both successes and challenges.
Although I have found the SAMR model helpful in framing my approaches
to mentorship and evaluation, it has identified contextual gaps (Hamilton,
Rosenberg, & Akcaoglu, 2016). My analysis and application of the SAMR
model, within the context of my own leadership experiences, include
representative examples and conclude with recommendations.

The Changing Face of Mentorship

Understanding and unpacking the many roles of department chair often
come as on-the-job training. Guides such as the work of Tucker (1984) or
Gmelch and Miskin (1995) might serve as resources, but they do not tell
the whole story. Both resources are helpful starting points for those taking
on the role, but the information provided is general. Many undertake
the job of administration based on success that they might have had in
research or teaching but not necessarily in administration (Riley & Russell, 2013). The resources available often introduce concepts of creating
budgets, handling the assignment of duties, recruiting faculty members,
or dealing with conflict and management, but they do not specifically
address leadership or mentorship (Hargrove, 2014). An important con-
tributor to mentorship success is the creation of relationships based on
positive interactions. Supportive relationships are crucial in the development and growth of new faculty members (Horne, Du Plessis, & Nkomo,
2016), but how do these relationships occur, and can they be part of the
administrator's experience?

The notion of mentorship as the "passing on" of knowledge, experience,
and information from a senior individual to a junior member is present
in all disciplines in postsecondary education (Smith, 2015; Stubbs et al.,

2016; Tejonidhi, Uma, Swathi, Margaret, & Vinod, 2018). This process can cover a range of topics, and the manner in which it is presented can also vary. Not all sharing of information is done formally and is often anecdotal, within specific contexts that allow the information to be applied. Senior professors have knowledge and power, which in turn can make the mentorship process a difficult experience for new or adjunct professors. Junior faculty members might have fear or show deference that does not contribute positively to the mentorship process. In addition to this potential imbalance in power, Savage et al. (2004) identify a shift in mentorship with a loss of socialization contributing to an erosion of the mentorship process. Institutions such as faculty clubs, which played a significant role in the past, have either changed substantively or are disappearing. As a result of this loss of traditional social venues for mentorship, there has been a rise in distrust and disconnection. Many new negative conditions are therefore emerging for early career professors, including a sense of loneliness or isolation and a perceived lack of support.

Impacts on Course Design, Development, and Teaching

The department chair often receives no training or preparation in the field of course design, whether face-to-face or online. When a department chair lacks mentorship expertise, the level of guidance in course design and development, as well as the quality of online learning, is affected. The development of expertise is often left to professors who have been assigned online courses as a result of a departmental or university initiative. They put in play the systems that they have experienced or know but often do so without mentorship or direction. This lack of oversight can lead to a professor who founders or feels unsupported.

As online learning is viewed more and more as an option for postsecondary institutions to reach underserved students and to expand their academic footprints, more attention needs to be paid to it to ensure that it is conducted properly. Along with the increase in technology development comes a range of resources available to both developers and instructors of online courses. What appears to be missing is mentorship beyond simply directing someone to a resource. Much like the manner in which effective teaching and learning are based on actions such as observation, discussion, and knowledge exchange, online learning is more than digitizing and posting content. Rather than simply directing professors to put courses online, there needs to be a systematic means of supporting them in course development. Roth (2015) argued that, even though universities and institutions of higher education often talk about what they plan to do, effective integration is not truly taking place. He identified that a large range of technology integration schema exists, giving many options, but he notes that these options are not being utilized. There is a need not just to make the frameworks or taxonomies available but also to show professors how to apply them.

One such framework (Figure 2.1) that can serve as a guide is the SAMR model put forward by Puentedura (2011).

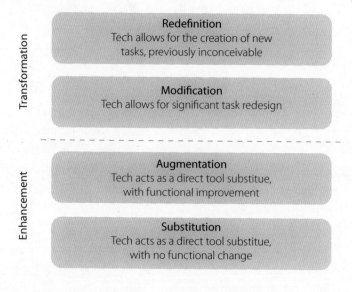

Figure 2.1 The SAMR model. Source: Puentedura, R.R. (2011).

The SAMR framework has been used primarily as a taxonomy for the integration of technology in teaching. The four stages (substitution, augmentation, modification, and redefinition) represent a continuum of integration to build toward a fully supported technology environment for instructors and students. Much like the application of Bloom's (1956) taxonomy, the initial steps are foundational and minimal. As individual professors progress through the four steps of SAMR, they increase the depths of learning opportunities and supports for students. SAMR is intended to ease instructors into their understandings of the change of methods for online learning.

For those new to the model, substitution is the level at which generally they start. Adding existing information to a learning management system (LMS) or meeting online instead of in a classroom might represent their entire concept of online learning. The next step up might be augmenting traditional face-to-face time with an online discussion area or online groups. Modification of assignments through digital options can be used to create content. Finally, facilitating time, place, path, and pace (Horn & Staker, 2015) to allow for a learning experience that truly would not have been possible without transferring the course to an online environment is viewed as redefinition. Together, these steps take anyone new to online learning into the process gradually, even over a long period of time.

Criticism levelled at SAMR might be valid for those looking to integrate technology and see it as a panacea (Hamilton et al., 2016). The linear nature, the lack of context, and the notion of "product over practice" (p. 434) might generate valid critiques, but using the SAMR model as a way of making sense of the shift to online learning is useful because at the heart of online learning is the move from one instructional approach to another. Rather than a process of prescribing the tools to be used, SAMR identifies how professors move their students into a deeper understanding of content. For certain types of content, a great depth of understanding is not necessary for a student to be successful in the online course. The opportunity to use SAMR to "navigate a complex landscape by seemingly simplifying a multifarious process" is helpful (Hamilton et al., 2016, p. 439).

I have found the SAMR model helpful in framing my approaches to mentorship and evaluation, but it has other applications. SAMR can be used to evaluate different areas of education. For example, Romrell et al. (2014) have used SAMR as a framework for evaluating mobile learning. This similar approach can be used to evaluate the transition from face-to-face learning to fully online supported learning. What they propose is done naturally in some situations, but truly to make a difference the modification and redefinition levels of SAMR should be reached.

Methodology

To share my experiences in mentoring and evaluating professors in online learning, I have chosen to use an auto-ethnographical approach. In this context, mentoring refers to my deliberate attempt to share my experiences to benefit those new to online instruction. Auto-ethnography is the method of sharing experience written from the perspective of the individual at the heart of the experience (Ellis, Adams, & Bochner, 2010). Often the subject is extremely personal, powerful, and guided by a significant incident or epiphany. Successful auto-ethnographic accounts rely on good writing and engaging the reader in the story. The purpose of auto-ethnography is to "inspire and create a connection" (Ellis & Bochner, 2000, p. 748). It is up to readers to make sense of what they are reading and to apply it in their current or future contexts.

To achieve educational success in the classroom, instructors must develop understandings of others' cultures. They need to make efforts to know their students. Sharing stories and listening to those of others provide much-needed insight. In addition to other key aspects of teaching, sharing personal experiences helps to support students to be successful in the classroom. The application of auto-ethnography helps to support the view that all stories contribute to increased understanding.

For the reader to understand my story fully, I need to deal with it in a somewhat systematic way, but rather than "search for facts what is presented is meaning based on an individual's experience" (Ellis & Bochner, 2000, p. 751). I present what I have experienced from a range of roles, contexts, and perspectives and how these experiences have shaped my approach to my role as department chair. I aim to examine critically the opportunities and challenges that I encountered in using an academic mentorship approach in combination with Puentedura's (2011) SAMR model for supporting and evaluating the design and delivery of online programs in graduate education.

After I present my experiences, I share the analysis of the work to tease out themes or recurring thoughts that might be useful. Similar to a grounded theory approach (Charmaz, 2014), my story is written and then analyzed for key outcomes. What occurs repeatedly or has prominence in my story has significance to me and hopefully will provide insight for others. Reading and reflecting on what I have done have comprised a large part of the process. Talking with others involved in my experience has helped me to draw out my actions and the impacts that I and others have recognized. All that I share leads back to the question "How does my work to mentor others contribute to the understanding of the department chair role?"

My Background

Unlike others, I took on the role of department chair with a vast range of practical experiences in course design (Schwier & Wilson, 2010; Wilson, 2013). I believe that these experiences have provided me with insights that help in mentoring and evaluating professors in their online teaching journeys. More than just "street cred," exposure to many non-traditional ways of delivering courses has allowed me to understand key roles such as student, designer, instructor, and administrator. Each opportunity has added to my understanding. Each failure or struggle has added to my learning. What follows is an overview of the work that has contributed to my understanding of the online course design process.

I have been involved with the design and development of innovative online instruction since the first day that I came to the University of Saskatchewan. Truly on my first day, May 1, 1995, I began work on a new televised course. It comprised four full-day telecasts to over 300 undergraduate teachers spread across the province. The design of the course included the use of voice interaction through existing telephone networks. From this initial experience, I was exposed to so many new ideas. I was not the instructor but part of a team of instructors, technicians, and designers. I was responsible for organizing large numbers of students, producing educational resources, creating message design, and providing student assistance. Not having much specialized training or guidance, we went with what we thought was good or what the students shared with us. I was able to see how addressing a range of learning styles was part of a successful learning experience. The synchronous and asynchronous nature of the experience showed me how both successes and failures could occur. This course was offered for four years, thus affording the chance to revise and reflect on it. We did not see what we were doing as course design, but in hindsight it was. I began to see that I was not only expected to bring my knowledge to the process but also given the opportunity to learn from it.

I next supported the offering of a blended interactive videoconference Master of Nursing program in which the instructor was at one location and a group of students was at another. The development team did not use the term "blended learning" at the time since the technology was so new. My job was to ensure that the technology was working to deliver the content and that the interactivity was facilitated. I learned how important it was to engage students in multiple locations and not to focus on the students who were the easiest to engage. This experience provided me with more insight into why we should break up content and have activities and student-led discussions instead of always relying on the instructor as the source of knowledge.

While supporting distance education, I began teaching undergraduate and graduate courses in a face-to-face environment. This was the first opportunity to develop my teaching style in a manner in which technology was not the mode of delivery. I was able to create a solid foundation as an instructor and to learn the basics without many of the variables that are parts of online environments. This experience helped me to develop my planning skills, prepare assessments and content, and give immediate feedback as part of a traditional classroom. This experience also permitted me to begin integrating technology slowly into my teaching. Using basic tools, I supported my students' learning within the safety of a face-to-face environment in case anything failed. Over time, I encountered new demographics and new opportunities to learn about learners. I began to experiment with blended courses using a range of videoconferencing tools. It was similar to working with the distance education students again but with a much more flexible system. This was an opportunity to fail and see once again how hard it is to play to two distinct audiences. The student feedback was clear and critical and represented the point where I decided on either face-to-face or online instruction but never a blend of the two.

My first graduate online teaching experiences were part of a program offered fully face-to-face for many years that morphed into an online program. The process involved slowly changing elements of a course or two at a time based on the needs of students. Each instructor had a course with which she or he was familiar and looked at ways to make the transition. We worked with one another to provide support, but there was no central or administrative direction, and each process was unique. The work was guided by principles of instructional design and teaching. We made many mistakes, and it became clear that, when a review of the program was required, a systematic look at what the individuals were doing was necessary. This review and a subsequent reapplication for program status allowed us to be more systematic and consistent in the redesign of the program. We looked for what had been successful and made it common among all of the courses. In the end, we had a battle-tested, coherent program.

Running parallel to my work designing courses was my experience as a distance education student. Enrolling in a doctoral program from Australia gave me the opportunity to see distance learning from a new perspective. This program used a basic text and voice model utilizing printed material, email, and audio teleconferencing. Communication with the instructor was primarily through email. There was no text-based discussion board, mailing list, or other means of interacting with other students in the program. There were semi-regular telephone calls, but the process was highly impersonal and did not promote engagement. This experience demonstrated to me how difficult it was to create quality technology-supported graduate programming. Poor program success rates reflected the inability of this approach to support graduate students who needed more than access to information. Only 2 of the 17 students who started the program in my cohort finished it at a distance. The experience was one of isolation and perseverance. I worked alone during my courses. There was little instructional connection until my dissertation work started, but even that was limited to email. The experience also showed me how the individual needs of students are not always considered in course design and delivery.

Throughout my time at the University of Saskatchewan, there has been a push to utilize innovative technology. I began my postsecondary career just as the Internet was becoming a ubiquitous way to support learning. My university was on board early with a learning management system, taking a chance as an early adopter, and as a result there was an opportunity to learn the basics before a wide range of online options became available. The first online courses used simple text-based forums or discussion boards to leverage skills that students already possessed. As each LMS iteration was released, a new tool or function was added. Although university support consisted of the provision of an LMS, users dealt with innovation that was evolving and sometimes not stable. We were moving from correspondence or distance education to online learning. Factors that we could not control began to materialize. Stop-gap measures such as copies of online materials had to be provided for students in areas with poor connectivity. Synchronous video was not an option initially, so telephones supplemented online discussion and electronic copies of readings. This experience showed me the dangers and rewards of taking chances in course design. If one was willing to put in the effort, then the return was positive but also came with the risk of pain.

On my campus are a number of excellent groups that have supported me over many years. I work with these groups regularly. I consult with them; they consult with me. I am often asked to pilot new software or options. As a result, I am on the bleeding edge and come face-to-face with issues that I might not have experience dealing with because they are in a context different from mine. This exposure gave me a chance to broaden my horizons and to see where I really stood on issues of course design and delivery. As an example, to look for ways to improve support campus wide, the distance education unit, in collaboration with the teaching and learning centre, wanted to create an online instructor's toolbox. They wanted to have material available and to curate what was already there. I thought that, if we truly were addressing the needs of instructors, then the material should be more interactive. My belief was based on what I was hearing from other administrative participants. They did not necessarily agree even though I was convinced that I was proposing a solution to an issue that they thought was relevant. The major sticking point was accountability. Who would respond? How would questions be answered? Was it okay to refer an instructor to another member of the team whose expertise was more suited to the requests being made? In the end, an excellent online resource was created to leverage the best materials available but without real-time instructor support. It was the best offering under the circumstances and gave me a chance to reflect on whether or not my ideas were appropriate.

My understanding of online learning has the benefit of many years of course design in a range of roles and situations. It is my hope that each time I have an experience I can bring it to my conversations with others and guide my own actions for the benefit of as many stakeholders as possible.

Becoming a Department Chair

When I became the chair of the Curriculum Studies department, I found myself wearing many hats, and along with this new role came many expectations. Early on in my appointment and even as I gained experience, I often found it challenging to manage the wide range of tasks encompassed by a department chair. It is a struggle to deal with all that is expected given little previous knowledge of a complex institution with detailed sets of procedures and processes. Expectations come from many sources. Deans and senior administrators expect you to represent institutional-level interests. Colleagues wish to maintain existing relationships or expand them based on your perceived new level of influence. Members of your department see you as an advocate for their personal program, research, and teaching needs. Along with these expectations, basic financial duties, personnel issues, significant numbers of meetings, collegial processes, and academic mentorship are all important aspects of the position. I have asked myself "What does someone like me entering the job really know?" I might have observed or participated on the periphery but never assumed direct responsibility for any of these tasks. I see myself as an instructor, researcher, and professor. I have to be organized to take on these roles, but my scope is narrow. I look after my personal piece of the university. Traditionally, for the most part, those who rely on me are undergraduate and graduate students. This is not to say that I took on the new role completely unsupported, and I have interacted with those who occupied the position before me.

When I started as chair of the department, attempts were made to transition me into the job, such as job shadowing, meeting with others across campus, or having informal coffee meetings. Limited professional development opportunities were provided to address the basics of leadership. Official university-sponsored department chair orientations took place. These initiatives are great for surface-level or immediate issues, but unfortunately for many department chairs their successors are often on leave or moving on to other administrative roles. A former department chair represents the most important source of insight and institutional knowledge about the role. Learning by doing has helped one's predecessor to gain understanding, and to have access to this understanding is deeply beneficial. I might be an anomaly based on my experience. I sheepishly share with others the supportive relationship that I have with the individual who held the position before me. There is secretarial and administrative support, and if one is lucky these individuals have been on the job for a while and know the important processes. They do not, however, have the same requirements or expectations as the incoming chair. They help the new chair do what needs to be done, providing of course that the new person knows what the heck that is.

On top of the many new administrative expectations, the individual is responsible for his or her own teaching and for that of everyone else in the department. The burden is potentially overwhelming. It can also be particularly tricky in a College of Education in which teaching has a high priority and profile. In my experience, some of the courses that I have been responsible for staffing are actually about effective course design. I try to find not only competent instructors but also those able to deliver effectively the subject where the actual instruction is the course itself. If this sounds confusing to you, it does to me as well. When we talk about "practising what we preach," there is no clearer example. Success or improvement in teaching is a significant aspect of a professor's career. I am now responsible for annual reviews, salary reviews, and tenure and promotion, and all of these processes are affected by success and growth in teaching.

Another task not likely to be on the radar for a new administrator is supporting course design. The new chair might have designed courses before, but there is a chance that her or his knowledge of the area is limited. The individual might or might not have extensive teaching experience or a background in online course design and delivery or familiarity with the many technological options available to instructors. Even though many tools, systems, and resources exist to help guide the process of course design and delivery, the experience will likely be foreign to most incoming department chairs. By extension, they might not know how to evaluate whether or not a particular professor is successful in delivering instruction at the graduate level or in other contexts. Tools can be used to evaluate instruction, but often they are unreliable or focused on aspects that do not give a clear picture of what is really happening. They act more like popularity contests and are not true indicators of instructional efficiency. Taking the results of these tools at face value can be dangerous in that poor approaches can be supported or go undetected.

Even if the new department chair is experienced in course design, there can be both advantages and disadvantages. I came to my new position with a wealth of knowledge and experience in course design in traditional face-to-face, technology-rich, and online contexts. When I reflect on my experience, I see examples of both. One advantage is that, by having made many mistakes, I am able to give honest and direct advice. "This is what didn't work for me, and this is how you might approach it to mitigate similar problems." My experience also helps me to ask the right questions so that I can more accurately evaluate an individual's performance.

Another positive that I find in any mentoring situation is that, when I share my experiences, including mistakes, the advice is more readily accepted. Through this engagement, a traditionally imbalanced relationship begins to level. It is less an administrator directing professors and more a collegial interaction. Through our dialogues, instructors realize that they are not alone or in a position unique to them. They can more fully appreciate that good and bad things will happen and that options exist to ensure that they will be fine in the end. This "transformation through dialogue" is a powerful part of the mentoring process. Once a process for sharing and learning is established, there is a great sense of relief in the instructor. I am also able to identify appropriate course designs based on content and similar audience. As schools of thought in course design come and go, and having been through a range of cycles, I bring a longitudinal perspective to my advice. There are also general characteristics of students in a program that I have noticed repeatedly, and it is beneficial to share them. When we meet, I am not telling the instructor what to do but giving him or her a peek at the next level. This process is much like working through the stages of the SAMR model. I see myself helping to sort through what instructors might have read in books and applying it to the student demographic particular to our program. Often, I have read the same literature, which helps me to navigate to the must-have advice or resource.

Possessing advanced knowledge can also have its disadvantages. I am often approached by others with questions for which I already know what works. I can see how mistakes are made because of a lack of consultation or understanding. It is important not to point out what is obvious to me with the aid of hindsight. Instead, a discussion needs to take place about the goals or intentions of the decisions that have been made. This process is easier when a trusting relationship exists and a "safe place" to unpack the experience is provided.

In most instances, I meet with instructors because they are not sure what to do. The range of experience in online learning is wide in any university, college, or department. Instructors who come to me are at different stages of growth in their academic careers and online learning experiences. Experienced designers and instructors might want to be in contact but do not require the investment and support that the inexperienced ones do. The experienced ones are generally more sophisticated in their approaches and might want to run new ideas past me to unpack them or receive feedback. For instructors at a basic level, not only are administrators supporting their pedagogical understanding, but also they might have a limited or non-existent understanding of technology and facilitation. As expected, this second group requires much more personal contact time. Their confidence and competence need to be nurtured.

I find it important to give professors the freedom to create courses that best suit their instructional approaches. Many academics have successfully learned using systems and processes that make sense to them and look for plans to make their work easy to carry out. In using the term "freedom," I mean not providing a recipe or a locked-down list of steps to follow. Rather than make all of the decisions for them, I hope that they are able to learn through their own skills and experiences. The latter situation can create an internal conflict for me. If total freedom is not good and no freedom also is not good, then I struggle with trying to determine how much freedom is appropriate. One has to keep in mind that the students' needs are crucial in any course design process. One does not want an instructor to try something that might endanger students' learning or make their experiences worse than the current approach provides.

There is also a need to remain current by undertaking innovation in instruction. I have heard from many students who have been caught in the vortex of course revisions or changes, and they are not always happy. They question why they are the test subjects. They might have a limited understanding that courses are always undergoing change and revision. I tell instructors to communicate with their students. Make it clear to them that they are participating in change for the better, but there will always be elements that need to be ironed out or might not work the first time through. One outcome I have observed is that communicating the uncertainty makes the students more aware of what is taking place. This concept is especially true if learners think that they are part of something new or challenging. The single act of communication or instruction to graduate learners often makes a significant positive difference. In my experience, students are more likely to tolerate uncertainty or be constructively vocal about it when they feel that they are part of the process. The comments on the course evaluations are different as well. The learners are less focused on the failings of the instructor and more constructive about the course design and delivery. This feedback is significantly more beneficial for all involved than comments about how the instructor dressed or whether he or she was competent with PowerPoint.

Yet giving complete freedom to professors is not always the best for a number of reasons. Instructors new to online or technologically supported learning do not fully understand the importance of engagement. They might think that students will learn from the materials that have been provided or the tools that are being used, but there is a need to have more and explicit engagement. Instructors' understanding of innovative learning might be low or not as current as required, and their struggle with technology can be obvious. There is fear or a lack of confidence that undermines their perceived levels of competence. Valid concerns exist when they have limited amounts of teaching experience. Although it might seem to be strange, it is not uncommon for newly hired professors to be given online courses. So, not only are they new to teaching in higher education, but also they have the added burden of designing and offering online courses in which mistakes can be magnified and the number of variables that need to be controlled is large.

To see how these experiences might be improved, I looked for a model that allows for the inclusion of more technology. I have used Puentedura's (2011) SAMR model (Figure 2.1) in my past teaching on integrating technology into teaching. I used the model to begin discussion and found it to be a successful way to ease anxiety and systematize the process for pre-service instructors. By using SAMR to support early career academics, I can show them where they are, and which possibilities lie ahead. If they are already at the modification level, then I can show them their progress. If they are just getting started at the substitution level, then the model can help them to realize that the first few steps are generally simple and easy to attain. Chunking the process of course development using SAMR creates possibilities that can alleviate many fears. Staging the process of growth makes the experience less intimidating. I take the time to connect with these individuals and treat our early work much like completing a needs assessment. They might not know what they do not know. They often approach the process in an unsystematic and sporadic manner, waiting for an emergency instead of planning ahead. This aspect of the mentorship process should take place early in the career of any new academic in order to support her or his efforts to enhance initial online teaching capacities and then to transform online teaching practices.

Introducing professors to a framework to systematize the process of transition is one of the more helpful ways of migrating from traditional face-to-face teaching to online teaching. In my experience, the SAMR model provides the instructor with just such an approach to the new form of teaching. Although it is the basic level of the SAMR model, the substitution of one form of delivery of information with another is a starting point. The simple act of shifting text-based content online is a starting point, but a lack of interactivity often creates a sterile learning environment for students. They might be asked to find, read, interpret, and share their thoughts on works without guidance. As a result, the complete absence of the instructor is an issue. Instructors who simply put their notes online and require their students to hand in assignments are not implementing an effective model for learning. This change can represent the substitution of the instructor for no live instruction or asynchronous interaction, but this is not to the benefit of the learner. Some professors might think that, when the design work is done in advance, it is up to students to work through the content. An instructor might approach the course as online self-study. It has been my experience that when these situations occur instructors are blissfully unaware of the revolt brewing below the surface. Students are generally vocal early on in the process. They contact the department chair to "fix things" or to send a message to the instructor. This situation provides an opportunity for delicate yet clear discussion of what is required of the instructor. The conversation might reveal a need for the department chair to reinforce the key elements of online instruction.

At the other end of the spectrum is the example of too much engagement by the instructor or students. Such an intensive approach can lead to unrealistic expectations of both the instructor and students. In the mind of the professor, the class can take precedence over everything else. The professor might expect students to be reading, connecting, and thinking about the course at all times. In the area of assessment, this instructional behaviour can take the form of an unreasonable number of posted readings, too many required postings, or excessive amounts of technology-mediated group work. A student might feel a need for support from the instructor at all times and might be able to access the professor through a range of technologies. I suggest to professors that, on the first day of class and in the syllabus, they make it clear that access is limited to certain times or that a 24-hour response rule is in place. Both situations represent significant differences from face-to-face instruction.

Department chairs are sometimes unable to use their knowledge and experience as administrators in their role of mentoring or evaluating. Even though they might be responsible for the assignment of teaching duties, they might not know how to navigate through the online or technology-supported teaching process. They might see value in using text and voice to support graduate students but do not know how to balance them or to determine the proper amount of resources to allocate to development. If they have little or no online teaching or technology experience, then they might have to rely on institution-wide supports. Use of these supports is not necessarily a bad option, but they add an extra layer of administration that can increase frustration for the instructor and delay the design process. As department chair, I might ask: "Do I rely on the local design and technology support systems? Do I put my faith in the teaching and learning centre? Will the centre support the needs and goals of my department? Does its agenda support all learner types, or is it wedded to a particular model?" The more the department chair knows the better she or he will understand course design at all levels, but at what point does the new department chair take the time to understand a process that might be foreign to her or him? I have been fortunate to have the support of well-trained designers and information technology (IT) personnel. I feel confident in directing other administrative colleagues and professors to these supports. I also recognize for a variety of reasons that other department chairs might not have such luxuries or confidence.

As I go through the process of mentoring and evaluating, I ask myself a number of questions: "What are my dilemmas?" "Where do I struggle in my work of guiding people?" I am often faced with the knowledge that a professor is weak in a particular area of instruction or might be looking for a convenient way to deliver their courses. Do I tell such professors what to do or guide them to a source of help? It is at this stage of support that Dewey's (1933) influence lands squarely on me. Reflection is so much a part of what happens—reflecting on what they might have done previously that was not successful, reflecting on what they have heard from colleagues and peers. Reflection is part of my approach to mentoring and supporting professors. Reflecting on my own course design failures helps me greatly in supporting the pursuits of others. I know that I have been in the same position and can empathize with them. I am still faced with the thought "Who am I to tell them what to do or how to teach?" These internal conversations are important. I believe that they represent a genuine desire to be better at what I do. If my dissonance level is low, then it might signal a lack of commitment or a need to step back and reprioritize what is taking place. I believe that this strategy is useful and appropriate for assessing all aspects of my job, not just teaching support.

To ensure that communication with professors of my department is clear and that I am as helpful as possible, I purposefully create an environment that allows professionals to feel physically and intellectually comfortable. My office is clean and tidy, a place where we can focus on the needs of teachers and students. I have big comfortable chairs in my office into which instructors can flop and share what is on their minds. The "Oh, crap!" chairs are important. The physical comfort that they provide is remarkable. Using these chairs was not planned, but they have become integral to the process of mentoring. Over time, professors feel more at ease, and deep conversations about teaching can result. The conversations are one on one. The professors engage me as newcomers or experts. The meetings are not interviews or training sessions. I keep materials such as books, articles, syllabuses, and other resources to take away, share, consult, or review. These resources become part of the dialogue and are directly related to the focus and flow of our conversations. We get to know one another in order to develop trust. We talk about whatever comes to mind. Stories that seem to be unconnected or inappropriate are actually foundational to understanding what is important to the instructor. The stories serve as a way for me to gauge the place or perspective from which the individual approaches teaching. This process reinforces to both of us that courses are not designed and offered without contexts. Even in cases in which the person is experienced, it is an especially important reminder. The ever-changing aspects of teaching life come into play, and we can discuss in depth how the previous class or session went. We can ask ourselves "What did my reflection bring forward to influence what is happening now or perhaps in the future?" I am as open and honest as possible, and this approach allows others to be the same with me.

What often arises from initial conversations with someone new to online learning or the use of technology is that there are unique aspects of graduate-level course design that need to be communicated to professors who work online. One of the first concepts that we discuss is the notion of pacing the course and its material. Graduate students often juggle professions, families, and other commitments. Discovering that the course you are teaching is not the focus of your students' lives can be unsettling to some instructors, but it is important to give students enough time to engage successfully with the content, complete the assignments, attend course meetings, and connect with their online peers. We also unpack the idea that expectations of graduate students must be realistic. Some students take a course only because it is convenient. They might need one more class to finish a degree and might not be studying in your discipline, and they will do the minimum amount of work required. Other students might not see the need to connect with you or other students regularly. For these reasons, instructors can spend a significant amount of time trying to make students love the process for which they are not suited or the content in which they are not truly interested. This can be a cold realization for new instructors but important for their understanding.

Most online courses will have students with varied background experiences. Certain students might not have learned to communicate using technology, or they might feel intimidated by it. They might prefer direct emails or phone calls to the instructor. This behaviour often runs counter to the development of an online community and a depth of understanding. Experiences shared with others through text-based technologies is part of successful online learning, and when students are allowed to keep their thoughts semi-private it reduces group learning. A student's current employment situation is also something that online instructors need to consider. Are there experiences that cannot be shared because of work requirements? It is up to the professor to ensure that this inability to divulge information fully does not affect assessment or evaluation. For students who are also busy professionals, there are times of the academic year when they cannot devote all of their time to classwork, such as around a fiscal year end or report card time. Keeping these outside pressures in mind is important. When I meet with instructors, I can communicate to them students' needs. Once instructors are made aware of these needs, it helps to take pressure off both them and students.

Instructors need to ask themselves "What do students understand and know or at least think they do?" So much of what happens in our learning environment is relational. We as instructors need to understand the creation of an environment that suits our students' relationships with each other, with us, and with learning resources. When I teach, in class or online, I see myself as the same person. I might need to be more animated, or speak more clearly than I do in person, but I am true to myself. Part of being an instructor is being comfortable with who I am. I believe that you will be exposed as a fraud quickly if you are not.

Another key piece of advice is keeping a focus on the needs of all those involved in the online course. Finding a balance among what the program and/or institution requires, what the instructor is capable of or aspires to, and what the student needs to be successful factors into the resources and energies directed to online course design and development. When a formal rubric or focus in determining or assessing what is crucial in the design of online courses is necessary, those who have never undertaken a course evaluation might be at a loss. Concerns about the quality of design and implementation might be addressed partly by the Online Learning Consortium (OLC) Quality Scorecard Suite Standards (OLC, 2014), but they might need to be modified or interpreted slightly differently to accommodate graduate students. Often students' needs are the last to be attended to (or at least students might think that this is the case). To address this issue, we cannot always use the power structure that exists in a postsecondary institution. The OLC makes its comprehensive tool available so that it can be used for programmatic review or applied at a course level. The tool reviews a range of aspects that makes up a quality online offering. As assessment and evaluation become greater parts of a professor's work, utilizing a proper feedback mechanism goes a long way toward identifying areas in need of change. The tool can serve as a focal point when difficult decisions or discussions need to take place about a professor's online course. It is also an example of how important it is to do something with information from an evaluation. If you are collecting performance or user satisfaction data, you need to be as consistent and systematic as possible. The tool, if applicable, can be used longitudinally to show growth both as an outside assessment and as a self-assessment. I use this tool periodically as a measuring stick to give myself perspective on courses that I teach or programs that I support. I can also share it with others to gain external perspectives and identify possible gaps in what I think is happening and what is actually happening. It is helpful since it is so much more than course evaluation, and it is especially useful for those not just overseeing online courses but also looking after entire online programs.

Administrators need to support all course development for professors. Generally, this support means advocating on students' behalf to deans and associate deans. As a department chair, you need to be an informed voice at the university level of programs of support and on resource decision making. In online or technology-rich course development, the range of supports and needs is greater. Proper levels of instructional technology, instructional design, and web development are needed. Training support contributes positively to the success of the instructor and the students. When these supports are not provided, it is the department chair's responsibility to advocate for them at college and university levels.

Instructors must be made aware of the strong external expectations related to online learning. There is often an assumption at the institutional level that online learning can be a revenue stream that engages large numbers of students at low cost. A simple digitization of a regular face-to-face course, especially one that is required in a program or applies to a number of programs, might be viewed as an easy option to engage massive numbers of students. Time and time again, I have had to crush the hopes and dreams of those who see online learning as an untapped revenue stream. They demonstrate their limited understanding of what online learning is and is not through their excitement about a potential windfall. They often argue that economies of scale with massive online open courses do exist. Some propose large online course offerings as another way to deliver effective learning. I point out to them that they would not put 1,000 students in a face-to-face classroom. Why would they think that doing so would work online, where the needs are greater and the efforts to create presence and community are challenging? Not only is this line of thinking wrong, but also it can be used to protect substandard course offerings. Unfortunately, the belief that quantity of students is more important than quality of instruction is still part of the postsecondary system. There will always be trouble spots with course implementation, but good initial design for supporting teaching and learning will always triumph.

The transition to online course status for any class must be systematic and measured. Just like the design of any good instruction, a number of factors need to be addressed. Educating upper-level administration on best practices has to be undertaken. This "pulling back of the curtain" will reveal how much really needs to be done to design and develop online courses properly. It is also an example of the importance of educating everyone involved in course design and delivery.

What Does My Story Really Say?

I need to contextualize all that I have shared in this chapter with the understanding that in my heart I am a teacher, and I want to see only the best for my colleagues and students in their teaching and learning experiences. Reflecting on what I have shared, I have to ask myself "What does this process do to me as a department chair or an instructor? What will happen when I go back to being just a regular professor?"

Professors should aspire to be more than better technicians; they should be dedicated to their craft regardless of the context. Most of us go through a teaching year or cycle working in multiple situations: graduate, undergraduate, online, and face-to-face. We have to be flexible in how we address our teaching. My need to share through this chapter has been inspired not by catastrophe or a significant moment but by a slice of the large pie that comprises being a middle manager in postsecondary education. I put forward for review my experiences for you to read, appreciate, and perhaps compare with your own contexts. There is no intent to generalize but a chance to experience what I have lived for a period of time. You might wish to compare it with your experience and apply it to your future work. By reading this, you have been exposed to a new way of understanding, and you can modify this approach or use a different metaphor or framework to achieve the same goal. Maybe reflecting on and writing about your own experiences will allow you to find your own strengths and weaknesses. I have found the process of looking back on what I have done to be revealing, difficult, yet satisfying.

My experience with technology-supported and online course development has shaped my approach to mentoring others in their quests to understand how best to migrate courses from traditional delivery or to create new courses from scratch. I have had the relative luxury of having used many successful and unsuccessful technologies, and I have designed many face-to-face and online courses. I have worked as an instructional designer and taught instructional design at the graduate level. I have also designed or redesigned a number of programs for face-to-face and online delivery. Despite this depth of knowledge, each situation needs to be approached differently. The topic will be different, and the instructor will have a different level of understanding.

I have faced similar struggles along the way and hope to share how I overcame them without dictating that others have to do likewise. I have no real template. There are many books that guide individual instructors on how they might approach the task, but for a department chair there is no manual for encouraging, guiding, and continually supporting new and experienced instructors in their forays into online and technology-supported learning. Clearly, there is no substitute for experience. The people who have tried and failed and then succeeded and then failed again are often the ones who have had the most success.

I hope that I have demonstrated that, when it comes to working with technology and online learning, there will always be change. My experience has shown me that those who believe that they have conquered a particular challenge and think that they can rest will be surprised to see administrative changes that force them to revisit their online courses and respond to those changes. The surprise can be pleasant or nasty, but all instructors should be prepared for it.

As a department chair, your relationships with professors in your department will change. Instructors in online and blended learning need to prepare for more mentoring than they might have anticipated. The familiar approach to teaching that many of them have enjoyed in traditional classrooms might be replaced by a feeling of inadequacy or helplessness.

As chair, you need to go beyond simply attaching people to courses based solely on their content knowledge.

Recommendations

There are some key considerations for those who are pondering a move into an administrative role or currently in one in regard to supporting online and technology-supported instruction. From my reading, writing, reviewing, sharing, and thinking, I can highlight information that I consider to be the most salient. When I reached this point in the writing process, I had to ask myself "What do I think is important to make administrators aware of so that they can be most successful?" Based on my experience, I do not believe that there is a universal approach to supporting professors. Each individual, context, and content area will be different. One certainty as a department chair is that the more you know the more you will be able to help others.

Your ability to provide support is dependent on how much time you are willing or able to commit to everyone engaged in online or technology-supported learning. Building strong relationships that value all individuals is crucial. Horne et al. (2016) apply the leader-member exchange theory to show how those who receive more attention are more likely to be successful and supported. Their research underscores the need to create an environment that supports mentorship (including putting comfy chairs in your office).

Before you take the job of department chair, ask what the expectations are regarding course or program development. You might want to use a model such as SAMR to bring structure to the process (Puentedura, 2011). There might be initiatives under way that you are expected to complete or champion. Your institution might have invested significantly in a tool or tools that your faculty members are expected to use. Is there a plan for professional development at the university level? Will you have to organize professional learning for your department? To ensure success, consult with, undertake research, and reach out to strong and experienced instructors or include them in meetings. You are the person responsible for keeping initiatives moving at the departmental level, including teaching assignments, and there is nothing wrong with taking advantage of supports.

In terms of assignments, do not give online courses to new professors or force them to use technology in their teaching. They need to become good instructors before they venture into online learning or the application of unfamiliar technologies. Train professors first in the basic technologies that they need to be successful, and then look at ways to engage them in the unique aspects of online teaching (Orr, Williams, & Pennington, 2009; Paloff & Pratt, 2011). If they show an interest in such teaching, have them shadow your experienced online instructors or co-teach with those using technology skilfully in face-to-face situations. Support programs such as the Distance Education Mentoring Program at Purdue University show potential for a systematic process of engagement to assist those new to online teaching (Hixon, Barczyk, Buckenmeyer, & Feldman, 2011).

Encourage your professors to develop a community in which they can find support and ask questions about teaching. The approach supplements the traditional senior-to-junior mentoring and works when groups are involved (Pololi & Evans, 2015). When faculty members develop a layer of support, it will help them to deal with feelings of isolation and benefit you as the department chair (Savage et al., 2004). Working with others going through a similar process can encourage them to reflect on what they have done in the past that has contributed to their success. This reflective process helps them to realize that they have a strong teaching foundation and helps to ensure that their confidence does not wane when they run into new challenges with online learning.

Instructors who teach online or use technology will have their own versions of success. As in traditional face-to-face instruction, there is not one correct approach. Communicating options, listening to and learning from others, and sharing what you have learned from them are key ways in which a department chair can support professors regardless of their level of experience with online learning. By being supportive and valuing online and technology-supported learning, department chair and instructor can share a successful experience.

Conclusion

The role of department chair is challenging and filled with many exciting opportunities to learn, with many surprises associated with each day. To be successful, you must attend to all areas of the role, especially when it comes to supporting faculty members. Any effort that you put into guiding, nurturing, and helping them to grow will create a more positive and productive environment. When managed properly, the unique challenges of graduate teaching will lead to an enriched teaching and learning experience for professors, students, and you as the administrator. All that I have presented here has resulted from reflecting on my range of experiences. The most important message that I hope you take away from this chapter is how much we can learn from reflecting on our practice.

References

Bloom, B. S. (1956). *Taxonomy of educational objectives: The classification of educational goals by a committee of college and university examiners.* New York, NY: Longmans.

Charmaz, K. (2014). *Constructing grounded theory* (2nd ed.). London, UK: Sage.

Dewey, J. (1933). *How we think.* Boston, MA: Heath.

Denzin, N. K., & Lincoln, Y. S. (Eds.). (1998). *Collecting and interpreting qualitative materials.* Thousand Oaks, CA: Sage.

Ellis, C., Adams, T., & Bochner, A. (2010). Autoethnography: An overview. *Forum: Qualitative Social Research/Sozialforschung, 12*(1). doi:10.17169/fqs-12.1.1589

Ellis, C., & Bochner, A. P. (2000). Autoethnography, personal narrative, reflexivity. In N. K. Denzin & Y. S. Lincoln (Eds.), *Handbook of qualitative research* (2nd ed., pp. 733–768). Thousand Oaks, CA: Sage.

Gmelch, W. H., & Miskin, V. D. (1995). *Chairing an academic department: Survival skills for scholars* (Vol. 15). Thousand Oaks, CA: Sage.

Hamilton, E. R., Rosenberg, J. M., & Akcaoglu, M. (2016). The substitution augmentation modification redefinition (SAMR) model: A critical review and suggestions for its use. *TechTrends, 60*(5), 433–441. doi:10.1007/s11528-016-0091-y

Hargrove, S. K. (2014). From faculty to chair. In P. Mosely & S. Hargrove (Eds.), *Navigating academia: A guide for women and minority STEM faculty* (pp. 119–136). Amsterdam: Academic Press.

Hicks, M. (2014). Faculty development and faculty support. In O. Zawacki-Richter & T. Anderson (Eds), *Online distance education: Towards a research agenda* (pp. 267–286). Vancouver, BC: UBC Press.

Hixon, E., Barczyk, C., Buckenmeyer, J., & Feldman, L. (2011). Mentoring university faculty to become high quality online educators: A program evaluation. *Online Journal of Distance Learning Administration, 14*(4).

Horn, M. B., & Staker, H. (2015). *Blended: Using disruptive innovation to improve schools.* San Francisco, CA: Jossey-Bass.

Horne, A. L., Du Plessis, Y., & Nkomo, S. (2016). Role of department heads in academic development: A leader-member exchange and organizational resource perspective. *Educational Management Administration & Leadership, 44*(6), 1021–1041.

Online Learning Consortium. (2014). Retrieved from https://onlinelearningconsortium.org

Orr, R., Williams, M. R., & Pennington, K. (2009). Institutional efforts to support faculty in online teaching. *Innovative Higher Education, 34*, 257–268. doi:10.1007/s10755-009-9111-6

Paloff, R. M., & Pratt, K. (2011). *The excellent online instructor: Strategies for professional development.* San Francisco, CA: Jossey-Bass.

Pololi, L. H., & Evans, A. T. (2015). Group peer mentoring: An answer to the faculty mentoring problem? *Journal of Continuing Education in the Health Professions, 35*, 192–200.

Puentedura, R. (2006). Transformation, technology, and education [Blog post]. Retrieved from http://hippasus.com/resources/tte/

Puentedura, R. R. (2011). A brief introduction to TPCK and SAMR. (Freeport workshop slides). Retrieved from http://www.hippasus.com/rrpweblog/archives/2011/12/08/BriefIntroTPCKSAMR.pdf

Riley, T. A., & Russell, C. (2013). Leadership in higher education: Examining professional development needs for department chairs. *Review of Higher Education & Self-Learning, 6*(21), 38–57.

Romrell, D., Kidder, L. C., & Wood, E. (2014). The SAMR model as a framework for evaluating mlearning. *Online Learning, 18*(2), 1–15. Retrieved from http://olj.onlinelearningconsortium.org/index.php/olj/article/view/435/105

Roth, R. L. (2015). Frameworks for integration of digital technologies at the roadside: Innovative models, current trends, and future perspectives. *International Journal of Learning, Teaching, and Educational Research, 13*(2), 37–54.

Savage, H., Karp, R., & Logue, R. (2004). Faculty mentorship at colleges and universities. *College Teaching, 52*(1), 21–24. Retrieved from http://www.jstor.org/stable/27559169

Schwier, R. A., & Wilson, J. R. (2010). Unconventional roles and activities identified by instructional designers. *Contemporary Educational Technology*, *1*(2), 134–147.

Smith, W. (2015). Relational dimensions of virtual social work education: Mentoring faculty in a web-based learning environment. *Clinical Social Work Journal*, *43*(2), 236–245.

Stubbs, B., Krueger, P., White, D., Meaney, C., Kwong, J., & Antao, V. (2016). Mentorship perceptions and experiences among academic family medicine faculty: Findings from a quantitative, comprehensive work-life and leadership survey. *Canadian Family Physician*, *62*(9), 531–539.

Tejonidhi, M., Uma, B., Swathi, H., Margaret, R., & Vinod, A. (2018). Exemplary faculty mentoring programme. *Journal of Engineering Education Transformations* [Special issue]. doi:10.16920/jeet/2018/v0i0/120941

Tucker, A. T. (1984). *Chairing the academic department: Leadership among peers* (2nd ed.). New York, NY: Macmillan.

Wilson, J. R. (2013). Course design using an authentic design studio model. *Canadian Journal of Learning and Technology*, *39*(1), 1 – 14. doi: https://doi.org/10.21432/T22S3P

Zawacki-Richter, O., & Anderson, T. (2014). *Online distance education: Towards a research agenda*. Edmonton, AB: Athabasca University Press.

Graduate Student Online Orientation Programs

A Design-Based Research Study

Jennifer Lock, Yang Liu, Carol Johnson,
Jane Hanson, and Alicia Adlington

Public institutions of higher education are offering and expanding their online and blended learning programs at an increasing rate (Allen & Seaman, 2016, 2017; Donovan et al., 2019). In conjunction with the ever-changing world of technology, online and blended learning environments are evolving from text-based settings to environments that are rich in multimedia and include both synchronous and asynchronous communication. In response to this evolution, instructional designers and faculty instructors are expected to conceptualize and develop online and blended technology–enabled environments using a combination of text and voice. An important consideration when creating these environments is how future students of these programs will be prepared to be successful learners—particularly in online, media-rich learning environments. A team of researchers at one western Canadian university used a design-based research (DBR) approach to investigate this question within the context of a graduate education program.

The purpose of this chapter is threefold. First, the need for, as well as the nature of, orientation and preparation programs to support online learners in higher education is examined. Second, findings from the first year of a two-year DBR study of an online orientation for graduate students in a Faculty of Education are shared. Third, drawing on the literature and from the analysis of the data from the study, implications for practice. and directions for future research are discussed and identified.

Online Learning

The delivery of online education is intended to increase access and convenience for students and break down barriers to higher education and collaboration through the use of technology. It was found from the 2018 Canadian National Online and Digital Education Survey that "83% of responding institutions offered distance education courses for credit" (Donovan et al., 2019, p. 6). This national study found that "over half of the institutions with fewer than 1,000 students (52%) did not offer online courses, while almost every institution with more than 10,000 students did" (p. 6). Donovan et al. (2019) found "in 2016–2017, 18% of all Canadian post-secondary students were taking at least one online course for credit" (p. 7). Furthermore, a steady growth was reported in online enrolment within Canadian institutions. As institutions of higher education in Canada trend toward growth in distance education programs, consideration needs to be given to how online programs are designed, delivered, and facilitated. This growth also requires students to have requisite skills with technology along with other soft or transferable skills that they may not have needed for face-to-face learning in the physical classroom.

Online learning exhibits key differences from face-to-face instruction. Unlike in the traditional face-to-face classroom, online learning does not require students to arrive at their class at a particular time and location to engage in learning. In the face-to-face learning environment, the majority of interaction between the instructor and a community of peers occurs within the physical space of the classroom. In contrast, the blended or online classroom requires students to unlock the door with a username and password. Within the online classroom environment, a new experience of learning takes place along with a new set of technological expectations (e.g., navigate to access content, engage in online classroom discussions, submit assignments to a digital repository, etc.).

One should not assume that all or most adult students are comfortable or proficient with technology, even those considered by Prensky (2012) as *"Digital Natives"* (p. 69). Prensky claimed that "students today are all 'native speakers' of the digital language of computers, video games, and the Internet" (p. 69). However, they might not be proficient in the use of technology for learning, specifically online learning (Johnson & Lock, 2018). As such, institutions of higher education must not make the error of overestimating student readiness for online learning. Many online post-secondary students are returning adult learners who might not necessarily be technologically savvy and might require instruction, coaching, and/or support on how to engage in the online environment. Students might also be required to work with a learning management system (LMS). As noted by Curran (2014), students in an online environment can encounter a steep learning curve that can be challenging if they are not familiar with the learning platforms and/or educational technologies used. Further issues such as "anxiety associated with using technology, being out of one's comfort zone" (Gillett-Swan, 2017, p. 21), can exacerbate students' frustration and hamper their success. In response to these issues, Chu and Tsai (2009) argued that

> Educators should pay more attention to giving enough practice time for adult learners to motivate them to engage in Internet activities that could enhance their confidence in utilizing technical learning tools. For program designers, the content provided is especially critical for adult learners, which should reflect and connect to their everyday life, and offer resourceful links for them to construct their own knowledge base. (p. 498)

In the absence of such comprehensive teaching and designing approaches, it is likely that adult learners might not succeed within an online environment. The digital barrier to learning, combined with both course expectations and learning how to use technology, might seem to be insurmountable to some students.

Deriving from an ongoing global research initiative of the New Media Consortium (NMC) the *NMC Horizon Report: 2017 Higher Education Edition* suggested that 21st century learning requires students to become proficient in the digital technology environment and that institutions have a role to play in supporting this development: "Institutions are charged with developing students' digital citizenship, ensuring mastery of responsible and appropriate technology use, including online communication etiquette and digital rights and responsibilities in blended and online learning settings and beyond" (Adams Becker, Cummins, Freeman, Hall Giesinger, & Ananthanarayanan, 2017, p. 22). Online learning therefore requires students to be equipped with the necessary skills to be able to work well in this new learning environment. It is important for institutions of higher education with online course offerings to have mechanisms in place to support students in developing their confidence and competence in order to be successful in online learning environments. These mechanisms can ensure that students have a successful transition, enjoy a positive online learning experience, and continue to enrol in online courses.

Orientation Programs for Online Learning

Low retention rates in online courses can be problematic when students are not equipped with learning strategies and the necessary soft or transferable skills (e.g., time management, self-regulation) to aid in their success. Institutions of higher education are beginning to provide orientation programs to support students enrolled in online learning courses. These programs can assist in addressing students' misconceptions about learning online and provide opportunities for students to learn strategies and skills to support them in being successful online learners. The challenge is to create a customized orientation that meets the needs of students, one aligned with the particular program's theoretical approach to online learning.

Studies suggest that students benefit from participating in an online orientation prior to the start of a formal program. Cho (2012) reported that familiarity with learning technologies is a major factor in students' success. With an effective orientation, students become more comfortable with using the technology (e.g., text-based discussion forums, video and audio for discussions and feedback, and synchronous conferencing), and they can focus their learning on course content rather than technology.

Additionally, Cambridge-Williams, Winsler, Kitsantas, and Bernard (2013) found that students who completed an online learning orientation program had a higher rate of graduation, and institutions that offered such programs had higher rates of retention. Koehnke (2013) further demonstrated that online orientation had significant statistical implications for those who completed such programs. Specifically, students who had online orientations had higher retention rates than those who did not. It is evident that orientation programs enable the success of students in online learning environments.

Some institutions of higher education have identified their online orientation programs as mandatory for students taking online courses. Although mandatory programs might be seen as being inflexible, they ensure that all students participate in activities that prepare them to learn online. For example, Richland Community College (RCC) provided its students with an optional, face-to-face orientation program from 1999 to 2009 (Jones, 2013, p. 43). RCC shifted its orientation into the online environment when it began to embed online courses into its programs; orientation became mandatory for students taking an online or hybrid course. These orientations ensured that students were equipped to learn successfully both in the traditional classroom and online.

As institutions of higher education look toward the development of content and activities for their online orientations, how these programs are developed depends on the individual institution's culture and program goals. For example, Mensch (2017) identified that Indiana University of Pennsylvania sought to prepare its students by developing their self-awareness of skills through an initial self-assessment. The university identified self-regulation and time management skills as markers for determining a student's fit for online learning. This highlights aspects of why an institution might develop an online preparation program focused on specific experiences or goals.

Adult learners, according to Curran (2014), "will find greater success in online programming if institutions commit to providing them with the introductory technology-skills seminars prior to starting their courses" (p. 1). As noted by Jones (2013), offering an orientation program to students new to online learning provides them with realistic expectations for their online course environment and provide[s] hands on practice with the technology that they will be using in their course. The orientation also provides the students with time to work out any potential technology barriers, without the worry of it affecting their academic coursework or grades. (p. 44)

When attention is not given to course design and orientation of learners to the online environment, "it is very likely that adult learners may not prevail within an online environment" (Bawa, 2016, p. 3). By providing such opportunities, students will "become more comfortable with the online learning environment" (Jones, 2013, p. 44). Therefore, the challenge for institutions of higher education is to design orientation programs that assist adult learners in developing their confidence and competence in learning within a technology-enabled environment.

Designing for Success Orientation Program

A large online graduate program exists within a Faculty of Education at one western Canadian university. Students who enrol in this program have a range of experiences and skill levels with technology and learning within technology-enabled environments. Students were previously offered two synchronous orientation sessions: one that focused on the academic and administrative aspects of their program and one that introduced them to the technology. Each orientation was from 60 to 90 minutes in length. The technology orientation introduced students to the theoretical approach and key features of the LMS and synchronous technology. Because the orientation was introductory and delivered primarily as a lecture, students had limited opportunities to experience and "play" with the technology prior to the start of their program. The students therefore experienced frustration in their first online courses; they struggled to balance skill acquisition related to the technology with the rigour of graduate-level learning.

In 2016, the research team received a two-year institutional Scholarship of Teaching and Learning grant. The focus was on studying the development of practical skills and knowledge in online learning for graduate students. The project was designed to explore the impacts of an online orientation program for new graduate students. The program was built upon the literature as well as a needs analysis with key educational stakeholders in our faculty; the team sought their input on current needs and recommendations for the orientation program. The development of practical skills and knowledge through the Designing for Success program should foster academic success for online graduate students in their professional programs of study.

Two key theoretical frameworks were used as a foundation for the research on and design of the Designing for Success orientation program. First, the conceptual model for the program was based on Garrison, Anderson, and Archer's (2000) Community of Inquiry (CoI). Second, the Universal Design for Learning (UDL), grounded on three principles of design, guided the designers to create opportunities within the orientation program for multiples of engagement, representation, action, and expression (Meyer, Rose, & Gordon, 2014). These two frameworks guided the design of the online environments (Desire2Learn or D2L for asynchronous and Adobe Connect for synchronous activities) and the nature of the learning tasks.

Community of Inquiry

Garrison (2006) explained that "the goal is to create a community of inquiry where students are fully engaged in collaboratively constructing meaningful and worthwhile knowledge" (p. 25). The community of inquiry is composed of learners and instructors "transacting with the specific purposes of facilitation, constructing, and validating understanding, and of developing capability that will lead to further learning" (Garrison & Anderson, 2003, p. 23).

CoI is composed of three key elements or presences (social, cognitive, and teaching) in which the nexus is the robustness of the educational experience (Garrison & Anderson, 2003). First, social presence is "the ability of participants in a community of inquiry to project themselves socially and emotionally, as 'real people' through the medium of communication being used" (Garrison et al., 2000, p. 94). Activities created in our Designing for Success orientation program to foster social presence included students posting introductions, sharing images of themselves, and communicating with each other for the purpose of getting to know one another. Within a community, it is the instructor's role to "set the tone and draw reluctant participants into the discussion" (Garrison & Anderson, 2003, p. 54). It is critical for students and their instructor to have conditions created "for sharing and challenging ideas through critical discourse" (Garrison & Cleveland-Innes, 2005, pp. 142–143) at the beginning of an orientation program.

Second, cognitive presence involves "the process of both reflection and discourse in the initiation, construction and confirmation of meaningful learning outcomes" (Garrison & Anderson, 2003, p. 4). Students were provided with opportunities to create and engage in the online classroom community in the orientation program. An online "café" was created in the discussion area for students to assist each other with any emerging course or technical questions and to encourage collaboration for problem solving. The instructor modelled the introduction discussion by posting an introduction and image of herself. The second instructor also posted her introduction by creating a short video clip. The instructors continued to model cognitive presence by providing timely responses and feedback to student assignments and emails. As a final activity, students took an online learner quiz and emailed to the instructor their reflections of themselves as online learners.

Third, teaching presence is "the design, facilitation and direction of cognitive and social processes for the purpose of realizing personally meaningful and educationally worthwhile learning outcomes" (Anderson, Rourke, Garrison, & Archer, 2001, p. 5). Within the community, both students and the instructor have roles in teaching presence. In our orientation program, teaching presence involved setting the curriculum and implementing it through various instructional strategies. Implemented strategies included audio and video in both content and assignment submission, discussion postings using text or audio, drop box for written assignments, email reflections to the instructor, quizzes, grade book entries, partner assignment using GoogleDocs, and ePortfolio. The content included a variety of text, audio, and video, all of which took into account various learning preferences of students. The course was designed to emulate the organization of the students' online academic course to increase familiarity with the online environment for their graduate program.

CoI helped to inform the design and facilitation of the online learning experience for Designing for Success. The three presences and their intersection helped to inform the design as well as the facilitation of our orientation program.

Universal Design for Learning

Universal Design for Learning (UDL) is "a framework to improve and optimize teaching and learning for all people based on scientific insights into how humans learn" (CAST, 2018). It is "a set of principles for curriculum development that give[s] all individuals equal opportunities to learn" (National Center on Universal Design for Learning, 2014, para. 1). Founded on neuroscience and educational research, UDL provides a comprehensive approach to designing learning to meet the diverse learning needs of students using multiple approaches and media (Meyer et al., 2014).

The UDL framework was used to direct the design of an online orientation environment guided by the three UDL principles: (1) providing multiple means of engagement; (2) providing multiple means of representation; and (3) providing multiple means of action and expression (Meyer et al., 2014). For multiple means of engagement, students had the opportunity to engage in synchronous and asynchronous discussions. They could engage in the tasks at various levels. For example, they could participate in the Adobe Connect orientation session and then go online to Adobe Connect to practise using the various features. The learning content was available in text, audio, and/or video form in order to provide multiple options for representation. For multiple options for expression and action, students had the opportunity to select from a list of ways to express what they learned. As an example, they watched a video on how to address procrastination; their associated task was to respond to a question about the video by using the audio or video feature in the D2L assignment drop box. UDL guided how various approaches and flexibility were built into the design of the online orientation program so as to support better the diverse learning needs of the adult learners.

Research Design

A DBR methodology was selected. It is a flexible methodology designed to "improve educational practices through iterative analysis, design, development, and implementation, based on collaboration among researchers and practitioners in real-world settings, and leading to contextually-sensitive design principles and theories" (Wang & Hannafin, 2005, pp. 6–7). The use of DBR is based on creating an intervention-based solution to a problem. This form of research, as noted by McKenney and Reeves (2012), "strives to positively impact practice, bringing about transformation through the design and use of solutions to real problems" (p. 14). This design allowed for the implementation of the innovation (Designing for Success) and the study of the iterations over time and with various cohorts. Ethics approval to conduct the study was received from the university's research ethics board.

Context

Based on research-informed practice, our graduate program orientation, Designing for Success, provided a consecutive seven- or 10-day online experience grounded on four goals: (1) to familiarize students with online learning tools used by the program; (2) to introduce students to best practices for online learning; (3) to prepare students for online graduate learning; and (4) to provide students with various supports and resources to assist them in learning online within a graduate program context. This program provided opportunities for students to experience synchronous communication (e.g., Adobe Connect) and asynchronous communication (e.g., D2L discussion forums, audio postings, video feedback). These opportunities modeled how students would experience using the technology in their programs (e.g., posting to a discussion forum), and allowed them to learn strategies to be effective online learners. The experience of using both text and voice within an online environment provides low-stakes learning opportunities designed to help students develop the necessary knowledge, skills, and strategies to be successful online learners.

The study is focused on the iterations of the Designing for Success program in relation to its design, implementation, and assessment. The first phase of the work involved designing and implementing the orientation program. An assessment of the program through surveys and interviews with students and instructors, along with D2L learning analytics, followed implementation. Follow-up interviews with students were conducted six months and one year after completion of the program. In the second phase, data from the initial implementation along with the follow-up data were used to inform the redesign of the program. The redesigned/ refined program was implemented, and assessment of its impact occurred through a second iteration.

Data Collection

All graduate students who entered online programs starting in the summer 2016, fall 2016, and summer 2017 academic terms were invited to participate in the program. In total, 112 students were enrolled in their choice of one of the four cohorts; of these students, 18 completed the survey, 6 participated in the interview at the end of their program, and 1 completed the interview after six months. Seven subset students gave consent to have their data (e.g., online discussion posts, messages, etc.) in D2L analyzed. Based on the statistics from the online management system (D2L), the research team drew data in terms of which content topic had been visited, frequency of topic views, quiz results, checklist progress, and which discussion boards were accessed and utilized. In addition, two instructors were interviewed as part of data collection for the first year. One instructor led the design of the D2L course shell and facilitated both the synchronous and the asynchronous components of the program. The second instructor worked as a consultant on the D2L course shell design and co-instructed in the synchronous sessions.

Data Analysis

Descriptive statistics were used to analyze the survey data to determine mean scores and frequency counts. Saldaña's (2013) first and second cycles of coding were used in analyzing the qualitative data from the participants' first and second interviews. With the first cycle, codes were assigned using key phrases from interview questions. The second cycle used the in vivo coding process in which words or phrases from transcripts were recorded as codes (Miles, Huberman, & Saldaña, 2013). The analysis involved finding repetition of the words or phrases that led to the development of patterns (Miles et al., 2013). The data were hand-coded by two members of the research team. D2L's learning analytics were analyzed using descriptive statistics of averages and frequency counts in relation to items accessed. Triangulation and member-checking of the data were used to support the integrity of the study.

Discussion of the Findings

From the analyses of the interview data, survey responses, and learning analytics, five themes emerged in regard to a technology-enabled environment that used a combination of text and voice to prepare students to be successful online learners: (1) the role of design in supporting confidence in learning in an online environment; (2) the use of modifications to course design to enhance the learning experience; (3) the role of the instructor in facilitating learning; (4) the impact of expectations of learning in an online environment; and (5) the development of confidence and competence for online learning.

Design

Data were collected on the design of both the asynchronous component (D2L online course shell) and the synchronous component (Adobe Connect) of the Designing for Success program. We used the data to examine the design feature of each technology.

Asynchronous Component

From the survey data, a subset of students (n=18) indicated that the inclusion of multimedia in the learning content was helpful in D2L. It provided them with a "fun" way to understand the essentials of online learning through easy-to-follow visual aids. As explored previously, developing an intuitive and easy-to-navigate online environment within a learning management system can be challenging. New users might not be familiar with the structure of or the terms used for specific features. This issue had to be considered not only in the navigation structure of the course in D2L but also in how the content was created and posted. From the survey data, the course design overall was found to be clear and easy to navigate. As noted by one student, the design of the D2L environment was "simple, intuitive, [and] well laid out. It seemed very simple to navigate and I was able to explore on my own very easily." According to the data, it had an "intuitive manner."

The orientation program was designed with modules meant to be completed on a daily basis. As noted by a student, "I enjoyed that the content area was broken down very clearly by day. I appreciated the checklist and wish my courses had this feature (they currently do not)." This student went on to indicate that she observed some inconsistency in the layout. For example, "there were one or two instances where an assignment was in one location and not in the other. For instance, you needed to go into the drop box in order to see the details of an assignment rather than in the daily postings where the other assignments were." The perceived inconsistency was designed purposefully to show students the various features of D2L. However, we discovered the need to articulate clearly to students the reasons for using different tools for learning tasks in order to provide clarity and minimize frustration.

A critical feature of the design was the succinctness of the content and support materials. For example, students appreciated the short informational slides, as indicated in the following interview: "I liked how the different slides were just one page, so you could just flip through the different pages." Furthermore, daily modules were used to structure the topics. One student commented on appreciating how each day's topic was specific and relevant to online learning.

Students appreciated the inclusion of multimedia, such as images and videos, describing it as a "break" from reading, and it allowed for "multiple perspectives" on learning. Multimedia were so positively received that one survey respondent requested that a future course include a learning task in which students create their own videos in order to gain hands-on experience with different media. One interview respondent noted that "I really appreciated that there were multimedia tools because I am a visual learner and the videos really helped me absorb the learning quickly. I am intrigued by the audio tool and cannot wait to try that in our classes." This demonstrates that the introduction of such an audio tool sets an expectation of its use in graduate courses.

Students from Cohorts Three and Four (n=5), who gave permission to have their D2L learning analytics reviewed, accessed and/or completed the activities within the orientation course. On average, these students accessed 92% of the topic content of the course. Some of the topics were visited four times or more per student. In Figure 3.1, we compare the rates of access for each student in the two cohorts. For example, the topic outlining how to use tools in the online environment (specific to the LMS used for the study) was visited four times by a participant from Cohort Three. The same topic was visited once, twice, three times, and once by each participant from Cohort Four. Topics accessed the most by the students were "Maximizing success for online learners"; "Are you ready to learn online?"; "Take charge of distractions"; "Time management for smart goals"; "Using planners"; and "Self-regulation." Table 3.1 provides an overview of how often students accessed the various topics.

Table 3.1 D2L learning analytics of content areas assessed.

Category	Topics	Cohort Three (n=1)	Cohort Four (n=4)			
		Number of times the topic was accessed by the student	Number of times the topic was accessed by each of the four students			
Strategies	Tools to use in the online environment	4	1	2	2	1
	Maximizing success for online learners	6	0	7	1	1

Category (cont.)	Topics (cont.)	Cohort Three (n=1) (cont.)	Cohort Four (n=4) (cont.)			
Strategies (cont.)	Tips for avoiding plagiarism	2	0	4	1	1
	How to avoid plagiarism— Harvard guide to using sources	1	3	1	1	2
	Are you ready to learn online? Five need-to-have skills for online students	3	1	5	1	2
	How do you know if online learning is for you?	1	1	4	1	1
	How students develop online learning skills	2	1	4	2	1
	Indicators of good online postings	2	1	4	1	1
	Take charge of distractions	4	1	3	7	3
	Netiquette: Ground rules for online discussions	2	2	1	1	2
Skill development	Time management and SMART goals	4	2	4	6	3
	Using planners	5	1	4	2	2
	Self-regulation: The other 21st-century skill	3	2	5	3	2

Students provided helpful insights into course design from the data collected. They identified the need for information about the university library as well as additional instructional and interactive videos (e.g., a video orientation to the layout of the course, opportunities for students to record video introductions). Such data helped to inform subsequent iterations of the course within the D2L environment.

Synchronous Component

From the survey data, overall student (n=18) perceptions of the synchronous Adobe Connect sessions were positive; the sessions were identified as being helpful. Some problems occurred, such as incorrect session links issued, system outages, and so on. These challenges became opportunities for learning; students indicated that they preferred to understand why a problem happened in Adobe Connect in order to prepare themselves better for future troubleshooting. In addition, the data suggested that an introductory session be separate from an "enrichment" session so that students could collaborate and/or have further practice using the Adobe Connect presenter tools. Some students experienced user or technical errors during Adobe Connect sessions (e.g., microphone issues, problems with Adobe Flash, etc.). These issues were typically addressed in the moment by one of the instructors, and at times the learning plan for the session was "paused" until all students could participate. Survey respondents recommended that such problems be addressed privately or separately with the student so as not to hold up the rest of the students in the session. It was also recommended that students view a "how to" video prior to their first synchronous session in order to anticipate and solve possible issues.

Respondents also recommended that practical discussions be incorporated into synchronous sessions for future iterations of the course. Students desired practical "play" time in order to learn more about various features of Adobe Connect and to be more confident in using them. One student commented that, for both D2L and Adobe Connect, they wanted access to "sandbox" versions beyond the orientation program: "It would be nice if it were open still to play around in it." This feedback was implemented beginning with Cohort Four; one formal Adobe Connect session was followed by a second session that allowed students, at their own convenience, to log in and experiment with the various features of the application in order to develop proficiency and comfort.

Students' perceptions and experiences of the synchronous sessions were positive; the learning activities were identified as helpful. Incorrect session links and user errors marred the experience for some, and this reminded the design team to check carefully and address such issues before students log in for their synchronous sessions. These issues, however, gave students chances to troubleshoot and anticipate challenges in their future studies. Overall, the data indicated that the design and facilitation of synchronous and asynchronous activities were successful and met project goals.

Modifications to the Design

Three major modifications were made to the design of the orientation program. The first modification was to the duration of the program. Students reported that a seven-day program was too short. They were unable to create community connections fully, especially given that many of them were enrolled in a wide variety of programs. As one student commented, "I think that maybe there just wasn't an opportunity to really build a relationship or community with the people in the class." Students appreciated the opportunity to introduce themselves, but they wanted more chances to talk with each other and work collaboratively. The program was therefore extended from seven to 10 days starting with Cohort Three. In addition, the instructors paid greater attention to opportunities for connection. Feedback showed that this change was well received. A student from Cohort Four remarked in her interview that she initially "couldn't understand why we needed 10 days to get acclimatized to the online part of the program." Yet later she was "happily surprised by the course content and the community connection." The student noted that the instructor played an integral part in the success of the program since she helped to define the expectations of the course, encouraged the students, and allowed them to connect with others when applicable. Given the experience, the student recommended that the instructor clarifies the intention with regards to the duration of the program along with the expectation that students participate in the program for 15 to 30 minutes per day.

The second modification was to allow students to have access to the D2L orientation program course shell after they completed the program. The research team initially assumed that students would not wish to return to view content after they completed the course. However, as evident in the learning analytics, the five students from Cohorts Three and Four who gave consent to view their data visited the course after the last day. One participant from Cohort Three visited the shell 25 times over a five-week period after the orientation program ended and their graduate studies began. Students accessed resources and materials by going back to the orientation program in D2L. As a result, the research team decided to provide students with unlimited access to the course shell upon completion of the orientation program.

The third modification was to the synchronous Adobe Connect content. A second instructor, a regular user of Adobe Connect, was added to assist with synchronous components of the orientation after feedback from the first cohort indicated that this was a weak aspect of our program. The co-teaching of subsequent cohorts provided a more supportive environment for the program instructor, and the students appreciated the unique perspectives that each instructor brought to the sessions. The addition of co-teaching helped to relieve some of the tension that the original course instructor had in facilitating the synchronous session. User error was addressed, and both instructors felt more confident delivering content to students.

In addition to these three major modifications, minor modifications were made to the D2L course design and to the activities of the Adobe Connect sessions in response to student feedback. The team found that it can be challenging to find the right blend of activities and pacing to meet the spectrum of novice to more advanced online learners enrolled in the program; students in each cohort presented various levels of knowledge and skill.

Role of the Instructor

The instructor of an orientation program plays a critical role. This individual needs to have a strong online presence in both synchronous and asynchronous environments, and a mentor-like presence helps to foster confidence in students. The instructor should make the orientation program interesting and both challenge and motivate students. Furthermore, an instructor should possess the ability to facilitate the activities in a way that students can move through components in a timely manner but be responsive to the various levels of knowledge of and skill with the technology.

The primary instructor for our Designing for Success program has several years of experience working with D2L. She both designs and teaches courses in the K–12 environment, and she has recently worked with postsecondary faculty members in designing and supporting their use of D2L. The instructor is also an alumna of the faculty's graduate program. As such, she has an awareness of the work required of graduate students. For this project, she worked collaboratively with members of the research team to design the asynchronous D2L environment and the synchronous Adobe Connect sessions. The instructor's experience and practice in addition to ongoing team consultation helped to inform the design of the learning environment.

Students indicated in the survey and interview data that they appreciated knowing that the instructor was both available and approachable during the orientation program. One student stated that it was important "just knowing that your instructor is there to support you if you're having a struggle through the online learning and being flexible." To support student growth and provide a positive experience, the instructor used the "24-hour rule" (i.e., responses to students' inquiries within 24 hours while the course was running). The instructor also tried to maintain a healthy online presence—posting content and responding to students in discussion areas and so forth—so that students knew she was there to provide support and assistance throughout the orientation.

Instructors were expected to be expert users of the technology when delivering an orientation program. The efficacy of such a program can otherwise be questioned by students, and frustration can occur when an instructor demonstrates user error. For our study, the instructor designed the initial one-hour Adobe Connect session to introduce students to online collaboration through synchronous technology. They engaged in an introductory activity and went on to explore features within Adobe Connect, such as the breakout room. The instructor was experienced in using the learning management system but was not as skilled in using Adobe Connect at the beginning of the research project. Interviewed students expressed concern about the lack of direction from the instructor, and they were unsure of what to expect from future synchronous sessions. One student commented that the instructor "showed us how to break into rooms," but once they were in the rooms they were given no direction on what they were supposed to do, and "We were all just sitting there in the rooms." After our own debriefing session about the situation, and given student feedback, we decided to have a second instructor assist with the synchronous sessions.

Instructor error also occurred on two occasions with the link to the Adobe Connect session. Adobe Connect is a free-standing communication application, and the instructor was required to create a session link within it and provide that link to students. In one situation, two different session links were posted in D2L for the session. Confusion occurred as a result, and some students could not access the session and had to be directed to the correct link. In the second situation, the link was provided, but a technical issue arose on the night of the session. The instructors had to create a new link and post it for the students. These two situations were problematic since they created confusion. One student recommended that the instructor or someone from the institution "try the link prior to the call to ensure that the link works well. I would be accessible 20 minutes prior to the call." Such preparation would allow the instructors to ensure that links are working, assist students with connectivity issues, and inspire confidence in students.

Impacts of Expectations

Students entering an online graduate orientation program have varied expectations, and not all expectations can be met realistically within the constraints of an online orientation. The goal of the team, regardless of students' expectations and prior knowledge, was to familiarize students with online learning within the context of a graduate program. We hoped that students would develop a deeper appreciation of what is expected of online learners.

We observed some variance in students' expectations of time commitment for participating in and completing the course. Some survey participants indicated that the team's recommendation of 15–20 minutes per day to complete learning tasks and readings was not realistic. Other respondents, however, indicated that these daily time commitments were appropriate. This variance can be attributed to students' skills with technology, personal commitments outside online studies, and limited experiences with online learning. Some students expressed frustration about perceived time commitments for online learning. As noted by a student in Cohort Four, "Not knowing how long I needed to spend on the work was a bit frustrating for me." This challenge cannot be completely resolved because of varying skills among students. For example, one student might complete a daily task in 10 to 15 minutes, whereas another might require double the amount of time. Expectations of time commitments in online studies might be tempered by helping students to understand that the amount of time spent on a task is in their control, and they can learn to develop a sense of how much time is required as they progress through their studies.

The asynchronous environment provides natural flexibility to students. They can determine when and where they are online and working through the activities. Students can therefore develop an appreciation of the flexibility but also might have to modify their expectations of the timing of responses from peers and instructors. As one student remarked, "there might be times where you can't respond to all your discussion posts in this time frame that is there, and . . . there's some flexibility available that you can maybe post later." Our team, for these reasons, introduced concepts of self-regulation and the need for scheduling in online learning. Students should experiment and develop their own schedules for such learning. For example, some might find that online learning works best in the morning or evening depending on their daily routines. Students also discovered that another advantage to asynchronous learning is the opportunity to read the postings, ponder what has been stated, and take time to compose responses. Students came to appreciate the opportunity to think, research, and reflect before responding online, an opportunity not always available in traditional classroom learning.

The design of the orientation program required students to interact with the content, the instructor, and their peers. It was not a matter of reading the content and completing a few tasks. Rather, working with peers in the synchronous and asynchronous environments was an expectation. One student reported that she collaborated and interacted the most in the discussion area in D2L. However, the partner activity "did not work well for collaboration as there weren't clear enough guidelines for communication expectations." It is a fine line between articulating expectations and overwhelming students with details. Students also need to be self-directed in meeting the expectations. They need to understand the impact if they opt not to participate and how it affects others in the class. Developing a greater understanding of learning within a CoI framework can be a new approach to learning for some students.

Another expectation in the online environment is timely instructor feedback. The instructor needs to have an online presence and establish a system for responding to students. It is somewhat challenging in that the instructor does not want to dominate the conversations or be online constantly providing feedback. Yet not having a presence or responding affects a student's online learning experience. A student in Cohort Four attributed her success in the orientation program to the instructor: "Her calm e-vibe was clear from the beginning and she listened well to our feedback. She created and held a functional learning space for the rest of us and I thank her for that." Providing timely feedback and being appropriately responsive to students help them to learn and move forward in their orientation.

Development of Confidence

Students indicated that they had become more aware of and developed understandings and skills that would help them to be more successful in their online orientation programs. They identified such skills and strategies as managing time and creating schedules, learning how to use new technologies, improving their computer skills, learning to navigate D2L and Adobe Connect, and collaborating online. As noted by one student six months after the orientation program, time management and self-regulation were two key skills for her. In terms of time management, "It just made me aware of what was to come. It prepared me in knowing what was going to be happening in the upcoming courses." In terms of self-regulation,

It made me realize I needed to prioritize and understand that certain sacrifices were going to have to be made, and certain things that I used to do had to be put aside until the coursework was done. I just prepared myself for knowing that there would be four or five hours in one day to write a paper and to focus on a paper and reading.

This student from Cohort One had also completed the six-month interview. She commented on her confidence about learning in an online environment:

I wouldn't say [that I am] 100% comfortable. I still am learning how to manage my time. Some weeks it's good, where I just know that on Monday I need to login and look at everything and make sure I'm up to it. But, if you don't have the drive and the momentum and you get tired, it will fall by the wayside. It's just constantly reminding myself to keep checking. I'd say I'm more comfortable since doing the orientation and doing some of the courses.

Students gained confidence both in using technology and in learning online through the activities required in the orientation program. For example, they spoke about gaining confidence in learning to use or enhancing their use of the technology within a safe environment. For some students, this environment allowed them to learn how to use different technologies (e.g., the checklist feature in D2L) without the fear of seeming to be inadequate to their peers and the instructor. The safe and judgment-free environment was well received by students. One remarked that the course "calm[ed] my nerves" and "built up my confidence." Another commented that "it was completely well worth the 10 days of commitment to get to a level of comfort with the tools."

In the follow-up interview six months after the orientation program, one student described how much more prepared she was for her graduate courses: "I think I was more prepared because the tips and tricks and the best practices that were provided in the orientation really helped me in getting myself organized for the courses." One strategy that she learned was to review the course outline before the start of the course. She noted all of the deadlines in her calendar and put reminders there one week before the due dates in order to promote self-regulation and organization. Another best practice that this student used "was to really reach out to speak to my prof or instructor if there was [sic] any kind of conflicts or I needed any more time in advance to do that. . . . I was prepared after taking the orientation." Overall, then, we found that the orientation program provided students new to online learning with opportunities to develop an awareness of what would be expected with online study and to develop confidence using the various features and strategies to support their learning.

Implications for Practice

In a review of and reflection on the findings, three implications for practice emerged. Each implication is reflective of one of the following three levels of inquiry: micro (teaching and learning), meso (institutional and collegial), and macro (global and theoretical).

Microlevel

At the microlevel, given the variance in graduate student skills with technology and prior experience with online learning, it is difficult to create an orientation program that meets the expectations of all students in terms of pacing and strategies. For example, some students advanced through the orientation program quickly, whereas others needed more time and sought more strategies to support their learning. "The delivery of an online course may be very foreign and difficult for a student who does not have a technical background" (Mensch, 2017, p. 2), so it is imperative that students with predominantly novice skills be oriented to both academic and technical expectations of online learning to ensure retention and success. Students who advance more quickly through the orientation might have more experience with the online learning environment. Mensch reported "that higher level students have probably had more experience in online classes" (p. 5). Alternatively, at an institution of higher education where there is no orientation program for online students, "many students' early experiences in an online classroom are done through trial and error" (p. 5). Mensch stated that, "If the university was to mandate that all online learners first pass a training course of what is expected from an online student, it is suffice to expect that the retention rates would improve" (p. 5).

What became evident in our study was that students might not have reached the highest skill levels. This reinforced the importance of integrating differentiated instructional strategies to accommodate better the array of adult learning needs:

> Differentiated instruction is responsive instruction. It occurs as teachers become increasingly proficient in understanding their students as individuals, increasingly comfortable with the meaning and structure of the disciplines they teach, and increasingly expert at teaching flexibly in order to match instruction to student needs with the goal of maximizing the potential of each learner in a given area. (Tomlinson, 2003, pp. 2–3)

From what we have learned, we need to be more intentional in how we provide additional support for students who require a greater degree of help. It would also be beneficial to allow more flexibility in pacing for those more advanced with the technology in future iterations of the program.

The work of an instructor in an orientation program is magnified in the sense that she or he not only needs to facilitate learning but also must be quick to problem-solve (e.g., troubleshooting issues with technology). Students look to the instructor as the one who demonstrates confidence and effective practice. The instructor is a role model during the orientation program. Yet it can be a stressful situation in which the instructor is vulnerable to criticism given that things might not function as well technically as one would like. The opportunity for co-teaching thus provides a forum in which "two or more individuals ... [can] come together in a collaborative relationship for the purpose of shared work ... [and] achieving what none could have done alone" (Wenzlaff et al., 2002, p. 14). We would strive to have both instructors actively involved in planning and facilitating the synchronous and asynchronous learning environments of the orientation program. Our goal would be a seamless approach. "From the students' perspective, there is no clearly defined leader—both share the instruction, are free to interject information, and [are] available to assist students and answer questions" (Bacharach, Heck, & Dahlberg, 2008, p. 11).

Meso-level

At the meso-level, students entering the orientation program expect realistic practice that models what they will be doing in their online courses. Tensions exist in orientation programs since some students expect more than an initial focus on online learning—that is, they expect to be oriented to graduate studies (e.g., tasks reflective of coursework). Although the research literature identifies the positive outcomes for orientation programs (Cho, 2012; Koehnke, 2013), it focuses on addressing the orientation of students to a new program as opposed to a singular focus on learning in an online environment. The instructor of the orientation should ideally have experience with graduate online teaching and be able to orient students in terms of the online learning environment and how and why the technology is used for various aspects of the course and in the program. At the same time, the instructor must be able to speak to and create experiences that reflect the nature of graduate learning. In an online orientation program, one learning outcome should be that "students learn how to write and read in an academic, online environment" (Fotia et al., 2010). In the orientation program, students learn what is expected, for example, of their discussion posts and responses, which they will utilize in their academic online courses.

The selection of an instructor or a team of instructors who can create and support both experiences will enhance the orientation for all students. In his study, Hew (2016) reported that the "accessibility and passion" of instructors comprise the second most important factor that students consider "in terms of their perceived ability to promote a satisfying or engaging online learning experience" (p. 321). The institution or faculty therefore needs to ensure philosophical alignment between program and orientation.

Macro-level

At the macro-level, careful consideration needs to be given to online student orientation programs as more and more institutions of higher education offer online programs. Online orientation programs will help adult students to become familiar with the culture of online learning. A lack of orientation programs for online learning can put students at a disadvantage. Derby and Smith's (2004) research suggested that students are more successful when they are offered orientation sessions for their online courses. With such sessions, Cho (2012) identified two issues. First, "the process of developing an OSO [online student orientation] is rarely shared among institutions" (p. 1052). Learning from and sharing with others help all institutions to support student learning better. Engaging in knowledge mobilization to share such practices helps other institutions to design and facilitate their online orientation programs for students. Second, it is commonly thought that such programs "focus more on administrative and technological issues than on students' learning in online environments perhaps because online orientation programs are not systematically designed from the perspective of student learning" (pp. 1052–1053). Institutions that design such programs need to examine the designs from students' perspectives to determine the necessary supports for students to develop their capacities to be successful in the online learning environment.

Limitations of the Study

Although there have been positive student findings from the four iterations of the study, limitations remain. First, there was a low rate of participation in the study. The low rate might indicate that students had a high level of satisfaction with the orientation program and opted not to provide formal feedback through the various data collection sources for the study. Information gleaned from the data cannot be generalized. We are using the information to inform the design. However, we are cautious not to create generalizations. Second, we are reporting on the first year of the implementation and the redesign that has occurred. As we move into the second year of the study, it will be important to continue the investigation of each iteration and to affirm what is working well and what needs enhancement. Third, there is an emerging tension in the interpretation of the purpose of the Designing for Success program. It has been created to familiarize students with online learning within one faculty's approach to graduate programs. We have tried to articulate clearly that low-stakes tasks are implemented to develop confidence and competence in online graduate learners. However, some of the participants expected that they would receive a more professional orientation to learning at the graduate level. Greater attention needs to be paid to the articulation of the purpose of the Designing for Success program both in advertising it for students and in the D2L and Adobe Connect learning environments.

Directions for Future Research

With the implementation of the second year of the two-year study, continued refinement through iterations of the study using DBR will occur. In terms of diversifying the study, it would be helpful to implement the orientation program in other graduate-level discipline areas. With an expanded offering of undergraduate online programs, this orientation program could be modified and implemented to support them. Studying the program to see if there are differences between graduate and undergraduate students in terms of orientation is important.

Given the focus on design using the UDL principles, it is important to investigate further the role and impact of multimedia in student learning. Beyond informational videos, the use of multimedia in both online discussions and assessments would help a shift away from the traditional text-based approach. A question to explore regards the nature of the learning that occurs when video is purposefully integrated into the learning in ways that foster greater interaction among students, peers, and the instructor. The potential and impact of intentional integration of multimedia in online environments for multiple means of engagement and representation need to be studied further.

Conclusion

The Designing for Success orientation program aims to orient graduate students to online learning. Through the iterative design process using DBR, we have implemented an evidence-informed and responsive practice to prepare students to be confident in working online while developing a deeper understanding of learning within technology-enabled online environments. The data inform not only the design of the online orientation but also the facilitation of online teaching and learning. Through this research-informed program, students are given the opportunity to develop and implement practical skills and knowledge needed for learning online. Interacting in a low-risk environment also helps them to develop expectations of what it means to be an online graduate learner in today's technology-enabled context of higher education.

Acknowledgements

This research was funded by a University of Calgary Teaching and Learning Grant.

References

Adams Becker, S., Cummins, M., Davis, A., Freeman, A., Hall Giesinger, C., & Ananthanarayanan, V. (2017). *NMC horizon report: 2017 higher education edition.* Austin, TX: New Media Consortium. Retrieved from https://www.unmc.edu/elearning/_documents/NMC_HorizonReport_2017.pdf

Allen I. E., & Seaman J. (2017). *Digital learning compass: Distance education enrollment report 2017.* Retrieved from https://onlinelearningsurvey.com/reports/digtiallearningcompassenrollment2017.pdf

Allen I. E., & Seaman J., with Poulin, R., & Straut, T. T. (2016). *Online report card: Tracking online education in the United States.* Retrieved from https://files.eric.ed.gov/fulltext/ED572777.pdf

Anderson, T., Rourke, L., Garrison, D., & Archer, W. (2001). Assessing teaching presence in a computer conferencing context. *Journal of Asynchronous Learning Networks, 5*(2), 1–17.Retrieved from http://cde.athabascau.ca/coi_site/documents/Anderson_Rourke_Garrison_Archer_Teaching_Presence.pdf

Bacharach, N., Heck, T. W., & Dahlberg, K. (2008). Co-teaching in higher education. *Journal of College Teaching & Learning, 5*(3), 9–16.

Bawa, P. (2016). Retention in online courses: Exploring issues and solutions—A literature review. *SAGE Open, 1*(11). doi:10.1177/2158244015621777

Cambridge-Williams, T., Winsler, A., Kitsantas, A., & Bernard, E. (2013). University 100 orientation courses and living-learning communities boost academic retention and graduation via enhanced self-efficacy and self-regulated learning. *Journal of College Student Retention: Research, Theory and Practice, 15*(2), 243–268.

CAST. (2018). Universal design for learning guidelines version 2.0. Retrieved from http://udlguidelines.cast.org/

Cho, M. H. (2012). Online student orientation in higher education: A developmental study. *Educational Technology Research and Development, 60*(6), 1051–1069. doi:10.1007/s11423-012-9271-4

Chu, R. J-C., & Tsai, C-C. (2009). Self-directed learning readiness, Internet self-efficacy and preferences towards constructivist Internet-based learning environments among higher-aged adults. *Journal of Computer Assisted Learning, 25*(5), 489–501. doi:10.1111/j.1365-2729.2009.00324.x

Curran, S. (2014). Traditional and non-traditional learners in online education. *The EvoLLLution: A Destiny Solutions Illumination,* February 26, 2014. Retrieved from https://evolllution.com/revenue-streams/distance_online_learning/traditional-non-traditional-learners-online-education/

Derby, D. C., & Smith, T. (2004). An orientation course and community college retention. *Community College Journal of Research and Practice, 28*(9), 763–773. doi:10.1080/10668920390254771

Donovan, T., Bates, T., Seaman J., Mayer D., Martel, E., Paul, R., . . . Poulin, R. (2019). Tracking online and distance education in Canadian Universities and Colleges: 2018. Canadian National Survey of Online and Distance Education. Canadian Digital Learning Research Association. Retrieved from https://onlinelearningsurveycanada.ca/publications-2018/

Garrison, D. R. (2006). Online collaboration principles. *Journal of Asynchronous Learning Networks, 10*(1), 25–34.

Garrison, D. R., & Anderson, T. (2003) *E-learning in the 21st century: A framework for research and practice.* New York, NY: RoutledgeFalmer.

Garrison, D. R., Anderson, T., & Archer, W. (2000). Critical inquiry in a text-based environment: Computer conferencing in higher education. *Internet and Higher Education, 11*(2), 1–14. Retrieved from http://cde.athabascau.ca/coi_site/documents/Garrison_Anderson_Archer_Critical_Inquiry_model.pdf

Garrison, D. R., & Cleveland-Innes, M. (2005). Facilitating cognitive presence in online learning: Interaction is not enough. *American Journal of Distance Education, 19*(3), 133–148.

Gillett-Swan, J. (2017). The challenges of online learning: Supporting and engaging the isolated learner. *Journal of Learning Design, 10*(1), 20–30.

Hew, K. F. (2016). Promoting engagement in online courses: What strategies can we learn from three highly rated MOOCs. *British Journal of Educational Technology, 47*, 320–341.

Johnson, C., & Lock, J. (2018). Making multimedia meaningful: Outcomes of student assessment in online learning. In E. Langran & J. Borup (Eds.), *Proceedings of Society for Information Technology & Teacher Education International Conference* (pp. 1484–1491). Washington, DC: Association for the Advancement of Computing in Education (AACE).

Jones, K. (2013). Developing and implementing a mandatory online student orientation. *Journal of Asynchronous Learning Networks, 17*(1), 43–45.

Koehnke, P. J. (2013). *The impact of an online orientation to improve community college student retention in online courses: An action research study* (Doctoral dissertation). Retrieved from ProQuest Database. (Accession No. 20133568654)

McKenney, S., & Reeves, T. C. (2012). *Conducting educational design research.* New York, NY: Routledge.

Mensch, S. (2017). Improving distance education through student online orientation classes. *Global Education Journal, 2017* (1), 1–6.

Meyer, A., Rose, D. H., & Gordon, D. (2014). *Universal design for learning: Theory and practice.* Wakefield, MA: CAST.

Miles, M. B., Huberman, M., & Saldaña, J. (2013). *Qualitative data analysis: A methods sourcebook* (3rd ed.). Thousand Oaks, CA: Sage.

National Center on Universal Design for Learning. (2014). About UDL. Retrieved from http://www.udlcenter.org/aboutudl/whatisudl

Prensky, M. (2012). *From digital natives to digital wisdom: Hopeful essays for 21st century learning.* Thousand Oaks, CA: Corwin.

Saldaña, J. (2013). *The coding manual for qualitative researchers* (2nd ed.). Thousand Oaks, CA: Sage.

Tomlinson, C. A. (2003). *Fulfilling the promise of the differentiated classroom: Strategies and tools for responsive teaching.* Alexandria, VA: Association for Supervision and Curriculum Development.

Wang, F., & Hannafin, M. J. (2005). Design-based research and technology-enhanced learning environments. *Educational Technology Research and Development, 53*(4), 5–23.

Wenzlaff, T., Berak, L., Wieseman, K., Monroe-Baillargeon, A., Bacharach, N., & Bradfield-Kreider, P. (2002). Walking our talk as educators: Teaming as a best practice. In E. Guyton & J. Rainer (Eds.), *Research on meeting and using standards in the preparation of teachers* (pp. 11–24). Dubuque, IA: Kendall-Hunt Publishing.

The Effective Use of Text, Visuals, and Audio in Online Graduate Learning

Jane Costello, Pam Phillips, Denise Carew, and Daph Crane

In this chapter, we share the reflections and experiences of four senior instructional designers (SIDs) as a form of self-study (Crafton, 2005; Grant & Hurd, 2010) at Memorial University of Newfoundland (Memorial). In our work, numerous instructional design approaches, including design considerations in using text, visuals, and audio in graduate online courses, emerged over time from literature reviews and discourses with content authors and fellow SIDs. These approaches and considerations might be relevant to others involved in online program or course development in higher education. Much of the material presented is also relevant to blended course offerings. We present a critical examination of considerations of and strategies for media and associated technologies in selecting an appropriately balanced mix of text, visuals, and voice for teaching and learning; the use of a team-based approach; examples of successfully implemented media blends; the role that SIDs played; and the supports provided to content authors in designing online graduate courses.

Design and Development of Online Graduate Courses at Memorial

We work at Memorial as SIDs in the Centre for Innovation in Teaching and Learning (CITL), which supports the development and delivery of courses and programs at the university. CITL also supports the implementation and administration of technologies that enhance teaching and learning both on campus and online. Memorial embarked on distance education in 1967 with credit-based distance courses offered at smaller centres around the province. Its long history of distance education influenced how the learning design and development team is structured today. This team has grown and evolved with the changing needs of students and instructors.

SIDs work across multiple academic units—any faculty, discipline, school, or department—as opposed to being assigned to just one. SIDs are paired with content authors (faculty members or lecturers) to develop and redevelop fully online undergraduate and graduate courses. The online course design and development process at Memorial can take up to nine months depending on the nature of the course. Memorial uses the Quality Matters Higher Education Rubric to guide course design and development and as a quality check. The academic unit identifies the content author, who enters into an agreement with the university, through CITL, to develop the online courses. Content authors might or might not teach the online courses. However, they are encouraged to use any content developed for their online courses in their on-campus teaching. SIDs also provide consulting services for on-campus courses when needed.

CITL's Approach to Online Course Design

Team-Based Design

A collaborative, team-based approach is used in developing online courses. This approach capitalizes on a broad range of skills and expertise. A typical course development team includes the content author; senior instructional designer; assistant to instructional designer (AID); copyright officer; video producer, including related team members, such as camerapersons and editors; and multimedia specialists. The SID is the team leader. The AID is responsible for web design and assisting in researching educational technologies. The multimedia developer creates dynamic digital animations, illustrations, simulations, games, and interactive media that address challenging concepts using storyboards developed by the instructional designer, AID, and content author. Audio and video production needs are taken care of by the video producer and her team. In some cases, the producer collaborates with multimedia developers on multimedia learning objects. Other team members, such as programmers and library staff, are added when required.

A Designing for Learning Perspective

Instructional design decisions "have a direct impact on delivery and influence student learning and engagement of all participants in the course" (Costello, 2013, p. 142). "Designing *for* learning" (Jones, Dirckinck-Holmfeld, & Lindström, 2006; Laurillard, 2012) is recommended. This relational view acknowledges that "designers have limited direct control over how their designs are enacted" (Jones et al., 2006, p. 51). Designers cannot design learning, for they "cannot control that which learners bring to the learning, only what is offered for them to use"; learners determine how the learning unfolds (Costello, 2013, p. 141). Designers can design learning environments. Activities for students to engage with content and resources can be designed in an online course, and assessment schemes can include the provision of marks for participation in activities or the assessment of their learning of course topics. Ultimately, it is up to individual learners if, how, and when they choose to participate in the learning experience designed. Ball and Cohen (1999) remind us of the essential need for continual "thoughtful discussion among learners and teachers [since] it is the chief vehicle for analysis, criticism and communication of ideas, practices, and values" (p. 13). Part of the responsibility of SIDs is to design venues for "analysis, criticism and communication."

Instructional Design as Reflective Practice

Similar to teachers who reflect on the impacts of their teaching practices on students and use their reflections to improve their practices, a reflective practice approach (Schön, 1983) is used in instructional design work.

SIDs continuously challenge preconceived constructs and explore innovative ways to enhance course design. In doing so, the examination of SID practice, while designing courses, builds on the foundation of their skills.

SIDs strive to be reflexive of the impacts of design decisions and recommendations (Grant & Hurd, 2010) for content authors, faculty members, lecturers, and students. One area where this is accomplished is through the thoughtful, critical examination of the instructional design considerations when selecting the most appropriate media mixes: text, visuals, and audio. Relatedly, SIDs identify challenges and questions that emerge from discourses with content authors, literature reviews, environmental scans, and research forays to find solutions to these challenges and questions. The research often involves evaluation of instructional or technological interventions in learning events and activities in the courses on which SIDs are working. The results of discourse and research are then shared with team members, other faculty members, lecturers, and SIDs to expand and improve the knowledge of instructional design and course design. In doing this, SIDs foster a community of practice to increase knowledge of course design (Wenger, 1998, 2015; Wenger & Wenger-Trayner, 2015) within the community while creating the best learning opportunities for students.

Factors that Influence Online Course Design

Course design must allow students to use their talents and help them to build on their weaknesses. This is done through careful planning and built-in guidance that encourages learner-centredness and deep learning (Fink, 2003). Knowing the learning population is one of the first steps in designing a course, in conjunction with context analysis (Stöter, Bullen, Zawacki-Richter, & von Prümmer, 2014). According to Knowles (1984), the careful planning of adult learning environments involves a strong overview of the course, including (1) identification of needs; (2) formulated learning goals, with well-defined expectations; (3) appropriate selection of resources (not too elementary but not too complex) with appropriate use of media that support a variety of learning strategies; and (4) evaluation of learning outcomes. These are essentially the basic tasks or steps in designing an online graduate course. Ally (2008) discussed components of effective online learning that should be considered when designing online learning materials such as learner preparation, activities, interaction, and transfer (p. 32). These, too, are incorporated.

SIDs' reflections on design practice have highlighted several factors that influence online course design and help students to be successful. Fink (2003) suggested that these situational factors relate to learning goals, teaching and learning activities, and feedback and assessment. Major factors are identified as the most relevant for discussion with the content author and development team during the planning phase of an online graduate course. These are discussed below.

Characteristics of Graduate Learners

Stöter et al. (2014) provided a summary of literature related to the characteristics of adult learners in higher education. Graduate students differ from undergraduate students in more than simply being older and more mature. Graduate students are organized, self-motivated, experienced, persistent, independent, computer literate, research skill orientated, able to demonstrate self-efficacy, and capable of being self-regulatory in their learning. Additionally, they accept more responsibility for their learning in terms of reading course material and contributing to, reflecting on, discussing, and assessing their learning experiences. This might seem like a tall order for any graduate student. However, any mature student will recognize that being stronger in one quality can make up for a weakness in another. Breunig (2005), referencing Frier (1970) and Hooks (1994), noted that "students are not empty vessels, but rather are individuals with life experience and knowledge, situated within their own cultural, class, racial, historical, and gender contexts" (pp. 117–118). Grant and Hurd (2010) recommended helping students to "develop skills and processes which are of relevance to their course of study as well as everyday life" (p. 5) rather than to learn content in isolation. Graduate students should build on their wealth of knowledge and experience.

Adult Learning in Online Environments

Most adults learn through a combination of activities in the cognitive, affective, and behavioural learning domains. Both the behaviourist theory and the cognitivist theory have been considered, and will continue to be, when designing online courses (Ally, 2008). Constructivist and constructionist theories are best suited to designing technology-supported, student-centred learning environments. Today the human dimension of online learning is of particular interest with a move from a technology-orientated to a pedagogical-orientated course; there is a "shift from what *technology* could do to what *learners* could do, to how they would enable their learning through the technology available to them" (Conrad, 2014, p. 383). Student-centred learning includes the ideals of "valuing student voice, promoting and practicing dialogue, shared decision-making, and valuing their previous experiences and their ways of knowing" (Breunig, 2005, p. 117). These learning environments promote active student engagement, group work, experiential learning, problem-based learning, social learning, co-construction of knowledge, and self-directed learning.

Papert (1990) stated that constructivism is the "idea that knowledge is something you build in your head. Constructionism reminds us that the best way to do that is to build something tangible—something outside of your head—that is also personally meaningful" (Constructivism section, para. 3). Technology can be used as a cognitive tool to construct rather than passively acquire knowledge, with the support of each other and the instructor.

Faculty Member Readiness

Faculty members and lecturers indicate their readiness by exhibiting a comfort level with technology. They are familiar with online facilitation and available to develop online courses. This readiness affects design decisions related to the learning activities and resources selected for inclusion (Bates, 2015; Dysart & Weckerle, 2015; Palloff & Pratt, 2011; Phillips, Hammett, St. Croix, White, & Wicks, 2017; Robyler & Doering, 2013).

Phillips et al. (2017) conducted a study of the technological, pedagogical, and content knowledge (TPACK) of faculty members and lecturers at Memorial using the instrument created by Schmidt, Baran, Thompson, Koehler, Mishra, and Shin (2009). The TPACK study asked participants to document their experiences with technology integration. The faculty members and lecturers surveyed noted that they changed their instructional strategies when teaching graduate students versus undergraduate students. They preferred to design their graduate courses to allow students to utilize their prior knowledge and experience as means of engaging in deeper learning. Knowing and effectively supporting their students can deter content authors from simply using "technology for disseminating information, rather than being challenged to use it in ways that assist students in building knowledge" (Dysart & Weckerle, 2015, p. 257). As facilitators, faculty members guide students through course content and the learning experience, thereby empowering them to embrace responsibility for their learning.

Geo-Socio-Economic Considerations

Campbell and Schwier (2014) suggested that the "sociocultural, geopolitical, and economic contexts" (p. 347) of the institution of higher education can influence course design decisions, including media selection and use. Contexts such as a growing international student body, considerations of indigenization, curricular goals of the institution or department, accreditation requirements, and accessibility standards do not drive course design but might influence it. Online learning environments can become spaces for students to effectively communicate in and contribute to analytical and global dialogues (Lundy & Stephens, 2015, p. 1058), thereby bringing their opinions to the world and exposing themselves to real-world relevance.

There is a growth in students entering graduate-level studies directly from the undergraduate level. This is possibly a product of the economy and credential creep (Bertrand, 2006). Many students see the attainment of higher credentials as a way to maintain their current employment positions or become eligible for promotions or pay increases.

Economic constraints at institutions of higher learning can influence course offerings, staffing levels, library holdings, and technology offerings and support systems. Academic support units, like CITL, must work within such constraints. Creativity often alleviates the challenges associated with these economic constraints.

Interaction

Interaction is active or passive communication with another student, the content, or the instructor (Moore, 1989). Anderson (2008) suggested that individuals' perspectives, attained via interaction, are central to constructivist-based learning. Interactivity fosters the development of learning communities and is achievable using multiple modalities (pp. 55–56). One model commonly used to design and explain learning communities is the Community of Inquiry (CoI) framework (Garrison, Anderson, & Archer, 2000), which highlights social presence and interaction in online courses. The basis of the framework is that learning occurs within the online community through the interaction of three core elements of presence: social, cognitive, and teaching (Garrison, 2009; Garrison et al., 2000).

The CoI facilitates the growth of an online community of practice supporting the development of "21st century learning skills (e.g. critical thinking, communication, collaboration)" (Phillips et al., 2017, p. 13), employing "social and participatory media" (Conole, 2014, p. 221). Although there is some debate about who originated the concept of Web 2.0, Aced (2013) noted that the term was coined by Di Nucci in 1999 and made popular by O'Reilly in 2003. By design, many Web 2.0 technologies make it easier for students to communicate and collaborate, and they provide new mechanisms for inquiry-based and exploratory learning (Conole & Alevizou, 2010; Evans & Haughey, 2014). Technology, such as Web 2.0 tools, makes communication and collaboration possible. The TPACK study conducted at Memorial revealed that, though there are many Web 2.0 tools for potential educational use, respondents did not seem to be aware of many of them. The study also revealed that newer technologies were not being used optimally (Phillips et al., 2017, p. 41). It is important for SIDs and content authors to explore how technologies can enhance teaching and learning.

Web 2.0 tools can facilitate interaction, providing "unprecedented access to information, new means of learner engagement, and dynamic asynchronous and distance learning options" (Lambert, Erickson, Alhramelah, Rhoton, Lindbeck, & Sammons, 2014, p. 7). A study on the use of Twitter (Rohr & Costello, 2015; Rohr, Costello, & Hawkins, 2015) revealed that it can be an effective means to encourage engagement and community in online classes. If designed appropriately, then some activities can encourage students to think critically while gaining exposure to authentic activities that they undertake in their daily lives, such as blogging, vlogging, and writing and/or presenting papers.

Copyright

Faculty members and lecturers are responsible for ensuring that all content not their own is identified and that appropriate permissions are obtained. This content includes materials that might be protected by copyright. Reviewing copyright guidelines and possibly linking to resources or creating your own are discussed in the planning phase. Copyright officers at Memorial assist content authors with this task.

Media

Consider all media formats—text, visual, and audio—early in the planning process. They can be combined in many ways to produce other formats, such as multimedia and video. These media types, their affordances, and their potential uses are discussed in the next section and constitute the focus of the remainder of this chapter.

Media Implementation at Memorial in Online Graduate Courses

Defining Media

Media comprise "anything that carries information between a source and a receiver" (Smaldino, Lowther, Russell, & Mims, 2015, p. 4), such as text, visuals, and audio, thereby facilitating communication and learning. Technology includes the tools, devices, software, and applications used to help develop and communicate the message. They stand alone "until commanded to do something or until they are activated or until a person starts to interact with the technology" (Bates, 2015, p. 201). Technology allows one to "control and integrate a variety of media" (Smaldino, Lowther, & Mims, 2019, p. 99), for example using a smartphone to access course content in the learning management system (LMS) or recording and editing a video using software.

Media and technologies give learners opportunities to develop digital, information, and visual literacy skills. Kereluik, Mishra, Fahnoe, and Terry (2013) defined digital and information literacy as the "ability to effectively and thoughtfully evaluate, navigate, and construct information using a range of digital technologies"; it also means effectively to "seek out, organize, and process information from a variety of media . . . [and] the responsible use of technology and media" (p. 130). Visual literacy, a component of digital and information literacy, involves being able "effectively [to] find, interpret, evaluate, use and create images and visual media" (Lundy & Stephens, 2015, p. 1058). The stronger a user's skills in visual literacy, the more benefit she or he can derive from it.

Types of Media and Technologies

The media used in online graduate courses include text, visuals, and audio or combinations thereof in forms of video and multimedia. It is important for content authors and instructors to be familiar with each type so that the best media and technology are selected for the learning situation.

Text is the most common way to present content. Content includes, but is not limited to, the course syllabus, module notes, lectures, and presentations. Course designers can organize, format, and present text in a number of ways using an LMS or other online technologies, such as blogs. Text can be presented alone or complemented with visuals that relate to the content.

Learners typically can recall and apply more information when resources include text and visuals. Visuals "engage students in the learning process, and images stimulate their critical and creative thinking" (Aisami, 2015, p. 542). They help to scaffold learning by enabling students to make connections and build on their background knowledge sets. Digital cameras and scanners ease capturing of visuals (Smaldino, Lowther, & Russell, 2012, p. 202), and editing software facilitates the manipulation of images. Levin's five instructional classifications for visuals include (1) decoration, to make instruction more appealing and motivating; (2) representation, to convey information quickly and easily; (3) organization, to help show relationships; (4) interpretation, to help explain difficult concepts; and (5) transformation, to help students remember information (Lohr, 2008, pp. 15–17). Well-designed visuals allow students to select or notice important information, structure information, and integrate new information and prior knowledge (Lohr, 2008). Kosslyn (1980) noted that visuals enable students to imagine things not evident in the content, thereby facilitating problem solving and comprehension.

Audio can be used to present content in ways that engage learners and make it easier for them to process the content. Audio involves hearing and listening. Similar to visual communication, an audio message is "effectively composed by a sender and deciphered by a receiver to develop the meaning" (Smaldino et al., 2012, p. 210). The ability of the instructor to organize and present an audio message, the technology chosen to record and play the audio, and the ability of the students to interpret the message are all factors that influence the effectiveness of audio in teaching and learning (Smaldino et al., 2012). Some common types of digital audio recording include music, voice, sound effects, and sounds in nature, which can be created for or accessed through a CD, streaming, a podcast, or Internet radio (Smaldino et al., 2019, p. 174).

Feedback on assignments provided via voice can empower student learning (Costello & Crane, 2015). Instructors can make notes while reviewing the student's work, record their feedback immediately via audio, and send it to the student. Students hear their instructors providing constructive criticism of their work using a medium that reduces the potential for misunderstanding of intention since intonation is discernible. Ice, Curtis, Phillips, and Wells (2007) found that providing audio feedback took less time than providing textual feedback and that students perceived it to be of better quality. Some learning management systems have built-in, audio-based feedback tools. Instructors can also use their own devices to record audio feedback and deliver it to students.

Video provides a higher level of fidelity than audio because it often combines visual and audio elements, possibly text, transitions, and special effects, all in a media format. Some video features that can help to enhance learning include "the ability to depict motion, show processes, offer risk-free observation, provide dramatizations and support skill learning" (Smaldino et al., 2019, p. 181). Videos can be streamed (embedded) in the online learning environment, or links can be provided for students to access them. Both video and audio are considered to be portable and multimodal.

Elin (2001), citing Feldman (1997, p. 24), stated that multimedia comprise the "seamless integration of data, text, sound, and images of all kinds with a single, digital information environment" (p. 4). Elin added that multimedia "can be accessed interactively by the user" (p. 4). The SIDs at CITL generally consider multimedia to be the combination of two or more media produced as an embedded stand-alone object. Interactive multimedia allow learners to engage with the content, using more than just navigational controls. Learners can respond to and manipulate aspects of the object, such as in a drag-and-drop activity. Multimedia that move on a timeline, allowing learners to use navigational controls to play, pause, and stop them, can be considered video or animation rather than interactive multimedia. It is important to keep in mind the twelve principles of good design proposed by Mayer (2005, 2009, 2014) when designing and using multimedia for learning.

Mixed media are two or more media combined on a web page, on a presentation slide, or in a document. Mixes of text, visuals, and audio can be used in lieu of a video mini-lecture. Having audio in the mix allows students to benefit from the nuances of intonation in the instructor's voice, thus helping to reduce the likelihood that the speaker's intentions will be misunderstood. Although video is generally seen as more favourable than audio, images with text and possibly an audio file can be a more effective way to present content. It is important that mixed media are designed with a specific purpose in mind and are not overused.

Presentation software helps students and instructors to produce and present content and instructional materials in multiple ways using combinations of text, visuals, and audio. Blogs and many other interactive social technologies allow instructors and students to post their thoughts related to a course topic and comment on others' posts, thereby generating discussion and co-constructing knowledge (Rohr & Costello, 2015). An ePortfolio allows and encourages learners to collect, reflect on, and share their work incorporating a variety of media in their learning (Baskin, 2008).

Synchronous online technologies can be used to bring instructors, students, and guests together for presentations, demonstrations, and dialogues. These sessions can be recorded so that students unable to attend them can watch the recordings later. Many students take advantage of recorded presentations to review material before tests and exams or as resources for their assignments. Johnson (2010) noted a similar result from a lecture capture study at Memorial. Students can also use synchronous tools to communicate and collaborate on course work outside scheduled sessions. In Memorial's LMS, the synchronous tool is embedded, thereby eliminating the need for additional links or passwords.

Many students have difficulty understanding what it means to reflect and be critical learners—to read, write, or think critically (Quitadamo & Kutz, 2007). King, Wood, and Mines (1990) claimed that there is little evidence of critical thinking at the undergraduate level and even less at the graduate level. Since critical thinking is often unfamiliar to students, they might need information, instruction, and activities that explain what it is and is not as well as means to practise and develop their critical learning skills. Media and technologies, when appropriately selected, can enhance understanding and help students to perfect these skills. Models or samples can spark creativity and interest and set expectations.

Selecting Media and Technologies

The effectiveness of online learning is influenced, in part, by careful planning and selection of the appropriate resources, including media and technologies. Bates (2015) identified content, content structure, and skills as elements to consider in choosing media (p. 228). Learning outcomes determine the content and skills that are desirable for students to develop. The nature of the course, teaching philosophy, learning environment, and amount of material presented inform content structure. It is important to analyze the learning situation and learning outcomes and to select instructional strategies, media, and technologies that can help students to achieve the outcomes. Some activities can be completed better without media and technologies. Prensky (2001), as reported by Anderson (2008), suggested that "different learning outcomes" are best attained by using "particular learning activities"; we learn, for example,

- behaviours through imitation, feedback, and practice
- creativity through playing

- facts through association, drill, memory, and questions
- judgement through reviewing cases, asking questions, making choices, receiving feedback, and coaching
- language through imitation, practice, and immersion
- observation through viewing examples and feedback
- procedures through imitation and practice
- processes through system analysis, deconstruction, and practice
- reasoning through puzzles, problems, and examples
- skills (physical or mental) through imitation, feedback, continuous practice, and increasing challenge
- speeches or performance roles by memorization, practice, and coaching
- theories through logic, explanation, and question. (pp. 62–63)

Although some media and technologies are better suited to specific learning situations, no one medium or technology is ideal for all situations (Bates, 2015; Martin, 2008). The successful implementation of media and technologies "depends on [our] ability to appreciate the requirements within the learning situation and select and use [them] to meet those needs" (Bower, 2008, p. 14). This reinforces the need for pedagogy to drive technology selection.

Although there are no rules about which specific medium and technology to use in any given situation, there are guidelines, rubrics, and models that can inform choices, for example Mayer's (2005, 2009, 2014) cognitive theory of multimedia learning, Koumi's (as referenced in Bates, 2015) xMOOCs (massive online open courses) video and print guide, Anstey and Watson's (2018) Rubric for E-Learning Tool Evaluation, Bates's (2015) ACTIONS model, Martin's (2008) Instructional Indicators model, Bates's (2015) SECTIONS framework, and Mishra and Koehler's (2006) TPACK model. Using these resources, SIDs help content authors to choose the most appropriate medium for the learning situation and its outcome. This involves identifying the characteristics, educational affordances, and design considerations of various media and technologies and then evaluating each "against the learning goals and outcomes desired, while recognizing that a new educational medium or application might enable goals to be achieved that had not been previously considered possible" (Bates, 2015, p. 223). Choose the technology that allows you to create the media to match the instructional strategies that support student learning and intended learning outcomes.

Before looking at successful implementations of media and technologies, we provide a brief survey of some of their advantages and disadvantages. Some identified advantages include students' access to courses at their own convenience (time, place, and pace); cost effectiveness of delivery; increased accessibility; relative safety compared with some real-life situations; and savings in terms of data storage since less physical space is needed to house digital materials. Some identified disadvantages include unintended or unexpected perceptions of visual materials because of a lack of awareness of differences in students' backgrounds and cultures; unintentional infringement of copyright; concerns about privacy and security among both students and instructors; and the absence of tactile and olfactory experiences because they are not relayed by technology (Anderson, 2008; Bates et al. 2017; Brineley, 2014; Dick & Carey, 1996; Gagné, Briggs, & Wagner, 1992; Mantiri, 2014; Smith & Ragan, 1993). Additionally, the creation of some types of media can challenge resources in terms of cost, skill, technology, and time needed to create them.

Examples of Successful Implementation of Media and Technologies

Media and technologies are used in online graduate courses at Memorial to help present content, enhance interaction, facilitate demonstration or performance guidance, assess work and provide feedback, and promote reflection. These uses emerged over time in discussions about media in online courses with content authors, other team members, and fellow SIDs. A description of each use along with a discussion of concepts and specific examples is presented below. Many of the examples can be found in the provincial learning object repository hosted by Memorial, Linney (https://linney.mun.ca).

Presentation of Content

The amount and format or organization of the text-based content are critical to giving students the best opportunities to learn in an online course. Page upon page of plain text and long weekly reading lists can be unmotivating for students. Dividing content into units or chunks using appropriate headings aids flow and makes the content more manageable for students. The use of white space provides eye relief and helps with readability. A research project led by the Nielsen Norman Group (n.d.), looking at people's eye movements while engaging with a web page, revealed that people are more likely to read concise and accessible content presented objectively that can be scanned.

Using different media and technologies to present text-based content can make it easier for learners to process the content. Using illustrations to depict abstract concepts often difficult for students to grasp is an effective use of media. Adding images to text is not a guarantee, however, of effective learning or "an improvement in learning" (Mayer, 2005, p. 31). Text does not always present troublesome concepts or abstract ideas effectively. Content authors are reminded to think of course participants and their expected levels of knowledge when selecting the images and details required.

A frequent practice employed in presenting content is the use of audio or video clips to introduce the instructor and the course. The instructor records a welcoming message that sets the tone for the course. Audio and video should be recorded at a proper level, the voice should be audible and clear, and transcripts should be provided to listeners and viewers. Provide user controls where necessary. The use of lengthy presentations through audio or video recordings conveying content typically communicated in a traditional face-to-face class lecture (the Socratic method) is discouraged. A few basics to think about when preparing scripts or outlines for audio and video recordings are keep the script short, up to six minutes (Guo, Kim, & Rubin, 2014) and use a conversational style of language to portray an approachable instructor. Succinct, focused videos tend to deter pontification. Speak at a normal pace with enthusiasm. Table 4.1 includes examples of how text-based content has been effectively presented in online graduate courses at Memorial. Examples include timelines, maps, caricatures, audio recordings, et cetera.

Table 4.1 Examples of presentation of content.

Example	Use
Historical timeline	History—timelines were used to represent and organize major campaigns during the First World War and Second World War.
	Education—the history of online education was presented in a timeline.
Static map	French-language course—a map of the world was created to depict the *francophonie du monde*, demonstrating the extent of French culture around the world.
Analytical model	Business—a visual of the situational strategic management analysis process displayed the inter-relationships of its steps.
	Economics—analytical models were used to simplify complex processes.
Procedural diagram	Nursing—a diagram was used to illustrate a nursing procedure. Students used the diagram in learning and mastering the task.
Caricatures of Canadian explorers	English—visuals of authors/explorers were used to give students a glimpse of who they were, increasing social presence, engagement, and interest.
Comic strip	Human Kinetics and Recreation (HKR)—comic strips relayed stories of personal experience of inclusion.
Illustration	Education—a "genderbread person" was used as a safe way to increase understanding of gender in the classroom.
Audio welcome message	Various courses—the instructor recorded a welcome message for students, introducing himself or herself and setting the tone for the course.
Multipurpose multimedia object	Education—a mandala was used to illustrate a concept and as a navigational tool. Each area of the mandala had a specific meaning and, when clicked, revealed a unique module with its own learning outcomes, resources, activities, and assessment.

When presenting content, ensure that it is accurate. The object's design conveys its meaning clearly, making it easy to interpret and process. Objects should be clear and concise, free of extraneous information, and easy to scan and read. Consider both responsiveness and Universal Design for Learning (UDL) principles, see Chapter 3 for a discussion of UDL. Finally, ensure that copyright has been cleared for all items.

Interaction

Interaction with content, other students, teams, or instructors can take place asynchronously or synchronously using media and technologies, such as email, discussion, video, audio, chat technology, or web conferencing. Interactions with others foster and strengthen social presence. Interactions with content can take place in a content page, a specially designed multimedia item, or a technology such as a simulation. Examples of the effective use of media and technologies to enhance interaction in online graduate courses at Memorial are presented in Table 4.2. Discussion forums, guest speakers, and video assignments are some examples.

One means to incorporate, and hopefully increase, interaction in online courses is through the use of guest speakers. They provide many benefits to students, such as support, professional networking, alternative voices, and real-life experiences (Costello, 2013, 2014; Costello & Rohr, 2016). Costello (2013) studied their use and found that they can offer professional connections to students and instructors alike, bringing a form of enculturation to the learning community as they connect theoretical studies to daily applications in real life (p. 143). Costello (2013, 2014) warns that guests ill chosen can present issues. For example, there might be an expectation of reciprocation; they might not know how to relate to the students at their level; the nature of the course might not be understood; and ill-timed guests might not receive the attention that they deserve.

To generate good discussions, use provocative questions versus yes/no questions, and topics for podcasts or vlogs must be broad enough for each learner to offer a unique perspective or to build on comments by others. Decide if synchronous sessions are to be scheduled before registration begins. The schedule should be provided at registration or just as the course begins. Make an effort to involve students in selecting the sessions' dates and times. Include guidelines for recording video for those unable to attend the sessions. Synchronous sessions can be facilitated using a variety of platforms. CITL refers to them as online rooms.

Table 4.2 Examples of enhancing interaction.

Example	Use
Discussion forums	Various courses—students used discussion forums to discuss readings, to collaborate on various aspects of the courses, and to establish rapport with each other.
Virtual classes in online rooms	Various courses—real-time classes were held using online rooms.
Guest speaker	Education—a guest speaker participated via online rooms and discussion forums to explore issues related to teaching mathematics from philosophical and pedagogical perspectives, providing an alternative perspective on critical issues in mathematics.
Weekly podcasts	Education—instructor-created podcasts were provided to students, who used them and other resources to complete their weekly discussions and assignments.
Student-recorded video assignment	French-language course—students recorded a video in response to a question, offering an alternative to the written response in discussions.

Demonstration or Performance Guidance

When learning a complex task, students develop skills, procedures, and techniques. It is critical that they know how to approach a task and its associated steps. Students also require guidance when completing tasks, as well as evaluation and feedback, as they work to master those tasks. Table 4.3 shows how media have been used effectively for demonstration or performance guidance in online graduate courses at Memorial. The examples include screen shots, various videos, and the RSA Animates style animations (Royal Society for the encouragement of Arts, Manufactures and Commerce). RSA style animations are time-lapsed video recordings of a live drawing of a concept described with audio.

Instructors can support students in completing a task "at the exact moment that they need help performing [it]" (Lohr, 2008, p. 6) through the use of media and technologies. For example, recording videos of students as they perform tasks can be very effective when evaluating their work and providing feedback on it. Videos can also be used to prepare students for outcomes prior to experiencing actual situations. This approach is especially useful for complex tasks in which students might need to watch the demonstration multiple times.

Approaches to tackling problems can be illustrated. Animation can also be used for demonstration and practice guidance. Animated presentations involve taking a series of pictures and putting them together to form the illusion of continuous motion. They are designed to present information quickly, clearly, and engagingly. However, animations can often become monotonous and annoying rather than engaging and useful. Therefore, it is important that they are designed with a specific purpose in mind and are not overused. Also consider duration and adaptability to various devices, and be sure to include user controls such as pause and fast-forward.

The choice of media for demonstration or to provide performance guidance depends on what students need, their expected prior knowledge, and the level of proficiency required. Ask yourself the following questions:

- Is the video of high quality? For example, is it clear and sufficiently detailed to be useful to the learner?
- Does it therefore support learning?
- Will the video be streamed or downloaded?
- Where will it be hosted?
- Does the video player include controls allowing the learner to play, pause, stop the video, et cetera?
- Are close-ups of apparatus used effectively?
- What technology will you use to edit the video?
- Do animations, when used, solve a learning problem?

Videos that do not have user controls might require students to watch an entire video, or most of it, to find a specific piece of information. When video-recording, focus the camera on the speaker, and avoid background distractions. Use a mixture of close-ups and pan or wide shots and multiple cameras if possible. Attain releases from participants. If on location, then attain permits. Consider the use of transcripts, and ensure that copyright has been cleared where necessary.

Table 4.3 Examples of demonstration or performance guidance.

Example	Use
Screen shots of statistical software	Nursing—the instructor captured screen shots from within a statistical software package to help students use it and resolve issues encountered when completing software-based assignments.
Screencast video of a data analysis	Business—the instructor explained actions while recording them as she walked students through an analysis of data on the Internet. These videos were saved and added to the LMS to support students' learning.
Recorded lecture	Business——the instructor recorded lectures, using audio-narrated slides, to explain financial calculations, using a step-by-step process to guide students' attempts to solve complex problems. User controls allowed students to pause and replay the material as needed.
Demonstration of procedure	Nursing—video is used to demonstrate, with verbal explanations, how to complete a physical nursing procedure.
Videos of role-playing scenarios	Business—a series of role plays depicting ways to interview and not interview potential employees was recorded. Students watched the videos and then discussed the scenarios online with the class.
RSA-style animations	Human Kinetics—RSA-style animations were created to introduce students to the concepts of health promotion and stigma. A lighthearted manner helped to relay core concepts to students.

Assessment and Feedback

Assessment is "a task whereby learners demonstrate what they know or can do," whereas feedback is composed of "the comments provided to learners on their work" (Costello & Crane, 2015, p. 212). Faculty members and lecturers determine to what degree students have met the course learning objectives by assessing their work. Assessment is formative, ongoing throughout the course, or summative, at the end of the course.

Many faculty members and lecturers perceive the assessment of student work to be an onerous task. Using media and technologies to complete assessments and provide feedback, in a timely and efficient fashion, will help students to learn. Teachers who give students feedback on assessment items increased their teaching presence (Shea et al., 2011). Costello and Crane (2013, 2015) provided a comprehensive review of media and technologies suitable for student-centred feedback in online learning. They discussed the relationship between feedback methods and technologies. Their review also covered methods, technologies, and types of feedback. Table 4.4 provides examples of approaches to assessment and feedback effectively integrated into online graduate courses at Memorial.

In discussing assessment options with content authors, it is important to consider various types of assessment and to encourage the use of audio, video, or other media to provide electronic feedback. Automated tutors, auto-scoring of assignments, reflective networks, and self-check feedback methods require extra time for initial planning, design, and set-up. Content authors can perceive spending this extra time negatively, but these assessment and feedback methods generally provide time savings in the long run.

When using media for assessment and feedback, include questions for formative and summative assessments. Opportunities to apply material rather than simply to recall information are preferred, as is the ability of students to use feedback for continuous improvement.

Table 4.4 Examples of assessment and feedback.

Example	Use
Embedded questions	Nursing—questions embedded in the content provided students with opportunities to pause, reflect on readings, and apply new knowledge.

Blog assignment and feedback	Nursing—students wrote their final papers in phases using a blog, allowing the instructor to monitor their progress as work evolved. The instructor provided constructive feedback on each phase in an efficient manner.
Reading self-checks	HKR—biweekly self-checks, using the LMS quiz tool, were used to confirm that students read the required material and understood it sufficiently to apply it to novel situations. Follow-up class-wide discussions allowed the instructor to address troublesome areas.
Synchronous online classes	Second-language course—online rooms provided a means for instructors to meet with students synchronously to provide feedback on their pronunciation and grammar in the target language.
Audio-recorded assignment	Second-language course—students were encouraged to complete one of the three assignments as an audio assignment.
Audio-recorded feedback	HKR—an instructor recorded audio feedback on students' assignments instead of typing it, improving efficiency while providing a constructive response. The students were appreciative and thought that this approach was more personal.
Interactive practice exercises	Nursing—an array of engaging, interactive exercises, such as drag-and-drop and scenario-based true-and-false activities, were used to check and reinforce students' understanding of concepts.

Reflection

Reflection requires students to think about their learning in terms of where they are, where they have come from, and where they hope to arrive. It is useful as a self-assessment practice, requiring that students plan, monitor, and assess their understanding and performance. They can reflect on personal situations related to the content or on what and how they are learning (i.e., metacognition). Social activity can be an essential part of reflective practice; by reflecting together, students can begin to understand their own learning in relationship to others' learning styles and experiences.

A straightforward way to encourage students to reflect is to design a *reflection box* on the course content page. Asking students to reflect on what they are reading or doing can make the content more meaningful and memorable. Examples of how media have been used effectively to promote student reflection in online graduate courses at Memorial are provided in Table 4.5.

Table 4.5 Examples of promoting reflection.

Example	Use
Blog reflections	HKR—an instructor used a class blog to share reflections, and students used it to make comments and share their reflections. Students were encouraged to draw from their personal experiences when possible and to relate them to the assigned readings. Instructors shared their personal experiences and related them to theories and concepts presented in the readings.
Blog fieldwork assignment	Biology field study course—the instructor used a class blog for students to upload their images related to their fieldwork and to share their experiences with the class. Seeing and reflecting on the work of their classmates proved to be an impetus for self-reflection and led to more creativity and deeper learning among students.
Twitter brand marketing assignment	Business—Twitter was used to teach students how to market their brands effectively. Students and the instructor tweeted reflections on course topics and advertisements related to the class. This authentic experience allowed participants to reflect and concisely to share their thoughts on the marketing examples that they encountered.
Storytelling using animated comics	HKR—the instructor told personal stories using animated comics to relay real-life experiences related to sensitive topics. Students were asked to reflect on the meaning and relevance of the story in relation to the course topics and their own lives.
ePortfolio for a reflective practice assignment	HKR—students used ePortfolio to record, reflect on, and creatively present evidence related to course topics and their personal learning goals. They synthesized course materials through critical reflection on learning "artifacts" (documents, images, videos, etc.).

When using media for reflections, ensure that the reflections relate to course content and outcomes. Learners should have the skills to take quality images to use in blogs and ePortfolios. Assignments should be broad enough that they are relevant when learners are completing them. Determine whether the ePortfolio platform will be useful and accessible to students following graduation.

Challenges Encountered

Selecting media and technologies for maximum benefit to the learner is not without challenges. SIDs in CITL at Memorial work with many amazing content authors knowledgeable in pedagogy, willing to work in a team environment, and enthusiastic about their online courses. Content authors' and instructors' sometimes limited experiences in using media in online courses present a variety of challenges. Many of them recur, and some are related to either course design decisions or challenges inherent in the media themselves. Nevertheless, it is the responsibility of the development team to design the best learning environment in which facilitators guide students to learn so that they can achieve the learning outcomes.

Time Commitment
Content authors have the challenge of developing courses beyond their daily instruction, research, and service responsibilities. Many of them comment that it takes more time to design and develop a course than they expected.

Media in Course Design
Content authors' lack of understanding of effective course design principles, including appropriate media selection and use, can lead to students who are not prepared for class, become bored, or display poor knowledge retention (Fink, 2013, pp. 26–28). Increased knowledge of how to design learning experiences could help to counter these issues. As noted in the Memorial TPACK study, though faculty members and lecturers were confident in their content knowledge and, to a lesser degree, their pedagogical knowledge, they were much less confident in their technological knowledge and how to integrate technology (and media) into their teaching (Phillips et al., 2017). They acknowledged their lower confidence in

"adapting their teaching style[s] to different learners . . . solving technical problems; knowing different technologies; and choosing technologies that enhance a lesson" (Phillips et al., 2017, p. 40).

Learning about media and technology, and their affordances for teaching and learning, takes time. Consequently, content authors often default to what they are familiar with, simply abandoning media and technologies all together.

Universal Design for Learning

Courses that do not consider UDL principles reduce the equity of access for all and increase the need for student accommodation. Knowledge of these principles requires time if they are to be incorporated effectively. Unfortunately, UDL and accessibility are often afterthoughts and thus counter to the UDL approach.

Responsive Design

As more instructors and students use mobile devices to interact with their online courses, it becomes increasingly important to employ responsive design in media and content delivery. Designing courses to ensure they are responsive on any type of device can affect design choices and development time and cost. Although free media and technologies exist, expertise is often needed to incorporate them into courses or to develop solutions from scratch.

Learning Outcomes

Learning outcomes are often a challenge to write at the correct level, for the right audience, and in terms of being measurable. In some cases, they are written after the course has been designed, including media selection. However, they should be written prior to consideration of which media to use. The media and technologies chosen are derived from the learning outcomes that shape the content, activities, and assessment in the course.

Alternative Assessment

Having the time and patience to learn about alternative approaches to assessment, the media and technologies that facilitate these alternatives, and their integration into a course is not a luxury afforded to all. Many faculty members revert to traditional and familiar approaches—papers and exams—yet they are not always the most suitable.

Accessibility

One challenge associated with all media relates to accessibility, though it is manifested in different ways for different media. Course content, including media, needs to be accessible through enabling technologies. Some media mixes are challenging to students with vision impairment. Visuals require alternative text for screen readers to make them accessible, necessitating graphic and web design skills. Audio and video require transcripts and possibly described audio or video, or closed captioning, to make them accessible. There can be technical issues for students when playing audio and video and interacting with multimedia.

Student Engagement

As previously noted, learning environments, experiences, and activities can be designed, but learning cannot. Although media and technologies might be carefully selected and incorporated into learning experiences, instructors have no control over whether or how students will interpret or use them.

Resourcing Media Creation

Creating multimedia objects requires a significant commitment in terms of human, time, and technical resources. Expertise is often required.

Open Resources and Copyright

Reusing resources created by others can be beneficial to student learning if they address the learning outcomes. However, some content authors require training and support in searching for, selecting, and integrating these resources; troubleshooting technical issues; and supporting students in their use. Although content authors are encouraged to use content developed for their online courses in their on-campus teaching, this sometimes presents challenges of copyright since typically it is cleared only for the online course unless otherwise requested.

Free Media and Technologies

Having the autonomy to select suitable free media and technologies can be a challenge for some instructors. There are implications when they use freely available online technology versus technology that the academic institution administers and supports. When instructors encounter issues with free technology, they are left to their own resources to problem-solve it, to teach students how to use it, and to prepare how-to job aids—all of which takes valuable time away from other responsibilities.

The Lack of Design Supports

Some content authors cherish the autonomy and flexibility to design learning experiences, resources, and media elements on their own. In doing so, they do not always incorporate sound design choices and sometimes resist available assistance. This results in less than ideal learning experiences for students. Bates et al. (2017) noted that this lack of support from educational technologists and instructional designers is one of the main barriers to the adoption of online learning.

The Art of Course Facilitation

Facilitating an online course is an art that takes time to master. It comes with practice and, to a degree, insight into one's teaching practice. Instructors can benefit from dialogue, guidance, and support in this area.

Course Sustainability

A course is never truly in a "finished" state. If the content, activities, and media are not sustainable after the process of development, then the instructor is likely to abandon those that present challenges as they arise. Instructors need to be trained on how to select media and use technologies. Provisions must be made for editing in order to maintain currency. Additionally, the use of online resources accessed through hyperlinks that constantly change presents a challenge to currency and maintenance in terms of the effort required to check them on a regular basis or to find alternative resources.

Recommendations

The challenges discussed above need to be addressed early in course design. It is important to design courses effectively so as to improve the likelihood that students will have "significant learning experiences, the kind that are being called for in many parts of society today" (Fink, 2013, p. 29). SIDs bring several recommendations to content authors' attention when planning online graduate courses and associated media while keeping learners' needs and course outcomes in mind.

Content Writing and Design

There is an art to writing content for online delivery; essays and monologues are not always needed. Course notes can paraphrase an assigned reading, add to it, or challenge students to think about it from alternative viewpoints. Use a consistent tone, voice, and tense as well as a standard style, such as that of the American Psychological Association or Modern Language Association, when designing and writing course content. To facilitate readability, break the content into small sections with appropriate headings. Enable learners to work independently by providing lectures or learning notes on course topics and opportunities for students to check their understanding and receive timely feedback. Incorporate multiple activities for students to interact with peers, the instructor, and the content. Notes also contribute to instructors' presence in online courses.

Selecting and using textbooks effectively in the course are important. It is recommended that content authors choose textbooks that support the course outline and topics rather than build a course around specific textbooks. As a means to reduce mistakes and the time required to keep courses current, refrain from using specific textbook page numbers in the content, except for assigned readings. This is crucial today with frequent textbook editions and multiple formats—such as e-book, published hard- or softcover book, audiobook, and open educational resources—available. When selecting a book format, consider its terms of use, the ability to print excerpts from it, restrictions on access to it and its related resources, and maintenance of websites where the resources reside. Where possible, use library holdings and open educational resources.

Online resources, though an economical choice for readings, are at the mercy of the owner of the website. Choosing reputable sites associated with an established organization will increase the chances that the links will remain durable. When choosing a video, consider the stability of the site where it is located, the quality of the video, how closely its content relates to course topics, and any copyright concerns. SIDs provide expertise in recommending the most suitable and sustainable media and technologies.

Enhancing Interaction

To increase interactions among students, content authors should design their contributions in ways that increase student participation. One idea is to encourage students to share assignments with their classmates, who can provide constructive feedback prior to final submission to the instructor for grading.

Design activities involving videos such that they foster active rather than passive learning. Students can interact with the content in several ways, by using guiding questions about the video, working with interactive features that give them control, integrating questions into the video, and making the video part of a larger homework assignment.

Rohr et al. (2015) suggest that the "course's philosophy, content, and participants' capabilities" (p. 257) should be taken into account when considering the use of Web 2.0 technologies. Topicality and close timing with other activities should be considered. Make students aware of how and why Web 2.0 is being used, whether "for communication of course logistics, reporting on current events, or other assessment-related activities" (p. 257). Because grading some activities takes time, finding ways to expedite the process, such as aggregators that compile tweets, are beneficial.

Demonstration or Performance Guidance

With students in mind, consider how course design, including the design and use of media and technologies, can assist in their understanding of abstract or difficult concepts. Paying special attention to these items is important since crowding too much information into a small area can make it difficult to read and process. Content authors should think about areas where media can foster deep learning by presenting concepts in alternative formats. This can also ensure that the media have a learning focus and are not distracting.

Assessment

Providing students with choices in how they demonstrate their learning can have positive impacts on their autonomy, flexibility, engagement, and self-directed learning. To increase choices, look beyond exam-focused assessment and consider learner-centred authentic assessment approaches. For example, students can choose audio-recorded responses to questions versus written responses or a video-based assignment versus a paper submission. Providing choices can ease concerns about accessibility. Accommodation of students' requests not to participate in work that employs Web 2.0 technologies can be considered on a case-by-case basis. In many such cases, alternative forms of technology or assessment can be used.

Faculty Readiness

Content authors are expected to have basic word-processing and email skills when developing online courses. The course development team will assist content authors in using the LMS and other tools used in the design, development, and delivery of the course. Some content authors come to CITL with clear content knowledge but little experience in designing and teaching an online course. Working on small chunks at a time, using design aids such as course maps, providing examples and guidance, and offering constant feedback aid the design process. Also, we recommend that content authors become familiar with the unique needs of online learners and how to facilitate a course online. Over time, they will develop the art of facilitation.

Support of Instructional Designer

Content authors, through post-pilot discussions and data attained from course development surveys, say that they have learned new ways to design their on-campus courses and use media and technologies after being guided through the development of an online course with an instructional designer. A participant in the TPACK study noted that "when developing for online [courses] we came up with new ways of doing things that we wouldn't realize . . . in a classroom environment; so it can be a catalyst for new ideas" (Phillips et al., 2017, p. 45). Fink (2003) also noted that learning solid design skills for developing courses can help to "integrate new ideas about teaching, solve major teaching problems, and allow institutions to offer better support for faculty and better educational programs for students (and society)" (p. 25).

Supports for Content Author and Instructor

It is critical to think of the types of supports required: during course planning and development, before teaching the first offering (pilot), during the pilot, when the pilot is complete and course design evaluation begins, and when the course is a regular online offering. Additional supports for the content author and instructor include teaching with technological resources, use of copyright-protected works, resources for troubleshooting technical issues, and resources for accessing and modifying an online course. The frequency and degree to which these supports are used vary depending on an individual's role in the online course (content author only, content author and facilitator, or facilitator only) and readiness to assume these roles.

Conclusion

In this chapter, we presented instructional designers' perspectives on the use of text, visuals, and audio in online graduate learning. At Memorial, it is the responsibility of the development team to design the best learning environment for facilitators and students using sound instructional design approaches. In setting the context of where and how SIDs work in CITL, we discussed and shared examples of the numerous considerations of how media are selected during course design. We also explored challenges often encountered and offered recommendations to avoid pitfalls.

Resource commitments (time, human, and technical) are required for the creation of media. Developers might wish to invest these resources in creating media that address troublesome concepts that have significant impacts on students' learning. Providing instructors with guidance and support in selecting media and technologies will facilitate their appropriate use.

Working with SIDs to increase knowledge of course design gets faculty members thinking about new ways of doing things in relation to planning and delivering their courses. Ultimately, faculty members might be served best by learning how to find open educational resources or to use technologies to create their own media, thereby being responsive to students' learning needs.

The degree to which working with an instructional designer to select and integrate media and technologies effectively in online courses is little understood in Canada. Our hope is that this chapter provides a glimpse of team-based course design and media selection from CITL SIDs' perspectives. The challenges of how to increase faculty members' and lecturers' knowledge of media and technologies, how to entice these educators to avail themselves of the supports provided, and how to address all pedagogical and technological needs still remain.

References

Aced, C. (2013). *Web 2.0: The origin of the word that has changed the way we understand public relations* [Conference session]. Representing PR: Images, identities and innovations, Barcelona International PR conference, Barcelona, Spain. -Retrieved from https://www.researchgate.net/publication/266672416_Web_20_the_origin_of_the_word_that_has_changed_the_way_we_understand_public_relations

Aisami, R. S. (2015). Learning styles and visual literacy for learning and performance. *Procedia: Social and Behavioral Sciences, 176,* 538–545.

Ally, M. (2008). Foundations of education theory for online learning. In T. Anderson (Ed.), *The theory and practice of online learning* (pp. 15–44). Edmonton, AB: Athabasca University Press.

Anderson, T. (2008). Towards a theory of online learning. In T. Anderson (Ed.), *The theory and practice of online learning* (pp. 45–74). Edmonton, AB: Athabasca University Press.

Anstey, L., & Watson, G. (2018, September 10). A Rubric for Evaluating E-Learning Tools in Higher Education. *EDUCAUSE Review*. Retrieved from https://er.educause.edu/articles/2018/9/a-rubric-for-evaluating-e-learning-tools-in-higher-education

Ball, D. L., & Cohen, D. K. (1999). Developing practice, developing practitioners: Towards a practice-based theory of professional education. In G. Sykes & L. Darling-Hammond (Eds.), *Teaching as the learning profession: Handbook of policy and practice* (pp. 3–31). San Francisco, CA: Jossey-Bass.

Baskin, P. (2008). Electronic portfolios may answer calls for more accountability. *The Chronicle of Higher Education.* Retrieved from https://www.chronicle.com/article/Electronic-Portfolios-May/20892

Bates, A. W. (2015). *Teaching in a digital age: Guidelines for designing teaching and learning.* Vancouver, BC: Tony Bates Associates

Bates, T., Desbiens, B., Donovan, T., Martel, E., Mayer, D., Paul, R., . . . Seaman, J. (2017). *Tracking online and distance education in Canadian universities and colleges: 2017.* Vancouver, BC: The National Survey of Online and Distance Education in Canadian Post-Secondary Education. Retrieved from http://contactpoint.ca/wp-content/uploads/2017/10/publicreport_2017_10_10.pdf

Bertrand, F. (2006). *A profile of master's degree education in Canada.* Ottawa, ON: Canadian Association for Graduate Studies. Retrieved from www.cags.ca/documents/publications/best_practices/CAGS-Master.pdf

Bower, M. (2008). Affordance analysis—Matching learning tasks with learning technologies. *Educational Media International, 45*(1), 3–15.

Breunig, M. (2005). Turning experiential education and critical pedagogy theory into praxis. *Journal of Experiential Education, 28*(2), 106–122.

Brineley, J. E. (2014). Learner support in online distance education: Essential and evolving. In O. Zawacki-Richter & T. Anderson (Eds.), *Online distance education: Towards a research agenda* (pp. 287–310). Edmonton, AB: Athabasca University Press.

Campbell, K., & Schwier, R. A. (2014). Major movements in instructional design. In O. Zawacki-Richter & T. Anderson (Eds.), *Online distance education: Towards a research agenda* (pp. 346–380). Edmonton, AB: Athabasca University Press.

Conole, G. (2014). The use of technology in distance education. In O. Zawacki-Richter & T. Anderson (Eds.), *Online distance education: Towards a research agenda* (pp. 217–236). Edmonton, AB: Athabasca University Press.

Conole, G., & Alevizou, P. (2010). *A literature review of the use of Web 2.0 tools in higher education: A report commissioned by the Higher Education Academy.* Retrieved from https://core.ac.uk/download/pdf/5162.pdf

Conrad, D. (2014). Interaction and communication in online learning communities: Toward an engaged and flexible future. In O. Zawacki-Richter & T. Anderson (Eds.), *Online distance education: Towards a research agenda* (pp. 381–402). Edmonton, AB: Athabasca University Press.

Costello, J. (2013). *Guest speaker impact on learning community* (Unpublished doctoral dissertation). University of Lancaster, UK.

Costello, J. (2014, September). *Educational considerations derived from a study of students' conceptions of guest speakers in humanities courses.* Paper presented at EARLI SIG 9, Phenomenography and Variation Theory 2014 Conference, Oxford, UK.

Costello, J., & Crane, D. (2013). Technologies for learner-centered feedback. *Open Praxis, 5*(3), 217–225.

Costello, J., & Crane, D. (2015). Promoting effective feedback in online learning. In S. Keengwe (Ed.), *Handbook of research on active learning and the flipped classroom model in the digital age* (pp. 212–230). Hershey, PA: IGI Global.

Costello, J., & Rohr, L. E. (2016, May). *Effectiveness of guests in large enrolment online courses as an instructional strategy.* Paper presented at Networked Learning 2016, Lancaster, UK.

Crafton, L. K. (2005). The scholarship of teaching and self-study in teacher education: Walking the walk. *English Leadership Quarterly, 28*(1), 3–6.

Dick, W., & Carey, L. (1996). *The systematic design of instruction* (4th ed.). New York, NY: HarperCollins.

Dysart, S., & Weckerle, C. (2015). Professional development in higher education: A model for meaningful technology integration. *Journal of Information Technology Education: Innovations in Practice, 14*(1), 255–265.

Elin, L. (2001). *Designing and developing multimedia.* Needham Heights, MA: Allyn & Bacon.

Evans, T. D., & Haughey, M. (2014). Online distance education models and research implications. In O. Zawacki-Richter & T. Anderson (Eds.), *Online distance education: Towards a research agenda* (pp. 131–149). Edmonton, AB: Athabasca University Press.

Fink, L. D. (2003). *Creating significant learning experiences: An integrated approach to designing college courses.* San Francisco, CA: Jossey-Bass.

Fink, L. D. (2013). *Creating significant learning experiences, Revised and updated: An integrated approach to designing college courses.* San Francisco, CA: Jossey-Bass.

Gagné, R. M., Briggs, L. J., & Wagner, W. W. (1992). *Principles of instructional design* (4th ed.). New York, NY: Harcourt Brace Jovanovich College Publishers.

Garrison, D. R. (2009). Implications of online learning for the conceptual development and practice of distance education. *Journal of Distance Education, 23*(2), 93–104.

Garrison, D. R., Anderson, T., & Archer, W. (2000). Critical inquiry in a text-based environment: Computer conferencing in higher education model. *The Internet and Higher Education, 2*(2–3), 87–105.

Grant, S., & Hurd, F. (2010). Incorporating critical pedagogy into the scholarship of teaching and learning: Making the journey alongside our students. *International Journal for the Scholarship of Teaching and Learning, 4*(2), 1–12.

Guo, P. T., Kim, J., & Rubin, R. (2014). *How video production affects student engagement: An empirical study of MOOC videos* [Conference session]. Association for computing machinery, New York, USA. doi:10.1145/2556325.2566239

Ice, P., Curtis, R., Phillips, P., & Wells, J. (2007). Using asynchronous audio feedback to enhance teaching presence and students' sense of community. *Journal of Asynchronous Learning Networks, 11*(2), 3–25.

Johnson, A. (2010). *Lecture capture project: Post-pilot report.* Unpublished report. St. John's, NL: Distance Education and Learning Technologies, Memorial University of Newfoundland.

Jones, C., Dirckinck-Holmfeld, L., & Lindström, B. (2006). A relational, indirect, meso-level approach to CSCL design in the next decade. *International Journal of Computer-Supported Collaborative Learning, 1*(1), 35–56.

Kereluik, K., Mishra, P., Fahnoe, C., & Terry, L. (2013). What knowledge is of most worth: Teacher knowledge for 21st century learning. *Journal of Digital Learning in Teacher Education, 29*(4), 127–140.

King, P. M., Wood, P. K., & Mines R. A. (1990). Critical thinking among college and graduate students. *The Review of Higher Education, 13*(2), 167–186.

Knowles, M. (1984). *Andragogy in action.* San Francisco, CA: Jossey-Bass.

Kosslyn, S. M. (1980). *Image and mind.* Cambridge, MA: Harvard University Press.

Lambert, C., Erickson, L., Alhramelah, A., Rhoton, D., Lindbeck, R., & Sammons, D. (2014). Technology and adult students in higher education: A review of the literature. *Issues and Trends in Educational Technology, 2*(1), 1–19.

Laurillard, D. (2012). *Teaching as a design science: building pedagogical patterns for learning and technology.* New York, NY: Routledge.

Lohr, L. L. (2008). Visual literacy for educators and performance specialists. In L. Lohr (Ed.), *Creating graphics for learning and performance: Lessons in visual literacy* (pp. 3–27). Upper Saddle River, NJ: Pearson-Merrill Prentice Hall.

Lundy, A. D., & Stephens, A. E. (2015). Beyond the literal: Teaching visual literacy in the 21st century classroom. *Procedia: Social and Behavioral Sciences, 174,* 1057–1060.

Mantiri, F. (2014). Multimedia and technology in learning. *Universal Journal of Educational Research, 2*(9), 589–592.

Martin, F. (2008). Instructional indicator's model. In A. Igoe (Chair), *Media Selection Models symposium.* Symposium conducted at Arizona State University, Tempe, AZ.

Mayer, R. E. (Ed.). (2005). *The Cambridge handbook of multimedia learning.* Cambridge, UK: Cambridge University Press.

Mayer, R. E. (Ed.). (2009). *The Cambridge handbook of multimedia learning* (2nd ed.). Cambridge, UK: Cambridge University Press.

Mayer, R. E. (2014). Research-based principles for designing multimedia instruction. In V. A. Benassi, C. E. Overson, & C. M. Hakala (Eds.), *Applying science of learning in education: Infusing psychological science into the curriculum* (pp. 59–70). University of New Hampshire Scholars' Repository. Retrieved from http://scholars.unh.edu/cgi/viewcontent.cgi?article=1286&context=psych_facpub

Mishra, P., & Koehler, M. J. (2006). Technological pedagogical content knowledge: A framework for integrating technology in teachers' knowledge. *Teachers College Record, 108*(6), 1017–1054.

Moore, M. G. (1989). Three types of interaction. *The American Journal of Distance Education, 3*(2), 1–6.

Nielson, J. (1997, September 30). *How users read on the web.* Nielson Norman Group, Fremont, CA: United States. Retrieved from https://www.nngroup.com/articles/how-users-read-on-the-web/

Palloff, R. M., & Pratt, K. (2011). *The excellent online instructor: Strategies for professional development.* San Francisco, CA: Jossey-Bass.

Papert, S. (1990). *A critique of technocentrism in thinking about the school of the future.* Retrieved from http://www.papert.org/articles/ACritiqueofTechnocentrism.html

Phillips, P., Hammett, R., St. Croix, L., White, G., & Wicks, C. (2017). *Teaching with technologies using the TPACK framework: A report of research conducted at Memorial University.* Unpublished report. St. John's, NL: Centre for Innovation in Teaching and Learning, Memorial University of Newfoundland.

Quitadamo, I. J., & Kurtz, M. J. (2007). Learning to improve: Using writing to increase critical thinking performance in general education biology. *Life Science Education 6*(2), 140–154. doi:10.1187/cbe.06-11-0203

Robyler, M. D., & Doering, A. H. (2013). *Integrating educational technology into teaching* (6th ed.). Upper Saddle River, NJ: Pearson.

Rohr, L. E., & Costello, J. (2015). The use of Twitter as an assessment tool in a large enrollment online course. *Online Learning: Official Journal of the Online Learning Consortium: Invited Papers/OLC 20th Anniversary Conference Special Issue, 19*(4), 25–36.

Rohr, L. E., Costello, J., & Hawkins, T. (2015). Design considerations for integrating Twitter into an online course. *International Review of Research in Open and Distributed Learning, 16*(4), 241–249.

Schmidt, D. A., Baran, E., Thompson A. D., Koehler, M. J., Mishra, P., & Shin, T. (2009). Technological pedagogical content knowledge (TPACK): The development and validation of an assessment instrument for preservice teachers. *Journal of Research on Technology in Education, 42*(2), 123–149.

Schön, D. (1983). *The reflective practitioner: How professionals think in action.* New York, NY: Basic.

Smaldino, S., Lowther, D., & Mims, C. (2019). *Instructional technology and media for learning* (12th ed.). Upper Saddle River, NJ: Pearson.

Smaldino S., Lowther, D., & Russell, J. (2012). *Instructional technology and media for learning* (7th ed.). Upper Saddle River, NJ: Prentice Hall.

Smaldino, S., Lowther, D., Russell, J., & Mims, C. (2015). *Instructional technology and media for learning* (11th ed.). Upper Saddle River, NJ: Pearson.

Smith, P. L., & Ragan, T. J. (1993). *Instructional design.* Danvers, MA: John Wiley & Sons.

Stöter, J., Bullen, M., Zawacki-Richter, O., & von Prümmer, C. (2014). From the back door into the mainstream: The characteristics of lifelong learners. In O. Zawacki-Richter & T. Anderson (Eds.), *Online distance education: Towards a research agenda* (pp. 421–457). Edmonton, AB: Athabasca University Press.

Wenger, E. (1998). *Communities of practice: Learning, meaning, and identity.* New York, NY: Cambridge University Press.

Wenger, E. (2015, April 15). *Communities of practice: A brief introduction.* Retrieved from https://wenger-trayner.com/wp-content/ uploads/2015/04/07-Brief-introduction-to-communities-of-practice.pdf

Wenger, E., & Wenger-Trayner, B. (2015). *Introduction to communities of practice: A brief overview of the concept and its uses.* Retrieved from http://wenger-trayner.com/introduction-to-communities-of-practice/

⑤ # Using Participatory Action Research to Support Pedagogical Processes in Postsecondary Online and Blended Spaces

Wendy L. Kraglund-Gauthier

Internet technologies extend an institution's ability to deliver courses to students who choose the option of studying at a distance for reasons of convenience, economics, time, and learning style. To meet this need and to capitalize on an underserved market, more and more postsecondary institutions incorporate online[1] courses and programs as parts of their curricula (Song, Singleton, Hill, & Koh, 2004). In a 2018 survey, more than two-thirds of 187 Canadian universities and colleges offered online courses for credit (Canadian Digital Learning Research Association, 2019), with online course enrolments increasing by approximately 10% per year in universities and 15% per year in colleges outside Québec (Bates, 2018, p. 11). Despite this increase, how experienced face-to-face faculty adjust to changes to their teaching practices when moving to virtual classrooms and how they deal with the impacts of online teaching assignments on their

---

1 Throughout this chapter, I use the term "online" to refer to the mode of course delivery: that is, using Internet technologies in fully online or blended courses. I use the term "virtual" to refer to the digital space of the online classroom.

academic identities within traditional postsecondary institutions remain undertheorized and under-researched.

As support for online learning slowly spreads throughout the academy, it is important to remain critically reflective on how "learning formats, pedagogical approaches and student achievement interact" (Lalonde, 2011, p. 408). Although an instinct might be to standardize practice in an attempt to reach a consistent quality, "shared practice does not entail uniformity, conformity, cooperation, or agreement, but it does entail a kind of diversity in which perspectives and identities are engaged with one another" (Wenger, 1998, pp. 128–129). Some faculty have not addressed the tendency to "teach the way they were taught" (Oleson & Hora, 2014), regardless of the new context; nor do they tend to share the challenges in adjusting to new processes openly. And, despite research to the contrary, some educators remain skeptical of the value and legitimacy of online courses and programs (Hanover Research, 2014).

In this chapter, I report the findings from a participatory action research (PAR) study designed to explore how changes to instructional methods, namely from face-to-face to online delivery modes, affected the pedagogical thinking and practice of faculty, how they situated their academic identities within the virtual classrooms and on the physical campus, and how they navigated the process of change. Related questions centred on whether online teaching has impacts on both the content and the process of teaching based on their pedagogical beliefs, which included, among other factors, the immediacy of voice and dialogue in the teaching and learning process.

The weaving of ideas herein reflects my own interpretations and ideas that emerged from the PAR process as I worked alongside participants and from my field notes and journal reflections as co-researcher, instructional designer, and fellow online instructor. My intention is for instructional designers to find meaning in how another instructional designer navigated the process of change alongside faculty learning to teach online. Other potential audiences are faculty who might see themselves reflected in the narratives of participants. Teaching consultants and administrators charged with the task of resourcing new and emerging online course offerings might find the lessons and recommendations useful to their own planning and budgetary processes.

Context of the Study

The research took place within the Faculty of Education at St. Francis Xavier University (StFX), a small, primarily undergraduate university in Canada. I use the term "faculty" to refer to an educator/instructor/ teacher/professor at the postsecondary level. I do not distinguish academic rank within this categorization. I use the term "sessional" to refer to individuals contracted to instruct on a course-by-course basis in the academic year. Other institutions might use the term "part-time," "contract," or "adjunct" employee. On the campus where this research was conducted, sessional employees receive one standard rate of pay, regardless of experience, and receive no employment benefits in addition to the contracted rate.

The results are from a moment in time, capturing a span of four years during which I led a PAR project with faculty transitioning to online teaching. As an instructional designer, I worked alongside faculty creating and modifying courses for synchronous and asynchronous online delivery. During this time, I became a novice sessional, delivering a Master of Education (M.Ed.) course a total of three times with face-to-face, synchronous, and asynchronous components and two Master of Adult Education courses delivered asynchronously. To contextualize the parameters within which the research was conducted, in the following section I describe the research setting as it was during the study.

Research Setting

StFX has an undergraduate population of approximately 4,800 students, of whom the majority attend classes on campus. Through its Department of Continuing and Distance Education, StFX offers a limited number of online courses at the undergraduate level, primarily from May to August, outside the regular academic terms of September to April. Other than a grandfather policy agreement within the Department of Nursing, faculty teaching online undergraduate courses do so beyond their regular teaching contracts. M.Ed. online courses are part of the faculty load. At the time of data collection, 16 of the 23 full-time M.Ed. faculty and more than 20 sessionals delivered courses at the M.Ed. level. The 16 full-time faculty had permanent office spaces at StFX, had full teaching loads across the programs, and maintained active research agendas. Most sessionals were employed full time in the public-school system as teachers and/or administrators; others were retired from teaching at public school or postsecondary levels or administrative positions.

To address student demand for alternative delivery methods, and because of budgetary restraints in challenging economic times, the M.Ed. program modified its course delivery to include online methods. Courses are delivered entirely face-to-face, entirely at a distance using asynchronous methods via Moodle, or entirely at a distance using synchronous methods via Blackboard Collaborate.[2] Others are delivered in a format that blends face-to-face, online asynchronous, and synchronous methods; face-to-face and online asynchronous methods; or face-to-face and online synchronous methods.

In the more than 10 years that the M.Ed. program has offered online courses, faculty have experienced changes in technology used to deliver programming. They have navigated new email and file storage protocols, a change from Learn to Moodle, and significant changes to their synchronous virtual classroom when ElluminateLive! was assimilated by Blackboard and became Blackboard Collaborate. The online faculty needed to learn how to think differently about delivering content and building community with their students. They had to move away from photocopied handouts and toward digital materials and make use of other collaborative features, including text-based discussion forums and file sharing. In synchronous courses, faculty and their students needed to learn to use technologies related to audio and video, chat conversations, and whole group and small group text-based discussions in breakout rooms; share applications and conduct web tours; and assign moderator

---

2 Blackboard is the software company, Learn is its learning management system (LMS) platform, and Collaborate is its synchronous virtual classroom.

status to or remove it from any participant. Their chalkboards became digital whiteboards, used to display images and slide presentations, and for some, this marked their first time using Microsoft PowerPoint.

Role of the Researcher

As an instructional designer, I am deeply committed to helping those creating course content to find their way through the technologies and changing academic institutional dynamics and emerge as effective facilitators in virtual classrooms. My role is to be responsive to the emerging and anticipated learning needs of faculty and to help them theorize the process of teaching online and exploring ways to build community. My becoming a novice facilitator was not part of the original research design, but its serendipitous inclusion enabled me to share authentically in the lived experiences of my research participants. There is no "neat dividing line" (Brennan & Noffke, 1997, p. 24) between my roles, and their intersections informed how I performed my role as researcher throughout the process; how I, the instructional designer, interacted with faculty developing and delivering online courses; and how I, the online sessional, designed effective learning environments and activities for my own students.

Insider research is not without limitations. Such proximity to the research can bias researchers' results. Insider research requires, as Friesen (2010) explained, awareness of and attention to merging inner subjectivity with outer objectivity. Existing relationships with research participants can influence their behaviour, and the researcher's tacit knowledge can lead to assumptions and misinterpretations of data (Denzin & Lincoln, 1998). Yet being an outsider is being an impartial observer of events that transpire over a term, an observer who does not engage in meaningful and informed conversations with participants as they explore their own issues with teaching online. How individuals navigate change and academic culture affects how technology is integrated (Paul, 2014); as an insider, I was aware of StFX's organizational culture in a time of pedagogical change.

Drivers of Change in Online Teaching Contexts

The shift from face-to-face to online teaching has instigated a great deal of change in the traditional bricks-and-mortar postsecondary institution that houses traditional communities of practice. Sutherland-Smith and Saltmarsh (2010) attributed the intense competition from global markets as one driver of change. Additionally, budgetary constraints and efforts to curb costs associated with physical infrastructure have resulted in some postsecondary administrators increasing their institutions' online course offerings (Rumble, 2014). Other drivers include pressures to respond to societal change and student demand (Bates, 2018; Canadian Digital Learning Research Association, 2019; Contact North, 2013) and to provide accessible programming (Canadian Council on Learning, 2009; The GO Project, 2008; Rumble, 2014). Laurillard (2005) noted that there are many drivers of change to online learning, yet aspects of learning quality are not dominant forces.

Understanding Change

Processes of change are rarely similar from one institution to the next because they are affected by unique variables in internal and external environments. Moreover, "change must always be viewed in the light of the particular values, goals, and outcomes it serves" (Fullan, 2001, p. 6). In light of research questions and results from data analysis, Fullan's (2001) model of change and Lewin's (1951) classic model of change can be adapted to an online context and serve as a foundation on which to explicate the process that participants experience as they move from a face-to-face to an online teaching environment. Moving to the latter environment requires change—not necessarily in terms of philosophical underpinnings of teaching and learning, but often in ways that one's pedagogical stance is set in virtual spaces (Conole, 2014). For some, this shift in stance necessitates a minor change; for others, the change is more substantial. An important element of unfreezing from comfortable processes and inviting change entails creating the conditions necessary for that change to occur.

Implicit to making the transition from teaching in face-to-face classrooms to doing so in virtual ones is the expectation that faculty will undergo a critical examination of the existing structures of their course materials and assessment activities for applicability in this new mode of course delivery. The theories of Rogers (1979) on how ideas permeate systems in terms of their technological advances and the changes required for faculty, administrators, and institutions to become initiated into new ways of thinking and acting in online spaces can be balanced with activities and outcomes of student learning, organizational capacity and agents of change (Fullan, 2001, 2013), and technological capacity (Rogers, 2003).

Purpose of the Study

This PAR was designed to increase understanding of the changes in teaching practice and pedagogical thinking that postsecondary faculty made as they transitioned from face-to-face teaching spaces to virtual ones, moving from classrooms dominated by dialogue and physical interaction to those that relied on solely text-driven interactions; a blend of face-to-face and asynchronous text-based communication; and a blend of face-to-face, text, and online synchronous dialogue. This understanding was gained after the administration of an anonymous questionnaire to StFX M.Ed. faculty (Part 1) and the implementation of a PAR process (Part 2) involving individual interviews (P1–6) and focus group sessions with six faculty (see Figure 5.1).

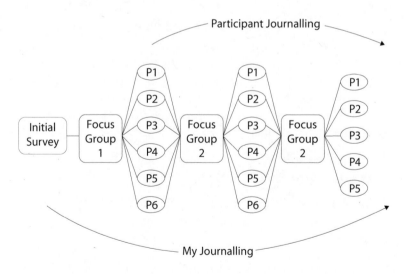

Figure 5.1 A visual representation of how data sets flowed through the research process.

Participants began journalling after Focus Group Session 1 and continued through four months of the academic term to end after their final individual interviews and the completion of their course.

With its emphasis on equal collaboration among participants working together to discover practical solutions that improve practice (Creswell, 2005, 2015), PAR was deemed the most appropriate research method. The PAR design provided the opportunity for participants as co-researchers to "step back cognitively from familiar routines, forms of interaction, and power relationships to fundamentally question and rethink established interpretations of situations and strategies" (Bergold & Thomas, 2012, para. 1). As per PAR, participants chose the focus of inquiry that they wished to explore as a group and as individuals and to gain knowledge from their experience. Throughout each of the components of Part 2, participants journalled their thinking and reflecting on experiences. My field notes spanned both phases.

Research Questions

Based on the tenets of PAR, the main thrust of inquiry emerged from the participants themselves (Bergold & Thomas, 2012; Creswell, 2015; Lewin, 1946; Noffke, 1994). Responses from the anonymous survey distributed during Part 1 were used to inform the nature of inquiry with participants during Part 2 and framed the questioning during individual interviews and focus group sessions. The following questions guided the research during both parts and framed my own journalling on the research process.

- In which ways do M.Ed. faculty change perspectives (i.e., in values, beliefs, and practices) on teaching and learning when they transition to teaching online?

- In which ways do M.Ed. faculty modify their pedagogy during the transition to teaching online?

- In which ways do M.Ed. faculty negotiate their identities during the transition to teaching online?

Significance of the Study

Online educational opportunities have burgeoned in the past decade, matching the pace of technological advances. In these virtual spaces, the shift from traditional modes of thinking about teaching and learning and ingrained concepts of face-to-face classroom communities of learners often need to shift to account for the differences found online. Other considerations include the alignment of online course offerings with the institution's operational practices and organizational culture. Although not yet matching this pace of opportunity and change, research does exist that explicates what students need from an online environment and from the faculty member (Bonnel, 2008; Friesen, 2010; Garrison, Anderson, & Archer, 2000). Far less research exists on what learning and supports faculty need to make the transition to teaching in virtual spaces, especially those where text takes precedence over voice.

What sets this study apart from other research is its focus on Faculty of Education members charged with the task of delivering educational content to in-service teachers enrolled in an M.Ed. program. Understanding the pedagogical constructs of virtual classrooms is important within the context of education programs in which faculty—trained and experienced in the processes of face-to-face learning—teach students trained and experienced in the same processes. This study helped to fill a void in the literature on teaching online, in particular in terms of how faculty themselves learn to navigate virtual classroom spaces and how they create or maintain their professional identities and connections to a community of practice with peers also experiencing change.

Methods

Data analysis involved using open coding techniques and themes (Creswell, 2005) from survey responses and from verbatim transcripts of individual interviews and focus group sessions and framed by the overarching research questions. My goal was to identify patterns emerging from the data without making explicit interpretations. These patterns became (1) *initiation* into teaching and learning online, (2) *early* and *later implementation* of teaching and learning strategies rooted in pedagogical practice, and (3) *institutionalization* of online teaching practices and pedagogy.

I viewed analyses through the lens of Fullan's (2001, 2013) three major stages of educational change: initiation, implementation, and institutionalization. I did this chronologically where possible in order to reveal participants' changes in patterns of thought and processes of learning over time throughout the action research cycles of the project that resulted in collaborative problem solving and knowledge generation (Bergold & Thomas, 2012; Creswell, 2015). Within these stages, I further organized data into three subcategories following Lewin's (1946) classic model of change. These stages of unfreeze–change–freeze are not distinct phases of time. Rather, as in any process of change, participants moved fluidly among them, sometimes jumping backward or forward depending on the particular issue and their own ways of facing the process of change and its inherent challenges. In the upcoming sections, I present the results from Part 1's survey and Part 2's focus group sessions and individual interviews and reflective journalling.

Results from Part 1

Twenty-two respondents shared their opinions on various topics related to both face-to-face and online classes (see "Appendix A: Selected Survey Questions"). Half of the respondents (11 of 22) were sessional faculty, and the remaining respondents were tenure-track (2) or tenured (9) faculty. Sixteen respondents held doctorates; five of them were sessionals. All respondents had prior experience teaching face-to-face postsecondary courses, and only 2 of 22 had no prior experience using Collaborate. Respondents' degrees of experience with synchronous teaching methods in virtual classrooms ranged from *novice* (zero to two courses; 12 of 22), to *emerging* (three to five courses; 3 of 22), to *experienced* (six courses or more; 7 of 22).

Overall, the results from Part 1 indicated that individuals who taught online felt institutional, program, and student pressure to do so. Institutional status affected respondents' transitions to teaching in virtual spaces. More sessional faculty commented negatively on their lack of choice in the decision, whereas tenured faculty commented on the necessity of having online courses in order to maintain enrolment numbers.

Comments also revealed respondents' concerns about increased pressures and decreased choices in the mode of instructional delivery. Like Paul (2014), they expressed concern about the requirement to change pedagogical processes within an institution steeped in tradition. Overall, the results aligned with the literature on change and diffusion of technology (Fullan, 2013; Rogers, 1979, 2003), meaning that the transition from teaching in face-to-face classrooms to teaching in virtual spaces was not smooth, regardless of respondents' expertise in instruction.

Of key import is respondents' recognition of the amount of time and effort expended during their transition to virtual classroom teaching spaces, reflecting Lewin's (1951) acknowledgement that developmental change is slow (Burnes, 2004). The respondents needed to rebuild their self-efficacy as educators and had to invest time in learning to navigate the technology. Respondents who had more experience in virtual spaces recognized the pedagogical possibilities of blending synchronous and asynchronous learning opportunities, especially in terms of deepening conversations and creating a sense of community among users when using audio and video applications.

Results from Part 2

Ten individuals volunteered via their online questionnaire submissions to be a part of Part 2; 6 of the 10 were accepted as participants based on the sole criterion of teaching via Collaborate during the data collection phase. While coding and analyzing transcripts from focus group sessions and individual interviews, I continued to be mindful of how the terms "novice," "emerging," and "experienced" referred only to participants' exposure to the teaching tools that comprise Collaborate's teaching and learning platform and not in terms of their actual years of experience teaching. In the following sections, I share some demographic data and excerpts from participants' initial individual interviews to provide both context and perspective. I have used pseudonyms to protect the identities of all participants and their students.

Dana: Sessional, Experienced User

Dana was within the age range of 60–69 years and had more than 30 years of experience as a junior high and high school classroom teacher and experience in administrative roles at the school and district board levels. He had taught for the StFX M.Ed. program for approximately four years and had delivered courses in physical locations, online, and in a blended format in which some of the classes were held at an on-site location and others were online. At the time of the first interview, Dana had taught a number of StFX's M.Ed. courses online, using the asynchronous components of Learn or a combination of Learn and Collaborate.

Dana enjoyed teaching with Collaborate: "It's almost as good as being there," he said, because of the immediacy afforded by voice capabilities. For him, the features of audio, video, chat, recordings, presentations, web tours, and group discussions were beneficial and an improvement on the more static LMS, in which he was "limited to typing in the discussions." In teaching, for Dana, the "aim is to keep it as interactive as possible and to . . . teach to facilitate the students' own learning." He reported enjoying the interactions among and with students in face-to-classrooms, but he also noted the challenge of connecting with some groups when they are "difficult to interact with or preoccupied with something else, [or] if the group was more wanting just to have something delivered to them, some absolutes delivered to them." Dana was also mindful of his learners' previous experiences, recognizing that "adults learn best when the topic is relevant to their needs or their issues in schools." He used discussions to focus on questions and needs. An indication of his pedagogical stance emerged in the following statement:

> I try to reflect a little bit on the principles of learning that Knowles developed, or wrote about, in my teaching within the M.Ed. program. I try not to lecture and preach but facilitate the students as they move through different topics in the course.

Jordan: Tenured, Novice User

Jordan was within the age range of 60–69 years and had more than 20 years of experience as a high school teacher and experience in administrative roles within the school and at the university. He reported having taught at the M.Ed. level at StFX for over 10 years, first in face-to-face classrooms only and then, when the distance education program expanded, in

Learn for approximately three years. In Learn, he and his students used the real-time chat feature to dialogue via typing rather than the asynchronous discussion forums. Jordan was relatively new to the synchronous format of Collaborate, having taught one course before the first interview, and he was scheduled to teach one course in the upcoming term. For him, Collaborate was, "such a step up; it's like almost being there but not quite."

Jordan characterized his face-to-face teaching style as "very amicable; I like having fun in class. . . . I am a task master. . . . I do believe in quality, but I do believe in the human side of it." When asked to explain what he liked about face-to-face teaching, Jordan said,

> I like the idea of tactile learning, you can touch things, you can do things. . . . I can go to the board on a moment's notice and draw big diagrams and connect things and map stuff which I can't easily do in other ways.

Jordan went on to state that he does not "like using technology in classrooms," explaining that he is "a walk and chalk kinda' person." For him, the concept of pedagogy is how he

> communicates theory, content, and practice. It's the communication process. . . . You have to be a walking example of perfect teaching. So, if I talk about fairness and equity, I have to do that in my actual classroom. My classroom has to be the mirror of what I say I do.

Pat: Tenured, Emerging User

Pat was within the age range of 60–69 years and reported almost five years of experience teaching in the public-school system before beginning to teach at the postsecondary level. After a decade as a liaison among a teacher-training program, the government, and public schools, she began to focus her work primarily on teacher education programs, a focus that had lasted over 25 years. Pat characterized her face-to-face teaching style as "very active, interactive, hands-on [with] development materials." The course content and her teaching style also contributed to the blended nature of the course. Pat said that she "wouldn't give up my 18 hours of face-to-face because . . . when the teachers do any activities that, for instance, are a demonstration of classroom activities—and, really, the participants have to live the activities out—[they put] things together." She also reported her strong preference for "hearing [her] students, knowing their feelings about what [she] was teaching through their tone of voice."

Pat's self-described teaching style linked strongly to her concept of pedagogy. Pat was quick to provide a personal definition that contained elements of a belief in constructivism and the value of lived experience:

> Pedagogy is not just talking about ideas; it's not just delivering. It's making people believe the experience and work through the experience. By working through that experience, they can actually understand what should be changed and what might be changed and what doesn't need to be changed and what are the benefits of certain types of procedures versus others.

Quinn: Tenure-Track, Novice User

Quinn's age fell within the range of 40–49 years. His public-school teaching occurred in high school classrooms, but Quinn had spent time in administrative positions as well. He had been teaching at the university level for over 13 years as a master's and doctoral student and then as a faculty member. Quinn had a wide range of experience teaching multiple topics and in different teaching environments, and his pedagogical beliefs, assumptions, and teaching methods evolved and were refined during these past experiences. With a stated preference for the lecture format, he was a "fan of intellectual capital [who] embodies that in teaching."

Quinn's M.Ed. teaching experience began in face-to-face classrooms six years prior to this research project. In time, Quinn gained more experience with online teaching, beginning first using a university-based LMS and then learning to use Learn's asynchronous discussion forums and functionality as a document repository to supplement learning in between scheduled face-to-face classroom sessions. At the time of the first interview, Quinn had taught two different courses using Collaborate and was scheduled to teach one again in the upcoming term. Class design included

Microsoft PowerPoint presentations and large and small group discussions, "like a real-world, face-to-face class."

Quinn characterized his face-to-face teaching style as "going between inductive and deductive teaching . . . depending on setting and what [students] are dealing with. I prefer a lecture format and transmitting knowledge and theory." Referring again to intellectual capital, Quinn noted how "giving content knowledge is important in university classes." He also noted the importance of varying approaches and altering instructional methods depending on the abilities of the learners, speculating that "most good teachers do that by nature." He enjoyed the setting of the face-to-face classroom, seeing it as a natural place in which one can see learners' "facial expressions, . . . if they are getting it or not, [based on] their . . . demeanour, their body language." He also noted the "clinical" nature of online discussion forums, in which tone, and therefore meaning from the vocalization of ideas, are lost.

Riley: Sessional, Experienced User

Riley was within the age range of 60–69 years and had more than 25 years of experience as a schoolteacher before moving to postsecondary teaching. She reported having almost 15 years of experience teaching in StFX's B.Ed. and M.Ed. programs in face-to-face classrooms, and she had spent some time in various administrative roles within the Faculty of Education. Riley had the most experience teaching in virtual classrooms compared with the other research participants. She was a part of the first cohort of early adopters (Rogers, 1979) when StFX's M.Ed. program introduced courses with online features, beginning first with Learn and then moving to Collaborate. She reported that she was often asked to share her knowledge and experience with faculty new to Collaborate. She permitted novice users to sit in on virtual classes and shared session recording links, and she responded to email requests for ideas and clarifications.

Riley characterized her teaching style as "facilitative," describing herself as "an oral person [who] likes to talk and not write." She also emphasized the importance of having "good ideas and a set of problems and providing students [with the time] to work on it." She described how she incorporated small group and paired activities involving literacy manipulatives such as word tiles and texts for cooperative learning. When asked what she enjoyed about teaching face-to-face, Riley ardently said "the people in the room. I like it when there are people together."

Taylor: Sessional, Novice User

Taylor had more than 25 years of experience teaching at public school and postsecondary levels. At the time of the initial interview, she was starting her first online course using Collaborate, but she reported using an LMS similar to Learn to teach two previous courses asynchronously. Taylor enjoyed the face-to-face classroom because she could:

> focus the energy in the room and see their faces and read their body language. . . . I have got people right there, and I have my connection with them. And I can see quickly if there is puzzlement or boredom or if they have tuned out because I can see the faces, and I can draw them in.

When asked about her teaching style, Taylor said emphatically that she was "*not* a lecturer." She elaborated on her teaching style and expectations:

> In my classroom, there is lots of discussion, but I am also very task-oriented. . . . I think that I want teaching to be hard in the sense that I really want them to think. I love knowing that is a strategy that works, and I try to do it in a way that is very active.

Taylor designed in-class activities that involved prewriting and talking in dyads or small groups, activities that "encouraged quieter students to talk." Like Quinn and Jordan, Taylor also "grabbed teachable moments [and] suddenly would be up at the board, explaining things," creating opportunities for learners to connect with the readings and with each other.

The six participants in Part 2 were similar in terms of their vast experience teaching within public and private K–12 settings and at the postsecondary level. After years of teaching similar content in face-to-face classrooms, they defined their teaching in terms of mechanical aspects of delivery, such as instructional activities and class designs rather than why they approached the subject matter in the ways that they did. Their personal definitions of pedagogy and their descriptions of teaching methods contained multiple references to the importance of dialogue as part of the learning process, especially dialogue that happened in the moment imbued with the richness of tone that a voice carries. Their demographics and approaches to teaching provided a lens through which to view the PAR data and informed the development of a framework to conceptualize faculty transitions from teaching in face-to-face classrooms to teaching in virtual ones.

Framework for Conceptualizing Transitions from Face-to-Face to Online Teaching

The Framework for Conceptualizing Transitions from Face-to-Face to Online Teaching (Kraglund-Gauthier, 2016, see Table 5.1) emerged from the analysis of data from Parts 1 and 2. It is rooted in Lewin's (1951) classic unfreeze–change–freeze model of change and in Fullan's (2001) three major phases of educational change: initiation, implementation, and institutionalization.

In Table 5.1, and described in detail in the following sections, the transition from face-to-face to online teaching is grouped in terms of three stages: initiation, early implementation, and later implementation. The fourth grouping is institutional practicalities and serves to capture the required technological, pedagogical, and administrative supports that participants considered to be necessary as faculty moved their teaching practices to online spaces. Data are further linked using Lewin's (1951) stages of change based on participants' responses to the main research questions involving pedagogical concerns, learning to use online tools, negotiating identity, and navigating the change in teaching methods from face-to-face to virtual classroom spaces.

Table 5.1. Framework for conceptualizing transitions from face-to-face to online teaching (Kraglund-Gauthier, 2016).

INITIATION PHASE _Unfreezing Practice and Preparing for Change_	EARLY IMPLEMENTATION PHASE _Adjusting to Differing Realities of Teaching Online_	LATER IMPLEMENTATION PHASE _Establishing Pedagogical Practices and Demonstrating Self-Efficacy_
Identify and address conflicts and concerns in terms of teaching mechanics	Acclimatize to the virtual space	Foster instructors' self-efficacy in terms of online instruction
Conceptualize teaching self in terms of professional identity	Identify ways teaching presence is enacted in online classrooms	Implement more complex online teaching tools and practices
Prepare for the role of an online instructor in terms of technological skills and content revision	Find balance between advance preparation and responsiveness to real-time learning	Identify and address students' needs in terms of learning and connecting to peers
	Undo engrained face-to-face teaching practices	Master tools and techniques that strengthen pedagogical beliefs of online teaching and learning
	learn new tools and methods that engage learners and enliven content	
	Gain comfort with teaching tools in virtual spaces	

INSTITUTIONAL PRACTICALITIES _Supporting Instructors Moving to Online Teaching_				
Recognize effort and innovation of online early adopters	Balance fiscal realities with faculty and student requests for online options	Identify champions to lead changing pedagogical options for teaching online	Establish and support a community of practice for online instructors	Support technological, pedagogical, and administrative needs of online instructors

Participants did not make definitive moves from one phase of change to the next. The initiation phase discussed below is just the beginning of the unfreezing process. It is common for elements of initiation to extend into the implementation phase. As additional tacit assumptions, habits, and routines were disrupted and brought into consciousness with the new teaching practice, participants underwent a smaller-scale unfreezing-refreezing process.

Within these stages of change, I filtered data analysis through participants' situated proficiency in Collaborate as "novice," "emerging," or "experienced" users. I do not use these terms pejoratively, nor are they meant to detract from participants' wealth of teaching knowledge and experience. Rather, I use the terms to indicate participants' positioning within their individual and institutional processes of change and their degrees of exposure to and comfort with the teaching tools specific to Collaborate and their experiences teaching online.

Initiation Phase: Unfreezing Practice and Preparing for Change

The initiation phase is a period of building readiness, not only for the task ahead but also for the process of change itself, regardless of whether the focus is on the innovation of change, as Rogers (1979) described, or on the individuals who are changing, as Fullan (2001, 2013) maintained. Regardless of the amount of experience participants had in face-to-face classrooms, transitioning to teaching in virtual classrooms involved another initiation into teaching. For some, the virtual space necessitated a change in perspective on the nature of teaching and how pedagogical connections with students and curricula are made, similar to what Fullan (2013) noted. Other participants realized that they needed to change how they taught and to adjust their assumptions about the nature of teaching and learning.

Participants characterized their entry into online teaching as a new beginning in which a degree of uncertainty formed as they began to unfreeze thoughts and actions related to teaching and learning. The disembodiment of the individual within the classroom (Friesen, 2010; Kang,

2007), and shifting pedagogical positioning in a virtual classroom of learners, left some participants unsure of their teaching methods and abilities.
In the following subsections, I explore four themes that emerged from
the data on participants as they underwent their initiations into teaching
online: emotional conflicts and concerns, professional identities, pedagogical concerns, and recognition of upcoming challenges.

Identifying Concerns about Teaching Mechanics

According to change theory, the initial period of unfreezing can be an
emotionally messy time, fraught with contrasting emotions of uncertainty
and anticipation. Participants went through a period of cognitive and
emotional dissonance as their values, beliefs, and pedagogical identities
were deconstructed and reconceptualized in their virtual classrooms. How
they processed these emotions and how they conceptualized their teaching abilities depended, in part, on their approach to managing change.
"Exposing one's vulnerability in learning is central to developing practice"
(Loughran, 2006, p. 29), and participants noted the importance of feeling
safe to make mistakes.

Because of their unfamiliarity with online tools when the teaching term
began, participants worried about not being fully familiar with the complete functionality of the learning platforms and about not being skilled
enough to use the technology to its fullest potential. They exhibited low
confidence, and the novice users were critical of their ability to manage
the change in the teaching environment and processes necessitated by the
new delivery methods. They expressed concern about their lack of technical pedagogical expertise, worrying that if they made technical mistakes
their students would not consider them to be competent. Quinn did not
"want to look inept or incompetent, because students will most likely
assume we don't know the content either."

Pat nervously checked classroom links and log-ins, even though she
knew that she and her students, like Jordan, were "at the mercy of the
evening's Internet connection." Even Riley, with her prior experience in
Collaborate, agreed with novice Taylor in feeling "more uncomfortable
starting each first online class than [she] ever did for a face-to-face one."
These comments reveal participants' feelings of vulnerability. Participants
felt in control of their physical classroom spaces and the activities that

they had planned, but they anticipated in the virtual space the absence of tangible confirmation that lessons would go as planned. They considered their physical presence an important component of their pedagogical practice and an integral element of their ability to manage the flow of the lesson. Their sense of disembodiment in the virtual classroom, or, as Friesen (2010) described it, the lack of a physical body as a part of the teacher self, was also experienced as an emotional disconnect from their teaching identities.

Conceptualizing the Teaching Self in Terms of Academic Identity

In terms of the concept of self that ties belief to action (Bandura, 1997) and the critique of self that ties self-efficacy to motivation and academic performance (Pajares, 1996), professional identity was linked strongly to how the participants taught. Quinn was confident in his instructional abilities in face-to-face classrooms, underscored by his admission of a certain lack of "real qualms or issues. It suits my style." He was prepared to take this confidence into the virtual classroom, explaining that, because of his "Socratic style" of instruction and content and his comfort with technology, he did not anticipate getting "caught up in trying to do too many things at once." Dana noted the tendency to teach in familiar ways, especially in face-to-face contexts, and recognized the comfort of familiar physical interactions: "It was sort of what I knew. [It] was the sort of modality that I knew, and grew up with, and that is what you sort of fall back on when you do your own teaching." Riley reported that she was "definitely more of a facilitator" in face-to-face classrooms, "different from the PowerPoint [she was] making" for her online class. Like Jordan and Taylor, she preferred a more fluid and responsive conversation with students rather than have them respond to her prepared highlights. Such comments reveal how participants' pedagogical beliefs were deeply rooted in their instructional activities and class designs and how determined they were to plant them in Collaborate. They were concerned more with learning simple yet effective ways to engage their learners with the content reminiscent of the physical classroom space than with pushing the technological boundaries of Collaborate and thinking differently about the virtual space.

Participants' professional and pedagogical identities were entrenched in being expert facilitators of student learning. Taylor noted that they held a "position of power and authority" as professors, and Dana observed that students looked to them "for answers, even technical ones, God help them!" Taylor worried about what her students would think about her knowledge and instructional abilities if "disaster struck online." She explained that the first session was important in order to set the tone for the class and "to make a good first impression." Rather than verbalize a lack of confidence in personal ability to cope with potentially different ways of teaching in an online classroom, Pat used her age of 60–69 years to explain her challenges with grasping technical concepts. She admitted to not liking change: "I have been teaching for 40 years; why do I need to do this now?" This comment reveals her vulnerability in redefining her role as a master educator in a virtual classroom. For Taylor, Pat, and Jordan, the potential of "looking foolish" as they learned to teach online deeply affected their identities as skilled, experienced faculty in face-to-face classrooms.

Participants' lack of confidence inhibited their abilities to learn new skills, and, as Bandura (1997) explained, their lack of self-efficacy in terms of online teaching negatively affected their beliefs in their abilities to create an effective learning environment online. Like Rogers (2003), participants' desires for positive outcomes were related to a need for concrete evidence that the innovation can improve instruction. Taylor explained that, in her experience in face-to-face classrooms, "if students were not comfortable in the space and didn't feel connected to each other, they were not likely to share deep reflections and their own pedagogical connections to practice." She predicted that she would have to spend a great deal of time community-building in her virtual classroom because she and her students would not be "cued by body language and physical presence." She was certain that her technological skills in Collaborate would limit community-building and considered it her "responsibility to manage the technology."

Early Implementation Phase: Adjusting to Different Realities of Teaching Online

The implementation of a new initiative often requires a shift from ingrained habits of thought and action to new perspectives and methods. In this research, the early implementation phase was a period of high expectations for instruction in the virtual classroom. In this phase, participants began to work through changes in teaching role, pedagogical stance, and relationship with students.

Acclimatizing to Virtual Spaces

As Kornelsen (2006) asked, "what is it about the presence of the person, the teacher, that contributes to the teaching-learning environment?" (p. 73). For some participants, a sense of teaching presence—what Lehman and Conceição (2010) described as "'being there' and 'being together' with online learners" (p. 3)—was tied to classroom management. For Taylor, the lack of a physical presence added to the challenge of maintaining control over the teaching milieu and learning activities of her students. She felt much more in control in the face-to-face classroom because she could "see every damn book opened, and I can eyeball them if they haven't got it opened." She missed the pedagogical influence afforded by her physical presence in the classroom and the immediacy of that presence and, as Friesen (2010) noted, its visual, non-verbal communication as confirmation of student engagement.

Without the accustomed feedback from body language and eye contact in physical interactions, Quinn, like Taylor, also could not "tell if [students] are engaged or not" in the virtual classroom. He wondered if his students "are paying attention. . . . I really can't tell because they are not there physically. Every now and then I'll see a happy face or a check mark, . . . but again it's not very much." His comments align with those emerging from other research. Major (2010), for example, noted the need for online faculty to rely on forms of electronic communication other than "sensory and expressive skills" (p. 2184) to connect with their students.

Major (2010) also acknowledged limitations in bridging what Moore (1993) termed "transactional distance": that is, the separation between online faculty and their students. In my research, it was evident that Taylor and Quinn had come to rely on the feedback of smiles, nods, and quizzical looks in face-to-face environments yet absent in virtual environments to reinforce their teaching practices and to communicate expected standards of learning. Lehman and Conceição (2010) explained this need to connect with students physically and pedagogically in terms of their Being There for the Online Learner model of ways to experience presence.

In Collaborate, personal web cameras stream live video from a maximum of six individuals out to viewers simultaneously. This additional visual emphasis can connect participants emotionally and help to animate the virtual space, thus adding to the social presence of faculty and students, as posited by Swan and Shih (2005). Although participants discussed the importance of seeing their students when teaching, some said that it was disconcerting to see one's own visage projected into the virtual space. As an experienced user and individual accustomed to speaking to groups as an administrator and community leader, even Dana was "too shy" to use his web camera. Taylor did not use her web camera either: "No, it makes me uncomfortable to see my face looking back at me." And Pat said that "I don't like the way I look and sound." When asked about the difference between being physically in front of a room of students and being in front of them via a web camera, Taylor stated that, "in the physical classroom, they can see me, and I can think I am projecting myself in a certain way. In a virtual class with my own face staring at me, I see myself the way my students see me." When asked whether they gave as much thought to these elements of identity and presence in face-to-face classrooms, all participants claimed that they did not, with Quinn explaining that it "felt more natural and wasn't something I have to really think about." Such comments reveal participants' feelings of disquiet and a lack of personal confidence as master faculty who must now teach in virtual spaces. Their physical bodies had become parts of their teacher identities, acting as "the marker that identifies us and that provides many ways to be either subtly or overtly expressive of who we are" (Friesen, 2010, p. 115).

Balancing Advance Preparation and Responsiveness with Real-Time Learning

Participants talked about the difficulty of balancing the need to have sufficient content prepared versus the need to respond to students' learning needs during class sessions. Rather than using course content prepared in advance and uploaded to a learning management system for students to complete within a prescribed time frame, participants in this study created their own syllabuses and outlined general course content and required assignments. They were flexible with specific instructional content based on the changing needs and experiences of students in their courses. They often adjusted materials based on students' experiences and needs related to course content. This meant that the instructors were constantly reviewing materials and resources in preparation for classes, regardless of how often they had taught the courses in the past.

Participants often mentioned the mechanical aspects of online content delivery rather than processes of teaching and conceptualizations of ideas. All participants believed that online courses needed to be more structured compared with the "freedom," as Jordan indicated, of "face-to-face to just go with the conversation and make notes on the whiteboard." They also discussed feeling more constrained by the platform and thought that they were less adaptive to their students' needs and to the evolving nature of scholarly conversations in their virtual classrooms. For Riley, the mechanical nature of so much advance planning to have something visual ready to load onto Collaborate detracted from the spontaneity of connecting "with students to draw from them." In 2017, 65% of institutions that participated in the Canadian National Survey of Online and Distance Education (Canadian Digital Learning Research Association, 2019) reported "moderate to extensive use of on-demand streamed videos" (p. 31). None of the participants in this PAR project recorded their own instructional videos to be included as course content, citing the challenges of time and technical editing skills as well as the importance of providing just-in-time content that reflected the learning needs of their students at particular moments in the courses. Their concerns about having the session designed and uploaded in advance contradicted Contact North (2013), which noted that the online context and accessibility of content have shifted the reliance from "limited content chosen by the instructor" (sec. 4, para. 1) to that which learners have found to connect to the topic under study. Participants' concerns with the inflexibility of the digital platform parallels Dron's (2014) argument that "the more we embed processes and techniques in our tools, be they pedagogies or machine tools, the fewer choices are left to humans" (p. 242).

On asking participants whether their experiences teaching online had led them to place more value on structure and teacher-directed activities, Taylor responded emphatically:

> I feel as though I am violating some of my deeply held principles—feminist pedagogy, participatory principles. . . . I feel more *structured*, more *teacher-directed*, and neither of those are words I would even have used to describe my teaching. And they are not words to which I have attributed high value in the past—certainly not part of my identity as [an] educator. (Focus Group Session 2)

This excerpt reveals the significant conflict that Taylor experienced while teaching online. Specifically, both she and Pat struggled with situating their valid knowledge for and in practice: that is, their immense knowledge gained through their prior teaching education and experience (Nussbaum & Ritter Hall, 2012), with new knowledge of practice that could lead to positive and educative online experiences for both them and their students.

Undoing Ingrained Face-to-Face Teaching Practices

Unlearning and relearning teaching roles and processes—that is, changing ways of thinking (Lewin, 1951)—emerged as a key component of participants' process of change during the early implementation phase (Fullan, 2001, 2013) of this PAR project. The intricacy of managing the different dimensions of technique, communication, and classroom dynamic in a virtual environment required an additional level of effort.

Participants needed to learn new technical skills and new teaching skills to manage the virtual environment. They needed to unlearn "that learning . . . is limited by time and space" (Nussbaum & Ritter Hall, 2012,

p. 50). They also needed to unlearn some of the tacit knowledge of teaching, such as reading a student's vocal tone and body language for cues about understanding the content and flow of the class, and more explicit knowledge in terms of content delivery and assessment.

Teaching in online spaces requires different approaches to the delivery and assessment of certain learning activities in face-to-face interactions, and as Dana noted "it may mean [faculty] have to do a bit more work in the beginning stages and put more time into thinking about how to deliver content" (Focus Group Session 1). Other participants agreed yet were also quick to point out, in the words of Jordan, that "the pay-off isn't exactly worth it sometimes when asked to take a familiar course and adjust it for online [delivery]" (Focus Group Session 1). As an experienced user and a long-time faculty member, Riley recognized her deeply ingrained habits of teaching, and her readiness to adopt e-learning technologies was affected by her uncertainty that they comprised an advantage over the process that they were designed to replace (Rogers, 2003).

Learning Tools and Methods that Engage Learners and Enliven Content

Novice and experienced participants noted their concerns about the quality of instructional content as they devoted more time to the mechanics of content delivery, including learning how to use presentation software and posting content and creating discussion forums in Learn. The time that faculty invested in learning to manipulate the online tools to strengthen the learning process was time that they did not spend on developing course content or grading student assignments. Taylor also mentioned how they "just want to teach and not worry about the tools they should be using" to deliver the material and have students connect with it. In the early phase, they were unable to identify the benefits derived from adopting the technological innovation, and they were unconvinced that Collaborate represented "a superior alternative to the previous practice that it would replace" (Rogers, 2003, p. 14).

As Pat and Taylor explained in Focus Group Session 3, they had their own pace of learning, and they had varying levels of ability to absorb new technical and pedagogical applications of the subject material. By the third interview, Pat had decided that "what I need is for someone to sit down with me for two days and do everything that can be done on the computer so I know what to do with the computer when things break."

Riley mused about learning new tasks and working with new tools for her synchronous class time, providing a revealing glimpse of how some faculty approach the mechanics of teaching online:

> I get the idea, now how will that work online? Pull in a video? I don't know I know how to do that. There are all those icons at the top of the screen that I need more practice with. And then I am thinking, "Well, I could go into that tutorial," but I don't actually think of doing that. I don't say "I am going to go spend some time . . . playing around." Maybe I will get better at that. At least it's in my head once in a while to go and do that, but I have never actually gone and done it.

Although classified as an experienced user after using Collaborate for more than six different courses, Riley was still unsure of what to do and was not yet motivated to learn more, despite recognizing that elements of the teaching environment and resources would add to the online experience and her comfort in delivering the content. Her reluctance reflects a typical response from a novice user of any technology in the initial phase of change (Rogers, 1979)—Riley had not yet accepted the innovation as an advantage. Participants were frozen in their thinking about how well they had performed the acts of teaching in physical spaces, and they were unable to imagine how the technology could enhance, rather than hinder, their work.

Gaining Comfort with Online Teaching Tools

For five of the participants, it was too much to manage the tools and the activities in the virtual classroom and still be attentive to the content. Acknowledging her inability to type well, Riley sounded apologetic as she explained how she told students that she "wasn't ignoring them but found it too hard to concentrate on what was being said, read the chat, and type responses at the same time." For Jordan, it was "easier in a real classroom because they just talked one at a time. Now one person is talking, and three or four are typing, and I wonder who is even listening when I am talking." Other participants struggled with the added element of text dialogue during synchronous presentations. As Taylor noted, it was as if the "missing element of me being physically present in the room gave [students] the sense they could do whatever they wanted, like chat while someone is presenting or scribbling on the whiteboard over someone's slides." Jordan said that sometimes the students "were like kids" in terms of their disruptive behaviour.

Participants explained how controlling or managing the discussion is different in a virtual classroom compared with a physical one. Two participants viewed the audible signal of a hand being raised as an interruption that caused speakers to lose their trains of thought. Pat recounted her issue with one student

> who takes advantage of holding the mic and will dominate the discussion for a longer time than I would allow in a class. . . . I feel a bit more reticent to lift my hand to cut her off. . . . I hold my hand longer than I would hold my tongue.

This sparked a conversation about the importance of classroom management and physical presence. In this conversation, participants failed to recognize that the same underlying concepts of classroom management and equitable learning spaces that they developed in their face-to-face classrooms could also be developed in their virtual classrooms.

Later Implementation Phase: Establishing Pedagogical Practices and Demonstrating Self-Efficacy

In the later implementation phase, participants became more comfortable teaching online and noticed and celebrated their progress. They became less frustrated when they bumped up against old ways of doing things that did not play out as intended in the virtual classroom. As participants adjusted to their "lived space[s]" (Friesen, 2010, p. 25), the later implementation phase also became a time of resolving emotional dissonance and coming to terms with the complex and challenging tasks of employing somewhat new ways of teaching familiar ideas and activities.

Fostering Self-Efficacy in Online Instruction

With ability comes confidence, and more confidence can translate into self-efficacy. This belief in one's personal ability to complete a task or accomplish a goal (Bandura, 1997) is crucial in the online realm, especially when an instructional designer is not available for assistance. Reflecting the work of earlier researchers in face-to-face contexts (Bandura, 1997; Pajares, 1996), participants thought that they were "getting better at it, the more classes I have behind me," as Dana put it. He was also student centred in his approach, believing that "all students can learn, and it is up to the teacher to find a way to work with that person in that teaching situation so that they do learn."

As an expert user, Riley had more confidence in her ability to navigate within Collaborate, whereas Taylor, a novice user of Collaborate, was not comfortable with the platform or with her virtual teaching presence. Taylor was "disappointed with [her] classes so far," believing that she was just not connecting with her students when she was worried so much about the technology. For both participants, their beliefs had powerful influences on their thoughts, actions, and behaviours as they navigated their personal processes of pedagogical change. As Kanuka (2008) argued, "our philosophy determines how we perceive and deal with our preferred teaching methods—which includes how (or if) we choose and use e-learning technologies" (p. 92). Comparatively, Pajares (1996) linked an individual's belief systems to self-efficacy.

Implementing More Complex Online Teaching Tools and Practices

In this final phase of change, personal concerns about the ability to manipulate the tools effectively and to troubleshoot technical issues were lessened. However, participants did note that the time it took to become comfortable in the virtual classroom was still an issue because it was time taken away from preparing content and being responsive to students' needs (Allen & Seaman, with Lederman & Jaschik 2012). Quinn—in a tenure-track position and obligated to publish research results and make conference presentations as well as carry a full teaching load of five courses per academic year—thought that he had less time to devote to learning how to deliver familiar content differently.

As researchers including Allen et al. (2012) and Bonk (2001) have noted, a faculty member's workload is often heavy, and "the different pattern of activities for online teaching can also mean a higher workload" (Bennett & Lockyer, 2004, p. 241). It was less of an issue for Dana to invest time in course development because he was retired from full-time teaching, and as a sessional he usually taught only one course per academic term. He also noted that, as he gained experience, he seemed to need less time to prepare his online classes, even after having to learn to use slide presentation software for the first time. Also retired from full-time M.Ed. teaching, Riley acknowledged that "the time spent thinking about how to do something in Elluminate is making [her] think more deeply about what [she] was doing."

As Bennett and Lockyer (2004) argued, as faculty make their way into virtual classrooms, they, instructional designers, and administrators should be cognizant of the time pressures of online teaching and plan accordingly. Additionally, following from the observations of Rogers (2003) that faculty members' personal approaches to change tend to be influenced by previous experiences of major change, if faculty are supported in the process of change, time to reflect on the pedagogical processes of teaching online is needed.

Discussion of the Findings

Results from this PAR project indicate that implementing online courses is not simply a matter of providing technological tools, training, and digital resources. It requires deep consideration of pedagogical processes and reflection on *how* and *why* departments and faculty make the decision to implement online learning and a focus on developing capabilities of facilitation that reflect adult learning principles (Bedford, 2014).

In light of the research questions and results from the data analysis, Fullan's (2001) model of change and Lewin's (1951) classic model of change were adapted to an online context and served as a foundation on which to explicate the process that faculty experienced as they moved from a face-to-face environment to a virtual environment. Despite critiques that Lewin's model of change is outdated and does not take into account politics and conflicts within organizations (Burnes, 2004), the research results reported here demonstrate an application of the phases of freezing, unfreezing, and refreezing as an explanation of the ways that faculty transition from face-to-face to online classrooms (Kraglund-Gauthier, 2016). Moving to the online delivery of education requires change, not necessarily in terms of philosophical underpinnings of teaching and learning, but often in ways that one's pedagogical stance is set in virtual spaces that offer a blend of voice and text in connecting with students. Despite being expert educators in face-to-face classrooms, they needed pedagogical, technological, and emotional support as they adjusted to the different realities of teaching and developed self-efficacy in navigating virtual classrooms. For some, this shift in stance necessitated a minor change; for others, it required a more substantial change.

Institutional status affected respondents' transitions to teaching online. Sessionals reported having little choice in the mode of delivery. Tenured faculty recognized the importance of online course offerings to maintain enrolment numbers but expressed concern about the requirement to change pedagogical processes within an institution steeped in tradition. Overall, the results aligned with the literature on change and diffusion of technology, meaning that the transition from teaching in face-to-face classrooms to teaching in virtual classrooms was not smooth, regardless of respondents' expertise in instruction.

Data analysis revealed that participants had to unfreeze established thinking and teaching practices during an emotional period in which they questioned their professional identities. Participants, especially sessionals who lived and taught at some distance from StFX, wanted pedagogical connections with colleagues and needed technological and administrative support that considered their schedules and physical locations. All participants sought recognition for their efforts as early adopters of online technologies and thought that the institution should identify and support champions able to meet program and student needs via their work as online faculty.

Faculty recognized a difference in their ability to teach in virtual classrooms that lack the concrete and tactile connections with learning objects such as molecular models or cue cards and the spontaneous conversations in small groups common in learner-centred classes. Faculty were thrust into the role of novice educator once again yet with the benefit of years of experience in applying pedagogical knowledge and facilitating student learning. Being in this novice role was uncomfortable and affected their academic identity and self-efficacy as professional educators.

Implicit to transitioning to teaching in virtual classrooms is the expectation that faculty will undergo a critical examination of the existing structures of their course materials and assessment activities for applicability in this new mode of course delivery. Rogers's (1979, 2003) theories of how ideas permeate systems in terms of technological advancements and the changes required for individuals to become initiated into new ways of thinking and acting in virtual spaces are balanced with outcomes and activities involving student learning. Other considerations are organizational capacity and agents of change (Fullan, 2013) and technological capacity (Rogers, 2003). In light of the literature on change and integration of technology (Fullan, 2013) and diffusion of technological innovation (Rogers, 2003), however, these results indicate a need for technical assistance and training resources.

Institutional Practicalities: Supporting Faculty Moving to Online Teaching

As postsecondary institutions attempt to maintain or increase course enrolments, their plans to expand course delivery via online modalities have been met with resistance from some departments and some individuals who might feel threatened by the increased competition from these virtual options (Anderson, 2008). For example, in 2018, 59% of faculty surveyed in Canada reported an overall lack of acceptance of online instruction (Canadian Digital Learning Research Association, 2019). In addition to considerations of how faculty transition through phases of change, institutions need to consider certain practicalities involved in supporting those faculty. Participants in the PAR noted the need for their institution to recognize the effort and innovation of the early adopters, to balance fiscal realities with requests for online courses, to support the pedagogical champions leading the institution's movement online, and to establish and maintain communities of practice that support the technological, pedagogical, and administrative needs of online faculty.

Objective monitoring and evaluative measurement designed for online teaching are needed (Anderson, 2008), especially as faculty move through the transitional phases of implementation. Furthermore, instructional designers, program administrators, and faculty must be aware of and address constraints that will limit or impede learner participation, such as economics, geography, social barriers, and the technology itself (Bates, 2005; Bell & MacDougall, 2013; Garrison & Cleveland-Innes, 2010). For example, courses designed using a blend of delivery methods including asynchronous text-based discussions and live or recorded audio or video components can address issues emerging from poor Internet connectivity and student scheduling of learning around work and family responsibilities (Kraglund-Gauthier, 2016).

Conclusion

This study helps to fill a void in the literature on teaching online, in particular in terms of how faculty learn to navigate in virtual classrooms and how they create or maintain their professional identities and connections to a community of practice with peers also experiencing change. The overarching significance of this work is a greater understanding of how faculty approach change, alter their thoughts and actions, and manage the preliminary process of transitioning to online course offerings.

Overall, it is evident that an application of Lewin's (1951) model of change can explain how faculty transition to teaching in virtual classrooms. Lewin's phases of freezing, unfreezing, and refreezing assessed within the context of Fullan's (2001, 2013) stages of change during the implementation of a new software tool or process can enlighten the work done by faculty and the instructional designers who work alongside them. Like the PAR design that requires a safe space in which to explore unknowns without concerns about being viewed negatively (Bergold & Thomas, 2012), participants' reactions underscore the need to validate emotional and instructional concerns, discuss training needs, and make these new boundaries between instructional support and technological support explicit for all, mirroring observations by Bonk (2001) and more recently by Allen et al. (2012) and Aldunate and Nussbaum (2013). Online teaching needs support to continue to develop.

The Framework for Conceptualizing Transitions from Face-to-Face to Online Teaching (Kraglund-Gauthier, 2016) is a way of conceptualizing and organizing what is known about online teaching in both voice-based synchronous and text-based asynchronous spaces from the perspectives of faculty, whose voices have been noticeably absent from the literature. When the framework is used as a discussion and planning tool, stakeholders can better understand faculty members' stages of change, pedagogical stances, technical skills, senses of academic identity (Clarke, Hyde, & Drennan, 2013; Feather, 2014; Wenger, 1998), and the practicalities within the institution (Paul, 2014; Rumble, 2014).

Instructional designers can use the framework to guide their work in developing online courses and to understand better instructors' pedagogical stances, technical skills, and senses of academic identity and the practicalities within institutions. At the microlevel, they can, as Campbell and Schwier (2014) noted, work with institutions to "articulate needs for professional development and help organizations to build the capacity to respond to needs and opportunities" (p. 370). Institutionalization and acceptance of online courses require support from respected champions of online teaching and learning, changes in organizational culture, and an environment in which a vibrant community of practice can flourish.

Appendix A: Selected Survey Questions

In addition to demographic questions, participants were asked to provide their feedback on a series of questions using a Likert ranking of 1=*Strongly Disagree* to 7=*Strongly Agree*.

8. Indicate the degree to which you disagree/agree with the following questions by placing a checkmark (✓) in the appropriate column.

NOTE: Face-to-face teaching refers to formal learning situations in which the facilitator and the students share the same physical location at the same time.

    a.   I enjoy learning new methods for *face-to-face (f-2-f)* teaching.

    b.   I enjoy learning new methods for *online* teaching.

    c.   I am able to attend to learners' needs in an *f-2-f* classroom.

    d.   I am able to attend to learners' needs in an *online* classroom.

    e.   I am confident I can accommodate individual learner differences in *f-2-f* classrooms.

    f.   I am confident I can accommodate individual learner differences in *online* classrooms.

    g.   I believe a sense of community can be developed in my *f-2-f* classroom.

    h.   I believe a sense of community can be developed in my *online* classroom.

    i.   I enjoy exploring new technology options for teaching *f-2-f*.

    j.   I enjoy exploring new technology options for teaching *online*.

    k.   I have the time to commit to learning new teaching techniques for *f-2-f* learning.

    l.   I have the time to commit to learning new teaching techniques for *online* learning.

    m.   I believe *f-2-f* classes are efficient ways for students to earn an M.Ed.

    n.   I believe *online* classes are efficient ways for students to earn an M.Ed.

    o.   I have a "Plan B" when I am planning *f-2-f* lessons.

    p.   I have a "Plan B" when I am planning *online* lessons.

    q.   I prefer to teach my *online* course from my office.

    r.   I prefer to teach my *online* course from my home.

s.   I have a reliable Internet connection when I teach my *online* course from my office.

t.   I have a reliable Internet connection when I teach my *online* course from my home.

Appendix B: Guiding Questions for Focus Group Sessions 1, 2, 3

Focus Group Session 1

1. In order to get to know a bit more about everyone in the group, please introduce yourselves and tell us something about your face-to-face and/or teaching experience.

2. What courses are you teaching face-to-face this term? What courses are you teaching online this term?

3. What are your opinions about teaching online compared to teaching face-to-face?

4. As part of an action research project, our sessions are designed to explore an issue related to online learning, determine ways to address that issue, and plan a course of action. Let's take some time to discuss the potential issues we can explore and determine which one to focus on this term. What are your thoughts?

5. How shall we move this issue further?

Focus Group Session 2

1. In our first focus group session and in my individual interviews with you, we have been exploring the issue of [*insert issue here*]. We decided to [*insert plan here*]. How is that going?

2. What information, skills, and/or assistance do you need at this point in order to move the issue forward?

3. Do we need to adjust the plan? Why? How?

4. What are you noticing about your own teaching style and orientation to online classrooms?

References

Aldunate, R., & Nussbaum, M. (2013). Teacher adoption of technology. *Computers in Human Behavior, 29,* 519–524. doi:10.1016/j.chb.2012.10.017

Allen, I. E., & Seaman, J., with Lederman, D., & Jaschik, S. (2012). *Conflicted: Faculty and online education, 2012.* Retrieved from http://www.insidehighered.com/sites/default/server_files/files/IHE-BSRG-Conflict.pdf

Anderson, T. (2008). Towards a theory of online learning. In T. Anderson (Ed.), *The theory and practice of online learning* (2nd ed., pp. 45–74). Edmonton, AB: Athabasca University Press.

Bandura, A. (1997). *Self-efficacy: The exercise of control.* New York, NY: W. H. Freeman.

Bates, A. W. (2005). *Technology, e-learning and distance education* (2nd ed.). New York, NY: Routledge Falmer Studies in Distance Education.

Bates, T. (2018). The 2017 national survey of online learning in Canadian post-secondary education: Methodology and results. *International Journal of Educational Technology in Higher Education, 15*(29), 1–17. doi:10.1186/s41239-018-0112-3

Bedford, L. (2014). The REEAL model: A framework for faculty training in online discussion facilitation. *International Journal of Teaching and Learning in Higher Education, 26*(3), 463–472.

Bell, M., & MacDougall, K. (2013). Adapting online learning for Canada's northern public health workforce. *International Journal of Circumpolar Health, 72,* 1–7. doi:10.3402/ijch.v72i0.21345

Bennett, S., & Lockyer, L. (2004). Becoming an online teacher: Adapting to a changed environment for teaching and learning in higher education. *Educational Media International, 41*(3), 231–248.

Bergold, J., & Thomas, S. (2012). Participatory research methods: A methodological approach in motion. *Forum: Qualitative Social Research/Sozialforschung, 13*(1), Art. 30. Retrieved from http://nbn-resolving.de/urn:nbn:de:0114-fqs1201302

Bonk, C. J. (2001). *Online teaching in an online world.* Englewood, CO: JonesKnowledge. Retrieved from http://www.jonesknowledge.com/pdf/faculty_survey_report.pdf

Bonnel, W. (2008). Improving feedback to students in online courses. *Nursing Education Perspectives, 29*(5), 290–294.

Brennan, M., & Noffke, S. E. (1997). Uses of data in action research. In T. R. Carson & D. Sumara (Eds.), *Action research as a living practice* (pp. 23–43). New York, NY: Peter Lang.

Burnes, B. (2004). Kurt Lewin and the planned approach to change: A re-appraisal. *Journal of Management Studies, 41*(6), 977–1002.

Campbell, K., & Schwier, R. A. (2014). Major movements in instructional design. In O. Zawacki-Richter & T. Anderson (Eds.), *Online distance education: Towards a research agenda* (pp. 345–371). Edmonton, AB: Athabasca University Press.

The Canadian Council on Learning. (2009). *State of e-learning in Canada*. Retrieved from http://en.copian.ca/library/research/ccl/elearning/elearning.pdf

Canadian Digital Learning Research Association. (2019). *Tracking online and distance education in Canadian universities and colleges: 2018*. Retrieved from https://onlinelearningsurveycanada.ca/download/556/

Clarke, M., Hyde, A., & Drennan, J. (2013). Professional identity in higher education. In B. M. Kehm & U. Teichler (Eds.), *The academic profession in Europe: New tasks and new challenges* (Vol. 18, pp. 7–21). *The changing academy: The changing academic profession in international comparative perspective.* New York, NY: Springer.

Conole, G. (2014). The use of technology in distance education. In O. Zawacki-Richter & T. Anderson (Eds.), *Online distance education: Towards a research agenda* (pp. 217–236). Edmonton, AB: Athabasca University Press.

Contact North. (2013). *A new pedagogy is emerging . . . and online learning is a key contributing factor*. Retrieved from https://teachonline.ca/tools-trends/how-teach-online-student-success/new-pedagogy-emerging-and-online-learning-key-contributing-factor

Creswell, J. W. (2005). Qualitative inquiry and research design: Choosing among five traditions. Thousand Oaks, CA: Sage.

Creswell, J. (2015). Chapter 17: Action research designs. In *Educational research: Planning, conducting, and evaluating quantitative and qualitative research* (pp. 578–597). Toronto, ON: Pearson.

Denzin, N. K., & Lincoln, Y. S. (Eds.). (1998). *Collecting and interpreting qualitative materials*. Thousand Oaks, CA: Sage.

Dron, J. (2014). Innovation and change: Changing how we change. In O. Zawacki-Richter & T. Anderson (Eds.), *Online distance education: Towards a research agenda* (pp. 237–286). Edmonton, AB: Athabasca University Press.

Feather, D. (2014). Defining academic: Real or imagined. *Studies in Higher Education, 41*(1), 110–123. doi:10.1080/03075079.2014.914921

Friesen, N. (2010). *The place of the classroom and the space of the screen: Relational pedagogy and Internet technology*. New York, NY: Peter Lang.

Fullan, M. G. (2001). *The new meaning of educational change* (3rd ed.). New York, NY: Teachers' College Press.

Fullan, M. (2013). *Stratosphere: Integrating technology, pedagogy, and change knowledge.* Don Mills, ON: Pearson.

Garrison, D. R., Anderson, T., & Archer, W. (2000). Critical inquiry in a text-based environment: Computer conferencing in higher education model. *The Internet and Higher Education, 2*(2-3), 87–105. Retrieved from http://cde. athabascau.ca/coi_site/documents/Garrison_Anderson_Archer_Critical_Inquiry_model.pdf

Garrison, D. R., & Cleveland-Innes, M. F. (2010). Foundations of distance education. In M. F. Cleveland-Innes & D. R. Garrison (Eds.), *An introduction to distance education: Understanding teaching and learning in a new era* (pp. 13–25). New York, NY: Routledge.

The GO Project. (2008). *Getting online: A research report on online learning for Canadian literacy practitioners.* Retrieved from http://en.copian.ca/library/research/goreport/goreport.pdf

Hanover Research. (2014). *The state of online postsecondary education.* Retrieved from https://www.hanoverresearch.com/media/The-State-of-Online-Postsecondary-Education.pdf

Kang, S. (2007). Disembodiment in online social interaction: Impact of online chat on social support and psychosocial well-being. *CyberPsychology & Behavior, 10*(3) 475–477. https://doi.org/:10.1089/cpb.2006.9929

Kanuka, H. (2008). Understanding e-learning technologies-in-practice through philosophies-in-practice. In T. Anderson (Ed.), *The theory and practice of online learning* (2nd ed., pp. 91–118). Edmonton, AB: Athabasca University Press.

Kornelsen, L. (2006). Teaching with presence. *New Directions for Adult and Continuing Education, 111,* 73–82. doi:10.1002/ace.229

Kraglund-Gauthier, W. L. (2016). *An investigation of post-secondary instructors' experiences moving from face-to-face to online teaching: Identifying changes to practice, pedagogical beliefs, and academic identity* (Unpublished doctoral dissertation). University of South Australia, Adelaide, Australia.

Lalonde, C. (2011). Courses that deliver: Reflecting on constructivist critical pedagogical approaches to teaching online and on-site foundations courses. *International Journal of Teaching and Learning in Higher Education, 23*(3), 108–123.

Laurillard, D. (2005). E-learning in higher education. In P. Ashwin (Ed.), *Changing higher education: The development of teaching and learning* (pp. 71–84). London, UK: Routledge.

Lehman, R. M., & Conceição, S. C. O. (2010). *Creating a sense of presence in online teaching: How to "be there" for distance learners.* San Francisco, CA: Jossey-Bass.

Lewin, K. (1946). Action research and minority problems. *Journal of Sociological Issues, 2*(4), 34–46.

Lewin, K. (1951). *Field theory in social science: Selected theoretical papers*. New York, NY: Harper & Row.

Loughran, J. (2006). *Developing a pedagogy of teacher education: Understanding teaching and learning about teaching*. New York, NY: Routledge.

Major, C. (2010). Do virtual professors dream of electric students? College faculty experiences with online distance education. *Teachers College Record, 112*(8), 2154–2208.

Moore, M. G. (1993). Chapter 2: Theory of transactional distance. In D. Keegan (Ed.), *Theoretical principles of distance education* (pp. 22–35). London, UK: Routledge.

Noffke, S. (1994). Action research: Towards the next generation. *Educational Action Research, 2*(1), 9–21. doi:10.1080/09650799400200010

Nussbaum, S., & Ritter Hall, L. (2012). *The connected educator: Learning and leading in a digital age*. Bloomington, IN: Solution Tree Press.

Oleson, A., & Hora, M. T. (2014). Teaching the way they were taught? Revisiting the sources of teaching knowledge and the role of prior experience in shaping faculty teaching practices. *Higher Education, 68*(1), 29–45.

Pajares, F. (1996). Self-efficacy beliefs in academic settings. *Review of Educational Research, 66*(4), 543–578.

Paul, R. (2014). Organization and management of online and distance education. In O. Zawacki-Richter & T. Anderson (Eds.), *Online distance education: Towards a research agenda* (pp. 175–196). Edmonton, AB: Athabasca University Press.

Rogers, E. M. (1979). New product adoption and diffusion. *Journal of Consumer Research, 2*, 290–301.

Rogers, E. M. (2003). *Diffusion of innovation* (5th ed.). New York, NY: Free Press.

Rumble, G. (2014). The costs and economies of online distance education. In O. Zawacki-Richter & T. Anderson (Eds.), *Online distance education: Towards a research agenda* (pp. 197–216). Edmonton, AB: Athabasca University Press.

Song, L., Singleton, E. S., Hill, J. R., & Koh, M. H. (2004). Improving online learning: Student perceptions of useful and challenging characteristics. *The Internet and Higher Education, 7*, 59–70. doi:10.1016/j.iheduc.2003.11.003

Sutherland-Smith, W., & Saltmarsh, S. (2010). Minding the 'P's for implementing online education: Purpose, pedagogy, and practicalities. *Australian Journal of Teacher Education, 35*(7), 64–77.

Swan, K., & Shih, L-F. (2005). On the nature and development of social presence in online course discussions. *Journal of Asynchronous Learning Networks, 9*(3), 115–136.

Wenger, E. (1998). *Communities of practice: Learning, meaning, and identity*. Cambridge, UK: Cambridge University Press.

Blended Synchronous Learning in One University's Graduate Programs in Education

Sawsen Lakhal

The work environment has changed significantly in recent years in order to cope with major trends in technical and technological progress (Valenduc & Vendramin, 2016). These changes require companies and social institutions to become increasingly competitive through, among other things, a highly skilled and innovative workforce. Education and training are key issues in facing these changes. Carey and Ferreras (2017) observed that "it's . . . about a workforce with new technical smarts and with a broader understanding of the big picture of workplace innovation" (para. 3). Consequently, many adults have to go back to postsecondary education institutions and some of them to universities to acquire additional skills in order to remain competitive (van Rhijn, Lero, & Burke, 2016). However, these adults have multiple responsibilities while attending courses, including professional and family responsibilities. Moreover, often they interrupt their studies for long periods of time. Because of these responsibilities, they cannot participate in face-to-face classroom sessions every week (Duarte, de Oliveira Pires, & Nobre, 2016). On the one hand, traditional face-to-face teaching and learning processes are more adapted to traditional full-time students; on the other, some online learning, in which all teaching and learning activities occur asynchronously, does not always meet the needs of adult students (Bower, Dalgarno, Kennedy, Lee, & Kenney, 2015), who often need to socialize with their instructor and other students enrolled in the course to remain engaged and motivated. To meet the needs of adult learners, to take into account their constraints, and to increase their access to higher education, universities have adapted their modes of course delivery. The development of information and communication technology and the availability of high-speed broadband Internet connectivity have allowed new opportunities in course delivery to emerge. Of these delivery modes, blended learning is one of the most promising and popular for adult students (Hill, 2012; Irvine, Code, & Richards, 2013) because it combines the benefits of face-to-face interaction with online flexibility and ubiquity (Lakhal & Khechine, 2016; McGee & Reis, 2012).

Blended Learning and Blended Synchronous Learning

Blended learning combines face-to-face learning with online learning in a planned and pedagogically valuable manner to form an integrated instructional approach (Garrison & Vaughan, 2008; Graham, 2006). In this mixed mode, faculty members and students work together to accomplish learning outcomes supported pedagogically by teaching, learning, and assessment activities and to offer a meaningful course environment to students (Lakhal & Khechine, 2016; McGee & Reis, 2012). Therefore, "blended education goes beyond just combining traditional and online teaching and learning. It involves a total redesign of traditional courses to include the use of technology for online communication, activities and delivery" (Kyei-Blankson, Godwyll, & Nur-Awaleh, 2014, p. 244).

Blended learning can take on different forms along a continuum, with a focus on face-to-face activities complemented by online activities, on the one end, and a focus on online activities complemented by face-to-face activities, on the other. Blended synchronous learning is one form of blended learning. It is defined as "learning and teaching where remote students participate in face-to-face classes by means of rich-media synchronous technologies such as video conferencing, web conferencing, or virtual worlds" (Bower et al., 2015, p. 1). "Multi-access learning" is another term employed to describe the phenomenon examined here. First introduced in Canada by Irvine et al. (2013), multi-access learning is defined "as a framework for enabling students in both face-to-face and online contexts to personalize learning experiences while engaging as a part of the same course" (p. 175). Often, moreover, some of the face-to-face sessions are replaced by online sessions for all students enrolled in the course. At francophone universities in Canada, blended learning is characterized as *hybride*, which means "blended" in English. Although researchers and practitioners define this phenomenon differently, essentially they are referring to the same mode of course delivery. This highlights the many ways in which modes of course delivery are described. In the rest of this chapter, I use the term "blended synchronous learning" (BSL).

In this chapter, I report on a scholarship of teaching inquiry into current practices in graduate programs in education using BSL in greater detail, as well as on the benefits of using this mode of course delivery and the challenges experienced by instructors and students, focusing on the use of video/voice and text. Given the recent interest and the scant published research in BSL contexts, the results reported here should provide faculties and higher education administrators with additional information and guidance, based on empirical data, in using this mode of course delivery in graduate programs.

In the following section, I present a literature review of blended synchronous learning, including its advantages and its challenges. I then discuss my experience with BSL. I provide a description of the sample and the procedure before presenting and discussing the results. I end the chapter with the implications of the study, its limitations, and future research directions.

Research and Literature Review

Theoretical and empirical research on blended learning is abundant and has been the subject of several literature reviews and meta-analyses (e.g., Bernard, Borokhovski, Schmid, Tamim, & Abrami, 2014; Boelens, De Wever, & Voet, 2017; Drysdale, Graham, Spring, & Halverson, 2013;

Halverson, Graham, Spring, Drysdale, & Henrie, 2014). However, little research has been done on BSL (Bower et al., 2015; Szeto & Cheng, 2016). Despite this paucity, one can extract from previous research some benefits and challenges of this mode of course delivery.

The references cited in the literature review deal exclusively with BSL. Some of the advantages and challenges are the same as those encountered in online learning, but others are exclusive to BSL.

Advantages of BSL

One acknowledged advantage of BSL is the increase in higher education student enrolment and the reduction in instruction costs. BSL can represent a solution for institutions of higher education with limited classroom space (Educause, 2010; Miller, Risser, & Griffiths, 2013). Another acknowledged advantage is accessibility. BSL provides students with greater educational access since it responds to their scheduling needs by offering flexibility in course attendance (Abdelmalak, 2014; Bower, Kenney, Dalgarno, Lee, & Kennedy, 2014; Bower et al., 2015; Cunningham, 2014; Francescucci & Foster, 2014; Miller et al., 2013). This is especially true for students who live far from university campuses (Bower et al., 2015; Bower et al., 2014; Educause, 2010) or who have work schedules and family responsibilities that make it difficult for them to attend weekly face-to-face sessions (Abdelmalak, 2014; Bower et al., 2014; Kyei-Blankson & Godwyll, 2010). Regardless of whether the student is enrolled in a face-to-face or an online synchronous course session, BSL gives him or her equal opportunities to interact in real time with other students and faculty members (Bower et al., 2015; Bower et al., 2014; Francescucci & Foster, 2014; Miller et al., 2013). Moreover, online students and face-to-face students might be able to get together in small group discussions (Bell, Sawaya, & Cain, 2014; Cunningham, 2014) and complete collaborative learning activities (Bower et al., 2014). Thanks to these interactions, BSL reduces feelings of isolation among online students (Cunningham, 2014) and allows them to get to know their classmates much better than if they were attending the course online asynchronously (Bower et al., 2015; Cunningham, 2014). BSL also promotes students' engagement in their learning (Cunningham,

2014) and produces similar if not more effective outcomes compared with traditional face-to-face courses (Kyei-Blankson & Godwyll, 2010; Kyei-Blankson et al., 2014). Finally, in BSL, there are better course and program completion rates for students who interact synchronously with other students and faculty members compared with those who rely solely on asynchronous communication (Bower et al., 2014).

Challenges of BSL

According to the authors reviewed, BSL has many challenges. They are classified into four subthemes: course design, management of online students and face-to-face students at the same time by faculty members, technological issues, and relationships between face-to-face students and online students. I summarize these issues in the following paragraphs.

Designing a BSL course involves much more physical and social preparation than courses in a single mode (Bower et al., 2014), for example face-to-face or online, such as setting up the rooms (both physical and virtual classes) in order to create meaningful learning environments. Faculty members can spend a lot of time anticipating interactions and collaborations between the two groups of students (i.e., face-to-face and online students) that do not occur spontaneously and have to be well planned (Bower et al., 2015). Otherwise, learning via videoconferencing would not be the same as in face-to-face classrooms because of inappropriate instructional planning (Szeto, 2014).

Another important challenge pertains to the management of online students and face-to-face students at the same time by faculty members (Bower et al., 2015; Bower et al., 2014; Francescucci & Foster, 2014; Hastie, Hung, Chen, & Kinshuk, 2010). In this particular context of learning, faculty members might have to slow down the teaching pace or overdone repetition in order to give additional explanations to online students, which can affect face-to-face student learning (Bower et al., 2015; Bower et al., 2014; Szeto, 2014).

A third challenge is related to students' levels of technological skill. If some online students lack technological skills, then faculty members might focus on them and spend much time troubleshooting technical problems (Bower et al., 2015; Bower et al., 2014; Cunningham, 2014). Moreover, issues with connectivity and technology can be barriers for online students in BSL (Abdelmalak, 2014; Cunningham, 2014; Francescucci & Foster, 2014; Kyei-Blankson et al., 2014).

Finally, some face-to-face students reported that interacting with online students was indirect, and therefore cooperative tasks were difficult to carry out in virtual environments; additional efforts were required to foster group interaction in the instructional process (Szeto, 2014). Communication and interaction seem to be more difficult between face-to-face students and online students than between face-to-face students (Bower et al., 2014). Moreover, some online students might feel less attended to and unwelcome in the course (Hastie et al., 2010), or they might perceive that their comments are not taken into consideration by face-to-face students. In fact, it is difficult to give free access to speaking rights to online students. They often have to indicate when they want to speak in text, and sometimes they are limited to written participation. Forming relationships with fellow classmates might be difficult for online students because they do not meet in person every week, making it more difficult to form relationships with face-to-face students (Francescucci & Foster, 2014) and thus to build up a social presence that would be helpful in learning (Cunningham, 2014). Therefore, social and emotional connectedness needs to be encouraged and fostered by faculty members in such a learning environment (Bower et al., 2015).

BSL in a Master Teacher Program

Transferring from a face-to-face mode to BSL presents universities with many advantages and challenges (Bower et al., 2015; Lakhal, Bateman, & Bédard, 2017). BSL has been used in the Master Teacher Program (MTP) in a Canadian francophone university because of its context in which face-to-face students are combined with online students and in order to expand teaching practices. The MTP is designed for practitioners to enable them to develop reflective and critical thinking on their teaching and to develop research expertise using methods of inquiry. These practitioners are teachers currently deployed in anglophone public and private colleges in Québec: Dawson, John-Abbott, Vanier, Champlain Lennox-ville, Champlain St. Lambert, Champlain St. Lawrence, Marianapolis, Centennial Academy, and Heritage. In Québec, public colleges are called *collèges d'enseignement général et professionnel* or *CEGEPs*, and private colleges are designated as *collèges*. They refer to postsecondary institutions exclusive to the system of education in Québec. They are exclusive in that the diploma of college studies, called *diplôme d'études collégiales*, is required for university admission.

The MTP grants three levels of a graduate degree: a graduate certificate in college teaching (GCCT), a graduate diploma in college teaching (GDCT), and a master's degree in college teaching (MCT). The MTP targets educational psychology, pedagogy, pedagogical content knowledge, and discipline-based learning with the aim of furthering the professional abilities and reflective practices of its teacher-participants. In an effort to serve anglophone colleges outside the Montréal region, BSL has been implemented since 2006 and is still in operation.

The MTP uses BSL, which requires students who live in the Montréal area to attend face-to-face classes, whereas students who live outside the Montréal region attend the classes synchronously online. Instead of using podcasts to reduce distant students' feeling of isolation, as suggested by Conrad (2014), desktop videoconferencing, which permits bidirectional communication, is deployed in each course session. Moreover, face-to-face session time is reduced and replaced with learning and assessment activities conducted asynchronously and, in some courses, conducted online synchronously between class meetings. The context of BSL use is different from contexts reported in the literature by Bower et al. (2015), Educause (2010), Irvine et al. (2013), Lakhal, Khechine, and Pascot (2014), and Miller et al. (2013) because students have no choice in the type of course participation; residents of the Montréal area must attend face-to-face classes, whereas students at a distance must attend courses online synchronously. Distance students who complete the MCT are asked to be present in class at four key times throughout the 45-credit program in order to have contact with their colleagues and to develop a sense of belonging to their cohort or class group. The travelling fees and hotel accommodations for these students are paid by the deans of the anglophone colleges.

Methodology

Participants

All course instructors in the MTP were invited to participate in the study during the 2017 summer session. Four of the 16 instructors agreed to participate in the semi-structured interviews. These participants were coded as T1, T2, T3, and T4. Participants were offered $50 as compensation for the time devoted to the study interviews. Table 6.1 outlines the demographic details of the study sample.

Table 6.1 Demographic details of the study sample.

	Characteristics	Participants
Gender	Male	1
	Female	3
Age group	45–50	2
	50–55	0
	55–60	0
	60–65	2
MTP graduate	Yes	2
	No	2
Number of years of teaching in the MTP	0–5	3
	10–15	1
Levels taught in the MTP	GCCT	3
	GDCT	2
	GCT	1
Number of courses taught using BSL	5–10	3
	10–15	1
Level of computer skills	Good	1
	Very good	3

Methods and Analysis

An exploratory case study was adopted for this research using qualitative data (Yin, 1994). Data collection comprised semi-structured online interviews using Skype software. Because the principal researcher was also the manager of the MTP, her research assistant was responsible for conducting the interviews and anonymizing the data, using a code for each participant. Ethics approval was granted from the ethics review board of the francophone university where the study took place. During the interviews, participants elaborated on their experiences with BSL in the MTP. The interviews lasted between 90 and 120 minutes and were recorded on video. The method used for data analysis was thematic analysis following the six stages of Braun and Clarke (2006): transcribing data, generating initial coding, searching for themes, reviewing themes, naming and defining themes, and producing the report.

Results and Discussion

Five major themes emerged from the data: (1) accessibility; (2) course organization, planning, and design; (3) teaching, learning, and assessment activities; (4) communication and interaction; and (5) technology. Table 6.2 presents these five themes and their subthemes. Within them, the MTP practices with BSL as well as the benefits of using this mode of course delivery and the challenges experienced by faculty members and students are reported accordingly. The advantages and challenges of BSL are summarized for each theme in the appendix.

Table 6.2 Themes and subthemes that emerged from the study results.

Themes	Subthemes
Accessibility	
Course organization, planning, and design	✓ Course organization
	✓ Course planning and design

Teaching, learning, and assessment activities	✓ Activities useful for students
	✓ Student-centred activities
	✓ Student engagement
	✓ Management of online students and face-to-face students
Communication and interaction	✓ Communication and interaction between face-to-face students and online students
	✓ Communication and interaction between instructor and face-to-face students and online students
	✓ Informal communication and interaction
Technology	✓ Software and equipment
	✓ Challenges with technology

Accessibility

In the case of the MTP, BSL provided access to higher education. The four instructors interviewed agreed about this advantage. Accessibility had two significations for study participants. On the one hand, BSL gave access to the MTP to students who lived in the Montréal region and were therefore supposed to attend face-to-face sessions but were not able to do so for exceptional reasons. These students were still allowed to participate in the course while benefiting from the interactions with their instructor and classmates in real time. Instructor T2 recognized that accessibility is "the main advantage. . . . I think about another teacher who ended up on bed rest with her pregnancy. Even though she was a face-to-face Montréal participant, she could still do the course because she could do it online" (55). On the other hand, BSL in the MTP allowed students from other regions to attend class sessions and to interact with their classmates in real time. These students were able to obtain a university graduate degree in education while remaining in their communities. Instructor T4 pointed out that "we are helping people that cannot otherwise get a university education at the master's level, and these are teachers" (106). As this instructor added, "we saw that they had had aspirations to do something like this, . . . get some more educational background in pedagogy and teaching, but there was no way for them to do it, so [this] was their opportunity" (121).

Distance education students appreciated the chance to take BSL courses and programs and to be in touch with colleagues from other *CEGEP*s. Talking about students from a distance, instructor T4 stated that "I think people really appreciate the chance to be doing that and to hear from their colleagues" (117). Moreover, participants observed that these online students were enthusiastic about attending class sessions and active compared with face-to-face students:

> From the beginning, we saw that they were very, very keen. They were the ones who would post things first. They were the ones to be more actively involved. The people in Montréal were . . . more laid back—"Oh, I'll do it tomorrow"— . . . whereas right after class these people would post things right away, and they were all excited. (T4, 121)

Some participants in the study wanted more choices for students living in the Montréal region in terms of course attendance in order to increase enrolment. For example, some students encounter issues because of traffic and road conditions, especially in winter sessions. These issues prevent them from enrolling in some courses, as instructor T1 indicated:

> Sometimes traffic, having to travel from [College A] to [College B]. Some people have decided not to take the course because of that. If we allow them to take it in blended format, then they would take it. If we force them to drive, then they won't. (3)

Some instructors even question why the university does not extend the program to other provinces. For example, instructor T3 argued that "we have students from all over, like in Québec, maybe open to other provinces. This program, by the way, can be very good for people from other places. I don't know why we keep it here in Québec" (97).

Previous studies also revealed that BSL courses provide students with greater educational access since they are available to those who live far from university campuses (Bower et al., 2015; Bower et al., 2014; Educause, 2010). Moreover, previous studies reported that BSL courses offer flexible attendance to those who have work schedules and family responsibilities that make it difficult for them to attend weekly face-to-face sessions (Abdelmalak, 2014; Bower et al., 2015; Bower et al., 2014; Cunningham, 2014; Francescucci & Foster, 2014; Miller et al., 2013). However, in the MTP, students do not have a choice in course attendance. Access to class sessions online is given to students from the Montréal area only in exceptional circumstances.

Course Organization, Planning, and Design

Course Organization. Besides class sessions in which online students are mixed with face-to-face students, two other types of activities are planned in using BSL in the MTP: face-to-face activities and online activities for all students enrolled in the course. The program committee chose to hold some face-to-face activities among all students for certain pedagogical purposes. Indeed, students are asked to be physically present in class in Montréal at four key times throughout the MTP. Regarding the role of these practices in enhancing the perception of social presence among students, instructor T2 claimed that, "when the people at a distance come in, those couple of days that we do in the program . . ., it helps as well to foster that bond" (34). Instructor T4 added that "we also have times within our program that everyone must be in Montréal, and the connections . . . at that point are tremendous, and then when you see them online you feel that much more connected to them" (106). Some activities in each course are held online for all students. Having face-to-face activities and online activities put all students on the same level. All students, whether they are from Montréal or other regions in Québec, are thus on the same page, so no one has an advantage or disadvantage. The inclusion of these activities also enables the program to offer a certain variety in course attendance. Talking about the two types of activities, instructor T4 revealed that "once again everyone is on the same level. You have these occasions throughout our program when everyone is face-to-face or regularly throughout the courses that everyone is online at the same time" (135).

Course Planning and Design. Planning and design in BSL courses are different from face-to-face courses or online courses. Indeed, instructors have to plan and design the courses in order to consider both online students and face-to-face students. For example, they have to create opportunities for all students to participate on their computers, so that those online and those in class contribute at the same level:

> You have to remember, it's like you've got two groups that you're always trying to make into one group. You need to be aware of both sectors and then try to blend it together to have the activities blended. (T4, 106)

There are advantages in having students online and students face-to-face in the same group. Indeed, giving access to students outside the Montréal region and mixing them with students from Montréal open the classroom up to other realities and, in the case of my study, to *CEGEP*s in other regions:

> The English colleges are fairly large ... and so we have a sense of what works in an urban environment in large colleges. When you talk about the English participants from smaller colleges that are rural, there's a whole other perspective there, and to be able to bring that into our context was really eye-opening I think for all of us. The exchange was really rich, and the different programs of course that they brought with them in the sense of what they were teaching was also very eye-opening for all of us, so very rewarding all around. (T4, 102)

However, BSL courses require more time to design than courses in other formats. Instructors also have to be familiar with the online aspect of the course. Indeed, for "a teacher that's not familiar with how it feels to be online, they may not realize the impact of their actions" (T1, 25).

It seems to be harder to design a BSL course than a face-to-face course according to instructor T2: "It's harder to design the course so that you can obtain the same learning and the same learning outcomes" (55). The planning also has to be more accurate. From the point of view of instructor T1, a BSL course works well when "it's super organized. We have everything down to five minutes, and we respect our timing. We always have our little schedule" (1). However, such accurate planning does not leave room for flexibility. The lack of flexibility results from the fact that activities have to be planned and available to online students on the Moodle page a few days before the class. A last-minute change to the teacher's plan cannot work in these circumstances.

These challenges were also reported in previous studies that found that a BSL course demands much more physical and social preparation than face-to-face or online courses (Bower et al., 2015; Bower et al., 2014), such as setting up the rooms (both physical and virtual classes) in order to create a meaningful learning environment. In fact, instructors might spend a lot of time anticipating interaction and collaboration between online and face-to-face students (Bower et al., 2015; Bower et al., 2014).

Teaching, Learning, and Assessment Activities

Useful Activities for Students. Instructors try to make sure that all teaching, learning, and assessment activities are relevant and useful for students. Students are always encouraged to discuss their concerns and experiences in class sessions. They are also invited to draw links between their experiences and theory. Instructor T3, for example, asks students "what can you take from this theory . . . and actually apply tomorrow when you go to the classroom, what can you do about it? Give me the scenario" (67).

Students should also be able to build on and use their learning in their own teaching. Talking about a learning activity, instructor T3 claimed that "it has to be very, very relevant to what they tackle every day" (58). Instructor T4 added that "it's targeted as what the participant's needs are. I really try to focus on that. What's going to make the most sense for you with this kind of assignment? How will it be the most useful?" (108). Thus, the activities carried out—whether synchronously or asynchronously— should be transferable to college teaching, preferably in the short term. Instructor T1 claimed that "what's really important is that they get to use what they're going to learn for something that's not two years down the line, for something that's coming, making the learning and the assessments useful to them right away" (7).

Activities presented to students in BSL meet the characteristics of educational approaches for adult students, as described by Stöter, Zawacki-Richter, and von Prümmer (2014). These authors revealed that learning for adults is characterized by, among other things, connecting new knowledge to their experiences and immediacy in application.

Student-Centred Activities. In the study, it was found that instructors used a variety of teaching and learning activities in order to meet different students' needs and characteristics and to make sure that all the course objectives are met. Instructor T4 claimed that "I really feel that our students are so diverse. Their intellectual abilities, their types of learning. . . . Anyways, there's just so many different types of learners and that you need the variety" (112).

Most of the time, instructors used student-centred strategies in order to encourage students to participate in their learning. Instructors act as a guide, even as a learner, and not the only holder of knowledge. They are part of the whole class and learn and share with the students. Instructor T4 argued that "I don't want to be seen as the sole source of knowledge" (117). This instructor also recognized that "I'm in there with them, I'm learning as well as they're learning, and how can we do this together? How can we collectively experience and learn whatever our topic is" (113). This advantage was also reported in previous studies according to which BSL allows instructors to use different strategies in order to meet different student learning preferences, approaches, and strategies (Abdelmalak, 2014; Kyei-Blankson et al., 2014). Moreover, the roles of instructors and students have to be conceived differently compared with those in traditional face-to-face courses. In BSL courses, the strategies of teaching and learning should be more student centred. Therefore, instructors should enhance students' participation in their learning and support interactions between face-to-face and online students (Asterhan & Schwarz, 2010; Bower et al., 2015; Bower et al., 2014; Hastie et al., 2010; Szeto, 2014).

Instructor T4 makes sure that all students participate in their learning, even the quietest ones. This instructor gives them the same opportunity to participate by calling on everyone in the class to go up to the white board (face-to-face students) and even at home (online students).

In the synchronous activities, group work is one of the most often used learning strategies in the MTP courses. The four instructors interviewed perceived this learning strategy as the most efficient. Moreover, it seems to foster the engagement of all students and a better understanding of the course content, whether students are online or face-to-face. Talking about group work, instructor T2 claimed that "it's to keep everybody active and engaged but also to have a better understanding of the content" (32). Group work also makes it possible to have discussions and encourage feed-back among students. In the MTP, group work has also been identified as a means to enhance a sense of belonging or social presence, as defined by Garrison, Anderson, and Archer (2000, 2001).

> When you allow them to do a lot of group work together, . . . they discover they don't live apart. They will travel together. They will group in somebody's office and all attend the session together. . . . It creates the sense of their belonging to a group. Then the group belongs to the class, and the class belongs to the program. (T1, 15)

In online synchronous activities, some instructors also seek students' participation. Instructor T2 claimed that, "when we're all online, I like to use the poll feature in WebEx, just to make sure that everybody is active and following along" (31). This instructor allows students to add to the PowerPoint slides during these synchronous sessions: "When they're online, . . . I give them the rights to write on the PowerPoint slide so that they can add [to it]" (34).

For the asynchronous activities, instructors employ all the features of Moodle, such as discussion forums, Wikis, quizzes, questionnaires, lessons, and glossaries. Some of these tools are employed for learning and others for assessment. Group work, with a mix of online students and face-to-face students, is used in these activities while taking advantage of these tools.

Asynchronous activities make it possible to provide continuity among synchronous activities in terms of learning and interacting among students and with course content. Instructors use the readings, the database activities, and the discussion forums in Moodle because they want students to think and to see what other students think about a given topic in order to integrate other viewpoints, not just the instructor's.

Student Engagement. To ensure that students are engaged in their learning activities, 20% of the grade in the MTP courses is devoted to engagement, which pertains to participation in course activities. Instructor T2 argued that this is "making sure that they are doing the work in the discussion forum. That they are contributing to the database. That they are contributing in class. [That] they are being vocal in class" (33). For instructors, measures of engagement, as an assessment strategy, are important because not all sessions are face-to-face. Some are done online asynchronously. Assessment of engagement ensures that students participate in learning activities in order to replace face-to-face or synchronous learning time. This was also reported in previous studies (Asterhan & Schwarz, 2010). Instructor T2 argued that "you've got so many hours now that are no longer in class. You got the hours that are now online outside of class. You've got to make sure that the students are doing it" (33). T3 elaborated:

> We have a forum in the course, so we have a little back and forth with ideas, sharing of ideas. Because I like to keep the class even though there's no classes, so you create this forum and people share. . . . It's not always effective, but it's something that creates some kind of learning experience outside. (75)

This type of engagement is particularly true in intensive course sessions, in which students are supposed to accomplish some learning activities online, more often than in regular course sessions. Students are expected to go online regularly, almost every day, to check the Moodle page, to contribute to the posts in discussion forums, to submit questions, and to respond to other students' questions. Instructors expect students to be visible throughout the course.

Engagement also means that students interact with each other and further their learning. For example, instructor T2 claimed that students not only have to post in forums but also have to reply to others in order to ensure continuity (32). For these activities, there needs to be clear time frames. Otherwise, some students do not participate promptly, and this could affect the learning of other students. As T4 noted,

> some people are so good with it, but then they posted, and no one respond[ed] to them or their partner who should have responded [and] didn't respond, and then they email me and say, "What do I do?" Those are the kind[s] of things that are problematic. (105)

Management of Online and Face-to-Face Students. It is difficult for instructors in BSL classes to manage online and face-to-face students at the same time. Some instructors might even forget that they have students online and focus on their face-to-face students:

> I'd be honest with you, sometimes it's very easy to forget students outside. It's so easy. . . . I always have to . . . remember you have these students that are outside, because it's so hard to disengage from the environment of the classroom. (T3, 60)

Instructors reported that they were unable to manage students online and face-to-face at the same time. This challenge was also highlighted by previous studies (Bower et al., 2015; Bower et al., 2014; Francescucci & Foster, 2014; Hastie et al., 2010). For example, in cases of trouble with technology, they cannot provide the support for online students and put face-to-face students on hold. Instructor T1 mentioned that "I can't do the technical support because it's only a three-hour period, and you just don't have time to say to all the others hold while I figure this out" (4). To overcome these issues, each instructor in an MTP course is paired with a teaching assistant. This solution has been adopted in other contexts. Teaching assistants have been employed to manage technology-related problems, respond to online student chat comments, and manage other issues (Bell, Sawaya & Cain, 2014; Bower et al., 2015; Bower et al., 2014). In the MTP, the teaching assistant is called a tech support. The four instructors interviewed agreed that the teaching assistant is a must in each BSL course because they are not able to manage the course alone. Instructor T2 commented that "you absolutely have to have tech support. You cannot do this without a proper technician" (56), and T4 claimed that,

> if I would be expected to do it all on my own, I'd be out of there very quick. You have to be on the ball, you have to know what's going on, you have to be there, and the teacher already has two elements, two mini subgroups of a whole larger group. You can't also do the tech support, you really can't. For three hours, it's not possible. (107)

The role of the teaching assistant is mainly to help include online students. This person is perceived to be the voice of online students as they use chat to ask questions, to add their comments, or to participate in class discussions. Talking about the teaching assistant, the four instructors interviewed agreed on his or her role. As T3 commented, "he is the actual frontline, the mouth for them" (77).

The qualifications of the teaching assistant seem to be an issue in BSL courses. As instructor T1 revealed, "the quality of the tech support, that has a huge impact too on making the class run smoothly" (25). Among other qualifications, the teaching assistant should have good troubleshooting skills.

Communication and Interaction

Participants in the study pointed out the importance for students to communicate and interact with each other and with instructors in order to enhance the three types of presence: social, cognitive, and teaching (Garrison et al., 2000, 2001). In previous studies, students enrolled in BSL courses were reported to experience high levels of social presence because of real-time communications with instructors and classmates (Bower et al., 2015; Cunningham, 2014). The Moodle features listed in the teaching, learning, and assessment strategies, such as reading, and discussion forums and Wikis enable communication and interaction among students. They are possible mainly through the use of text. Moreover, group work, one of the learning strategies used the most often by instructors in the MTP, allows students to work together, exchange ideas, and construct knowledge. Some instructors use "breakout rooms" with VIAand WebEx, which are two desktop web conferencing systems, when the groups are composed of face-to-face and online students. In these situations, students have to use their cameras and headphones as they rely mainly on voice and video to communicate and interact with each other.

Communication and Interaction Between Face-to-Face and Online Students. In class sessions, some instructors encourage face-to-face students to communicate and interact with online students by means of the chat room on WebEx. It also allows for immediate feedback. This is known as backchannel communication among students. This advantage was also reported in previous studies (Bower et al., 2015; Bower et al., 2014; Francescucci & Foster, 2014; Miller et al., 2013) and requires a degree of letting go from the instructor on behalf of the students. Along these lines, instructor T1 reported that, "in the class . . . , we allow them in WebEx to chat with each other so they can send private messages through one another" (12). However, not all instructors permit students to interact with each other using WebEx. Communication and interaction among students are vital in the context of BSL in order to ensure that online students develop a sense of belonging to the group and do not feel isolated and excluded, especially in class sessions in which there is a mix of face-to-face students and online students. Instructor T4 added that "we have to remember the people online, so we have to just engage them and make sure that the people in class are also working with the people online" (120).

Communication and interaction among face-to-face students are easy, but for online students additional efforts need to be made. Accordingly, instructor T1 recognized that

> when [you're] sitting next to somebody, you tend to talk with that person and discover something. . . . If we don't allow communication, it's the same like I just said, the exclusion, the people online, we need to make the effort to link them to the people in class. (10)

Talking about communication and interaction between online and face-to-face students, instructor T4 added that, in sharing their experiences, it is easier for face-to-face students compared with online students: "It's easy for them, and once again it's harder for the ones at a distance because you can't just casually chat with someone. . . . It's definitely more difficult for the people online" (118).

Face-to-face students have to show openness to online students and indicate that they really want to connect with them. Talking about face-to-face students, instructor T4 claimed that "we all collectively recognize that there's people at a distance that need to be included and that the group in class is aware. Each of them individually [is] also aware that there's these people at a distance" (101).

Not every student is ready to be an online student. Some students are not comfortable with the online aspect of the courses. Instructor T4 recognized that "within the blended learning we need to think that everyone online is not necessarily comfortable online" (135). Sometimes online students do not participate in the course. They are not there even if they are logged in. The visual anonymity makes it easier for online students to disengage from class discussions (Francescucci & Foster, 2014). Talking about a situation that happened in a course, instructor T4 related that "every once in a while someone [had] gone off to do their laundry or something. I mean you can't tell. They've logged on" (115).

Online students have to possess some specific skills. One of the best online students in the program was described by instructor T2 in these words:

> She'd have her webcam on. She would always jump in. She never hesitated. When you said "Okay, those of you online, have you got something to add?" she would always jump in. She was always using her hand or the emoticons. She was always writing on the board. She's probably one of our best online learners. (35)

To help students become good online learners, some training should be provided to them at the beginning of the program, as mentioned by instructor T2: "One of the things we need to do as an MTP program for everybody who's going to be online, they need a primer. They need a tutorial or something before they start" (36). For example, a module on Moodle or some videos should be available to these students.

Synchronous communication and interaction between online and face-to-face students can also be possible in group work. While using this learning strategy, some instructors mix online and face-to-face students. Group work with such a mix was also reported in previous studies (Bell et al., 2014; Cunningham, 2014). Instructors in the present study believed that it was their responsibility to create occasions when online students could work with face-to-face students. Instructor T2 argued that, "when I'm doing the group work, I'm always trying to mix them up so that the online people are working with the face-to-face people too" (42). Moreover, instructors can ensure that students have the chance to work with different colleagues instead of always having the same students in each group. Instructor T2 revealed that "I keep a long list of who's worked with who each class so that I make sure that the two people in Gatineau who already share an office aren't always working together" (32).

Finally, in order to optimize the mix between online and face-to-face students in group work, the number of each should be equal according to instructor T2: "Half the students were face-to-face, and half the students were online, so it made blending the groups very easy" (27). Instructor T4 preferred to have four or five students online, which corresponded to a quarter to a third of the class:

> There's 15 to 18 people generally in our classes, so we're looking at four. Four is a great number online. Four, five, that kind of number, like maybe a third. Quarter to a third are online. That's a good ratio. When you only have one person online, that's more problematic, I find. (101)

To arrange the groups when instructors do not have enough students online, some of them might ask students from the face-to-face group to be online intentionally.

Some instructors are reluctant to mix online and face-to-face students in groups because they reported that face-to-face students are against this. Talking about group constitution, instructor T3 reported that, in order to eliminate the irritants, "people in the classroom are going to create groups, people in Sherbrooke, in Gaspesie, in Québec City are going to be as a group themselves" (81).

Communication and Interaction Between the Instructor and Face-to-Face and Online Students. In class sessions, instructors have to ensure that face-to-face and online students have the same chance to step in. To make this happen, they have to be inclusive and show openness to online students in their attitude and their position in the classroom. Instructor T1 acknowledged that "the teacher has to be inclusive as well in their mind and think of the people that are online. The enthusiasm of the teachers too is really important to make them want to pursue, to continue [their learning]" (14). Talking about online students, instructor T4 added that "I really make an effort to individually acknowledge their presence and expect that they will be contributing to the class" (117). Instructor T1 advised to "always turn to them and try to include them and not just as an afterthought" (11). Instructor T4 took a position in front of the camera so that, even when speaking to the group in the room, T4 always looked at the camera.

Instructor T4 believed that it is harder for online students to be involved in class discussions. Moreover, some online students might feel less attended to and not welcomed in the course or that their comments are not taken into account by face-to-face students (Hastie et al., 2010). Instructor T4 made additional efforts to facilitate their interactions by giving them priority:

> They're having a little bit harder time . . . than everyone in class, so then they get a little bit of a privilege every once in a while. If I'm asking for some feedback on something or asking a question, I often will start with the online participants first—anyone online [who] want[s] to address this question first, that kind of thing. (113)

This challenge was also reported in previous studies (Francescucci & Foster, 2014). Despite the efforts made by instructors to include online students, their ability to gauge online students' understanding of the course content is a challenge in BSL courses. With face-to-face students, instructors can always see non-verbal attitudes of the students and determine if they understand the topics being taught. This is not the case with online students. Talking about face-to-face interactions, instructor T3 reported that, "in the classroom, it's much easier because you talk about body language, and you can talk about things that they see and they feel" (61), as opposed to interactions with online students. For this instructor, interactions with face-to-face students are "more direct, . . . you're feeling the atmosphere in the class, body language. I'm very into body language involvement, expression, tone of voice. Again, electronically, things are not transmitted as they are" in physical classrooms (79). This challenge was also reported in previous studies (Cunningham, 2014). Some instructors might feel guilty about online students. Instructor T3 recognized that "you feel you don't give enough to them, and you want to nurture them as much as other people" (76).

Informal Communication and Interaction. It is more difficult for online students to have informal communication and interaction and to create relationships with face-to-face students and instructors because they are not present in person during discussions before class or on a break:

> One of the things that they said at a distance is that they missed the pre-class discussions. They missed the break discussions. They missed the jokes that happened at the coffee machine. They missed those stories that the teacher and the students talk about in between. They miss out on that. There's definitely less opportunities for that to happen. That's huge. It's got nothing to do with academics. It's got nothing to do with pedagogy. It's [got] nothing to do with the content of the course. (T2, 38)

This challenge was also reported in previous studies, according to which it is more difficult for online students to form relationships with fellow classmates (Francescucci & Foster, 2014) and to build up a social presence that would be helpful for learning (Cunningham, 2014). Therefore, social and emotional connectedness needs to be encouraged and fostered by faculty members within such a learning environment (Bower et al., 2015). Online students make some efforts before and after class to be part of the group. Often they stay connected online after the class in case they hear something new from their classmates.

The instructor can also make additional efforts to ensure that online students do not feel left aside. For example, instructor T2 explained how he acts on this matter:

> Before class starts . . . , I always say hello to everybody online and make them come up so that they can say hello to everybody. . . . I stay online after class all the time. I'll put the headsets on so that it's not the whole class hearing and say "Do you guys have any questions? Is there anything that wasn't clear?" (39)

Other strategies can be used through technologies that allow students to connect with each other. For example, the use of cameras by online students in group work to allow face-to-face students to get to know them better is advised by some instructors. Other instructors encourage them to complete their profiles in Moodle in order to obtain general pictures of them.

Technology

Software and Equipment. The use of technology is necessary in BSL. Technology makes it possible to run online synchronous course sessions for all students. The technological tools used in face-to-face sessions are also used with a mix of online and face-to-face students. For asynchronous activities, Moodle with all its features is used, which presents some advantages. It enables instructors to keep track of students' learning. Instructor T1 claimed that "you . . . can go explore, and you get a lot of data that way. You can track your students and know what they've done and not just turned on Moodle and did nothing on it" (5). Moreover, it allows instructors to post course session records so that all students can access class sessions that they could not attend or for the purpose of review. This advantage was also reported in previous research in other contexts (Bower et al., 2015; Bower et al., 2014). Instructor T4 indicated that "we can record these sessions [so] that, if someone is sick or they're just not able to get there, they can review the class. . . . That's a benefit of the courses being blended because then they're taped" (106–107). Technology also enables online students to attend class sessions with face-to-face students in real time. In the MTP, VIA and WebEx are used to permit backchannel communication between face-to-face students and online students on the one hand and between online students and the teaching assistant on the other. In addition, cameras and microphones are necessary in the classroom to allow online students to see and hear face-to-face students and instructors. To make group work more efficient, and to avoid noise in the principal classroom, some instructors who mix online and face-to-face students need two or three additional small rooms, all equipped with cameras and computers. They might send some of the face-to-face students in these rooms to work with online students. In this context, talking about room settings, instructor T2 claimed that, "ideally, you'd have one big room with two or three small rooms on the side all with computers. All with hanging microphones from the ceiling. All with at least two webcams in the room at each end" (55).

Colleges where course sessions take place are different in terms of configuration and room setting. Instructor T4 reported that "every college is different, so the expectations and the room configurations are different" (135). Unfortunately, some of them are not well equipped for BSL. In this regard, instructor T2 claimed that "we didn't have the proper equipment. [It] . . . is always problematic when it comes to equipment" (29). More equipment is requested for teaching in some colleges. The equipment can be

> as simple as [a] microphone, as simple as headphones, as simple as [a] camera, there's no budget. I don't get it. Why do we sometimes have to bring them up? This is [an] elementary aspect that, like you have fingers and you have eyes, so it should be in the needs for [a] blended learning class. Before we talk about all the pedagogy, these are simple tools that we have to have there. Sometimes this is broken. (T3, 99)

Other technological tools have to be explored, such as the use of social media tools (Twitter, Facebook, etc.) and mobile learning, as described by Conrad (2014), in order to enhance interactions in BSL.

Challenges with Technology. According to the four instructors interviewed, technology can be a challenge in BSL for different reasons. It evolves quickly, and instructors have to be open to adapting to the changes. According to the instructors interviewed, technology has to be reliable. When it is not adequate, it prevents online students from participating with face-to-face students, and it hinders their sense of belonging to the group. Talking about online students, instructor T2 claimed that "you want to integrate them as much as possible with the people in the classroom, [but] we had so many technical problems that semester. We couldn't put them with the people in the class" (29). Moreover, students' access to the Internet can be a challenge, especially for those outside the Montréal region. This issue has also been reported in previous studies

(Abdelmalak, 2014; Cunningham, 2014; Francescucci & Foster, 2014; Kyei-Blankson et al., 2014). For example, talking about students in Granby, about 80 kms from Montréal, instructor T2 added that "Granby is talking about the rural environment and how the students in the rural environment don't necessarily have access to good wifi" (28).

Problems with technology can have other negative effects, such as delaying the beginning of a course session: "People online that login late [means that] . . . we can't troubleshoot" (T1, 3). Instructors might also have to stop a course session, as noted by instructor T1: "We had VIA, and it wasn't working, even with WebEx. All of a sudden, a session quits. We have to put everything on pause" (3).

Instructors' levels of technical skill can also be a challenge in BSL. Some instructors are comfortable with technology, whereas others are not, as reported by instructor T4:

> As a teacher, I need to be very comfortable with Moodle. I need to be very comfortable with WebEx. I really feel that because I used it in different ways . . . I understand it, but not everyone is that comfortable with that. (135)

Students' levels of technical skill can likewise be a challenge in BSL. Talking about some students in a particular course, instructor T1 revealed that

> they were so afraid of technology. It was very difficult to get them to break the barrier. . . . I'd say the biggest difficulty is always the difference in skill levels. Some are very, very low; some are very high or more high. . . . When you have a class of 28, it's really difficult to have eight people that can't help themselves. (3)

These challenges have also been reported in previous studies (Bower et al., 2015; Bower et al., 2014; Cunningham, 2014). It is essential for instructors and students to learn to use technology adequately. Some training and videos should be provided to them in this regard.

For instructors, it is important to have a technical person available while running class sessions, especially on weekends. The availability of this person is essential to running course sessions smoothly. Instructor T1 claimed that "having a technical person we can access weekends ... would be really interesting. ... A chat somewhere or somebody that could come in and see what we're experiencing, troubleshooting" (26). Since these course sessions are held in different colleges, the training and the availability of technical persons might vary. Moreover, these technicians are not always informed about MTP needs in regard to BSL. Instructor T1 claimed that "we're experts in our fields, but the technic[ians] of the locales, when you're working in several schools, they're not trained. Nobody has given them any kind of info" (27).

Implications

The results of this study help to enrich existing knowledge of BSL in higher education. This knowledge, based on empirical data, can give faculty members and higher education administrators additional information on the use of this mode of course delivery if they wish to implement it in graduate programs. It can also help instructors who aim to use BSL in their courses to make better decisions based on the MTP instructors' experience with this type of course delivery. At a more local level, the advantages can be exploited, and the issues raised by the MTP instructors can be addressed in order to implement a stronger model of BSL in graduate programs.

Limitations and Future Study

The findings of this study cannot be extended to broader populations or transferred to other contexts because of the small sample size. Indeed, these findings might present some bias because of the characteristics of the four instructors interviewed. Another limitation of this study pertains to the data collected. Indeed, the practices, advantages, and challenges of BSL in the MTP are reported solely according to instructors. The interviews with them are part of a larger study in which distance education students, students in the Montréal area, teaching assistants, and technical persons will be interviewed in order to obtain their points of view and to clarify the results of the study presented here and the themes and subthemes that emerged from the data. Moreover, observations of BSL class sessions and analyses of pedagogical documents such as course plans, teacher evaluation reports, and program evaluation reports will take place.

Conclusion

The aim of this study was to report on current practices in the MTP with BSL as well as the benefits of using this mode of course delivery and the challenges experienced by faculty members and students, focusing on the use of video/voice and text. To my knowledge, this is the first study conducted on this topic in a university in Québec. Indeed, previous studies on practices in BSL courses were carried out mainly in Australia, where this type of course delivery seems to be popular in universities (Bower et al., 2015; Bower et al., 2014; Cunningham, 2014; Hastie et al., 2010), and in the United States (Abdelmalak, 2014; Bell et al., 2014; Francescucci & Foster, 2014; Miller et al., 2013). The other studies carried out in French-speaking universities in Québec focused mainly on the determinants of students' use of desktop videoconferencing (Khechine, Lakhal, Pascot, & Bytha, 2014; Lakhal & Khechine, 2016; Lakhal, Khechine, & Pascot, 2013) and on students' satisfaction and learning outcomes (Lakhal et al., 2014) in BSL courses. The results of this study show that BSL in the MTP has many advantages but also faces challenges that have to be addressed. Some of these challenges were also reported in previous studies, but others are more specific to the context of this study, such as the variability in room settings and the availability of technology and technical persons from one college to another. The success of BSL courses is highly dependent on technology; thus, issues related to colleges have to be corrected. Moreover, instructors have to improve the inclusion of distant students, and some training could be provided to them to assist them in this matter.

Appendix: Advantages and Challenges of BSL

Advantages	Challenges
Accessibility	
✓ Students from Montréal have access in exceptional circumstances.	✓ There are more choices in course attendance for students from Montréal.
✓ Students outside the Montréal region have access to the program.	✓ The MTP should be opened up to students from other provinces in Canada.
✓ Students from a distance can get a master's degree while remaining in their communities.	
Course organization, planning, and design	
✓ Online and face-to-face activities for all students make it possible to place them all on the same level and to enhance the perception of social presence among distant students.	✓ Instructors have to consider online and face-to-face students in course organization.
✓ Online, face-to-face, and blended activities offer a certain variety of course attendance.	✓ Instructors need more time in designing BSL courses than online or face-to-face courses.
✓ The mix of online and face-to-face students opens up the classroom to other realities.	✓ BSL courses are harder to design than face-to-face courses.
	✓ The planning of a BSL course has to be more accurate, which does not leave room for flexibility.
Teaching, learning, and assessment activities	
✓ Students can discuss their concerns about college teaching in class sessions and draw links between their experience and theory.	✓ It is difficult for instructors to manage online and face-to-face students at the same time.
✓ Students can build on and use their learning in teaching their own students.	✓ It is necessary to have a teaching assistant in each course session.
✓ Activities should be transferable to college teaching in the short term.	
✓ Instructors use a variety of teaching and learning strategies to meet students' needs and characteristics.	
✓ The instructor acts as a guide and not the only owner of knowledge.	

✓ Online asynchronous activities enable continuity with synchronous activities.

✓ Activities such as group work enable the engagement of all students, allow discussions among and feedback from students, and enhance social presence.

Communication and interaction

✓ Communication and interaction between face-to-face and online students are possible by means of chat on WebEx.

✓ Communication and interaction between face-to-face and online students are possible in group work.

✓ Formal and informal communication between face-to-face students and the instructor is easy, but for online students some additional effort needs to be made.

✓ Some online students are not comfortable being online.

✓ The mix of online and face-to-face students is efficient in group work only with a certain number of students online.

✓ Some instructors are reluctant to mix face-to-face students with online students.

Instructors' ability to gauge online students' understanding is limited.

Technology

✓ Technology enables instructors to keep track of students' learning.

✓ Technology makes it possible to post course session records to enable all students to access class sessions that they could not attend or for review purposes.

✓ Technology enables online students to attend class sessions with face-to-face students in real time.

✓ Some colleges are not well equipped to run BSL courses.

✓ Technical persons are not available in some colleges.

✓ Instructors have to be open to the evolution of technology.

✓ Technology has to be reliable.

✓ Online students' access to the Internet can be limited, especially for those outside the Montréal region.

✓ Instructors' and students' levels of technical skill can be an issue.

References

Abdelmalak, M. (2014). Towards flexible learning for adult students: HyFlex design. In M. Searson & M. Ochoa (Eds.), *Proceedings of Society for Information Technology & Teacher Education International Conference, 2014* (pp. 706–712). Chesapeake, VA: Association for the Advancement of Computing in Education.

Asterhan, C. S., & Schwarz, B. B. (2010). Online moderation of synchronous e-argumentation. *International Journal of Computer-Supported Collaborative Learning, 5*(3), 259–282.

Bell, J., Sawaya, S., & Cain, W. (2014). Synchromodal classes: Designing for shared learning experiences between face-to-face and online students. *International Journal of Designs for Learning, 5*(1), 68–82.

Bernard, R. M., Borokhovski, E., Schmid, R. F., Tamim, R. M., & Abrami, P. C. (2014). A meta-analysis of blended learning and technology use in higher education: From the general to the applied. *Journal of Computing in Higher Education, 26*(1), 87–122.

Boelens, R., De Wever, B., & Voet, M. (2017). Four key challenges to the design of blended learning: A systematic literature review. *Educational Research Review, 22*, 1–18.

Bower, M., Dalgarno, B., Kennedy, G. E., Lee, M. J., & Kenney, J. (2015). Design and implementation factors in blended synchronous learning environments: Outcomes from a cross-case analysis. *Computers & Education, 86*, 1–17.

Bower, M., Kenney, J., Dalgarno, B., Lee, M. J. W., & Kennedy, G. E. (2014). Patterns and principles for blended synchronous learning: Engaging remote and face-to-face learners in rich-media real-time collaborative activities. *Australasian Journal of Educational Technology, 30*(3), 261–272.

Braun, V., and Clarke, V. (2006). Using thematic analysis in psychology. *Qualitative Research in Psychology, 3*(2), 77–101.

Carey, T., & Ferreras, S. (2017, May 23). *Industry 4.0: Accelerating evolution in employee capability and institutional agility*. Retrieved from https://forum.academica.ca/forum/industry-40-accelerating-evolution-in-employee-capability-and-institutional-agility

Conrad, D. (2014). Interaction and communication in online learning communities: Toward an engaged and flexible future. In O. Zawacki-Richter & T. Anderson (Eds.), *Online distance education: Towards a research agenda* (pp. 381–402). Edmonton, AB: Athabasca University Press.

Cunningham, U. (2014). Teaching the disembodied: Othering and activity systems in a blended synchronous learning situation. *International Review of Research in Open and Distance Learning, 15*(6), 343–351.

Drysdale, J. S., Graham, C. R., Spring, K. J., & Halverson, L. R. (2013). An analysis of research trends in dissertations and theses studying blended learning. *The Internet and Higher Education, 17,* 90–100.

Duarte, R., de Oliveira Pires, A. L., & Nobre, Â. L. (2016, October). Increasing adult students' learning opportunities with flexible learning pathways: Evidence from a technology and industrial management graduate course. In *2016 2nd International Conference of the Portuguese Society for Engineering Education (CISPEE)*(pp. 1–6). Portugal: Institute of Electrical and Electroneers Engineers.

Educause. (2010). *7 things you should know about the HyFlex course model.* Retrieved from https://library.educause.edu/-/media/files/library/2010/11/eli7066-pdf

Francescucci, A., & Foster, M. K. (2014). Virtual interactive real-time instructor-led (VIRI) learning: The case of synchronous blended learning in introductory undergraduate course. *Journal of Higher Education Theory & Practice, 14*(2), 36–45.

Garrison, D. R., Anderson, T., & Archer, W. (2000). Critical inquiry in a text-based environment: Computer conferencing in higher education. *The Internet and Higher Education, 2*(2–3), 87–105.

Garrison, D. R., Anderson, T., & Archer, W. (2001). Critical thinking and computer conferencing: A model and tool to assess cognitive presence. *American Journal of Distance Education, 15*(1), 7–23.

Garrison, D. R., & Vaughan, N. D. (2008). *Blended learning in higher education: Framework, principles, and guidelines.* San Francisco, CA: John Wiley & Sons.

Graham, C. R. (2006). Blended learning systems: Definition, current trends, and future directions. In C. J. Bonk & C. R. Graham (Eds.), *The handbook of blended learning: Global perspectives, local designs* (pp. 3–21). San Francisco, CA: Jossey-Bass/Pfeiffer.

Halverson, L. R., Graham, C. R., Spring, K. J., Drysdale, J. S., & Henrie, C. R. (2014). A thematic analysis of the most highly cited scholarship in the first decade of blended learning research. *The Internet and Higher Education, 20,* 20–34.

Hastie, M., Hung, I., & Chen, N. (2010). A blended synchronous learning model for educational international collaboration. *Innovations in Education & Teaching International, 47*(1), 9–24.

Hill, P. (2012, November–December). Online educational delivery models: A descriptive view. *Educause Review, 47*(6), 84–97.

Irvine, V., Code, J., & Richards, L. (2013). Realigning higher education for the 21st-century learner through multi-access learning. *Journal of Online Learning & Teaching, 9*(2), 172–186.

Khechine, H., Lakhal, S., Pascot, D., & Bytha, A. (2014). UTAUT model for blended learning: The role of gender and age in the intention to use webinars. *Interdisciplinary Journal of E-Learning and Learning Objects, 10*(1), 33–52.

Kyei-Blankson, L., & Godwyll, F. (2010). An examination of learning outcomes in HyFlex learning environments. In J. Sanchez & K. Zhang (Eds.), *Proceedings of E-Learn: World Conference on E-Learning in Corporate, Government, Healthcare, and Higher Education 2010* (pp. 532–535). Chesapeake, VA: Association for the Advancement of Computing in Education.

Kyei-Blankson, L., Godwyll, F., & Nur-Awaleh, M. A. (2014). Innovative blended delivery and learning: Exploring student choice, experience, and level of satisfaction in a HyFlex course. *International Journal of Innovation and Learning, 16*(3), 243–252.

Lakhal, S., Bateman, D., & Bédard, J. (2017). Blended synchronous delivery modes in graduate programs. *Collected Essays on Learning and Teaching, 10*, 47–60.

Lakhal, S., & Khechine, H. (2016). Student intention to use desktop web-conferencing according to course delivery modes in higher education. *The International Journal of Management Education, 14*(2), 146–160.

Lakhal, S., Khechine, H., & Pascot, D. (2013). Student behavioural intentions to use desktop video conferencing in a distance course: Integration of autonomy to the UTAUT model. *Journal of Computing in Higher Education, 25*(2), 93–121.

Lakhal, S., Khechine, H., & Pascot, D. (2014). Academic students' satisfaction and learning outcomes in a HyFlex course: Do delivery modes matter? In *Proceedings of World Conference on E-Learning in Corporate, Government, Healthcare, and Higher Education 2014* (pp. 1936–1944). Chesapeake, VA: Association for the Advancement of Computing in Education.

McGee, P., & Reis, A. (2012). Blended course design: A synthesis of best practices. *Journal of Asynchronous Learning Networks, 16*(4), 7–22.

Miller, J., Risser, M., & Griffiths, R. (2013). Student choice, instructor flexibility: Moving beyond the blended instructional model. *Issues and Trends in Educational Technology, 1*(1), 8–24.

Stöter, J., Zawacki-Richter, O., & von Prümmer, C. (2014). From the back door into the mainstream: The characteristics of lifelong learners. In O. Zawacki-Richter & T. Anderson (Eds.), *Online distance education: Towards a research agenda* (pp. 421-458). Edmonton, AB: Athabasca University Press.

Szeto, E. (2014). Bridging the students' and instructor's experiences: Exploring instructional potential of videoconference in multi-campus universities. *Turkish Online Journal of Educational Technology, 13*(1), 64–72.

Szeto, E., & Cheng, A. Y. (2016). Towards a framework of interactions in a blended synchronous learning environment: What effects are there on students' social presence experience? *Interactive Learning Environments, 24*(3), 487–503.

Valenduc, G., & Vendramin, P. (2016). *Le travail dans l'économie digitale: Continuités et ruptures.* European Trade Union Institute, Institut Syndical Européen, Working Paper, Brussels.

van Rhijn, T., Lero, D. S., & Burke, T. (2016). Why go back to school? Investigating the motivations of student parents to pursue post-secondary education. *New Horizons in Adult Education and Human Resource Development, 28*(2), 14–26.

Yin, R. K. (1994). *Case study research: Design and methods* (2nd ed.). Newbury Park, CA: Sage.

Supporting Authentic Higher Education through Sustainable Open Learning Design

Kathy Snow

According to Tony Bates (2017), a leading Canadian researcher in the field of online learning as well as one of the key investigators of the Canadian National Online Digital Learning survey, which interrogates the implementation of technology for learning within postsecondary institutions, two key issues arise from the 2017 Canadian National Survey of Online Learning that have implications for open learning in higher education. First, many institutions in Canada lack clear documented strategies for open education. Second, where strategies are found, the most effective are those tied to the strategic mission and vision of the particular institution. It is particularly challenging in small teaching-intensive universities to set aside funds and personnel for formal strategic planning specific to open education and the creation or adoption of open resources. In this chapter, I examine the development of a strategy for open education at Cape Breton University (CBU) through a series of small-scale developments that might offer insights for similarly scaled universities in their own processes of sustainable open education policy development.

First, I frame the discussion presented here in a review of current literature related to open education and a definition and typology of institutional approaches. Next, I examine the importance of positioning: to what degree does the purpose of opening education affect the design of open education? This is aligned with the mission of CBU, which acts as a case study for policy development in context. Next, I share illustrations of open education approaches chronologically, discussing each in turn in relation to the impacts on faculty time, teaching experience, and resource needs. I then present analyses through comparisons of approaches, illustrations of the common themes that arose from each example, and how they contributed to the long-term strategy for open education implemented in 2016–17. Finally, I discuss implications for the future, with the aim of presenting evidence for other small universities evaluating their own open education strategies. The central bias presented by the case example, rooted in the mission and vision of the university, is relationship building—students with one another, students with the university, and the university with the local community. The development of the open education strategy fundamentally guided by relationship building and how CBU was able to balance this goal against institutional constraints form the thesis of this chapter.

Framing the Issues

Universities and other postsecondary institutions have been exploring methods of open education adoption since its inception; however, open education still tends to be an aberration rather than the norm (Hylen, van Damme, Mulder, & D'Antoni, 2012; Dhanarajan & Abeywardena, 2013; McGreal, Anderson, & Conrad, 2015). According to the Canadian report on postsecondary education, more than 85% of postsecondary institutions offer some form of online education, but only 35% report using open resources (Bates, 2017). In the subsequent results from 2018, greater insight into this statistic is offered and illustrates that it is particularly challenging for small universities to approach systemic or large-scale adoption of open education initiatives. It is also important to note that the definition of open, or opening, is variable and that institutions interpret opening from positions that reflect these variable definitions. Therefore, defining open, and positioning the case in the context of the operationally supported approach to open learning, are discussed in light of the current literature and form the basis of analysis of the success of the case in developing a sustainable approach to open education.

Defining Open Education

Open education is not a new concept, for both academic institutions and commercial enterprises have been interested in open learning design since the 1970s, and, depending on the purpose of being open, a variety of definitions of open have been developed (Fraser & Deane, 1997). As a concept, open is defined by McGreal, Anderson, and Conrad (2015) as "the provision of activities, programs and policies of access and the development of resources and MOOCs [massive online open courses]" (para. 1). This is a good basis for defining what open resources are, but the design and delivery of open education are far more complex.

In 2011, the Open Educational Resources (OERs) movement, jointly led by UNESCO and the Commonwealth of Learning, has posited that conceptualizing open in the educational sector should include only the design, development, and provision of "teaching and learning resources . . . that permit no-cost access, use, reuse and repurposing by others with no or limited restrictions" (McGreal, Miao, & Mishra, 2016, p. 1). Public postsecondary institutions generally define open more broadly as providing resources and educational content for free or at least at low cost (Campus Alberta, 2015; eCampusOntario, 2016; Jones, 2016). The development of OERs or open textbooks is an approach taken by some institutions, such as Open BC Campus (https://open.bccampus.ca). However, the current literature in Canada suggests that institutions think about open education practices such as open pedagogies that facilitate inclusion and access for all to transform learning (Camilleri & Ehlers, 2011; Carey, Davis, Ferraras, & Porter, 2015). Perhaps the difference between an open learning product and an open learning experience is best exemplified by the divergent pathways that MOOCs, probably the most high-profile open education initiative, have taken. In my observation, the term "MOOC," as bandied about university campuses, has become synonymous with any fully online open course; in some minds, achieving mass enrolment in such a course is the gold standard for success. Although the origins of MOOCs are contested (Clarà & Barberà, 2013; Daniel, 2012), currently two major types of MOOCs are distinct. On the one hand, "cMOOCs" refer to connectivist-style MOOCs, wherein the purpose is to provide open access to "all who want to learn with available resources" (Daniel, 2012, p. 3), through an open pedagogy or experience. On the other hand, "xMOOCs" tend to be developed by either elite or private universities and are generally based on an instructivist perspective in education (Jones, 2016). They are thus based on the creation of a learning product that can be reused—an OER. Furthermore, xMOOCs focus on finding a market and seeking a return on investment (Jones, 2016). Therefore, xMOOCs, though advertised otherwise, are a step back in my view from the more widespread (and accepted) understanding of open as offering either cost-free or low-cost access to educational resources and activities. Alternatively, cMOOCs present a vision of learning that relies on group learning and concepts of crowd teaching (Dron & Anderson, 2014). According to Siemens (2015), one of the initial developers of MOOCs, a cMOOC focuses on networked learning and on participant autonomy and creativity that appear to be at the opposite end of the spectrum from xMOOCs with regard to educational philosophy. There is also the understanding that a cMOOC is platform independent, using any technology that can connect people and the products of their learning, which can include social media, a learning management system (LMS), or email aggregators.

The associated costs of the development of high-quality, reusable resources of these types do not necessarily fit departmental budgets. For instance, faculty members have identified the need for open initiatives that fit into regular practices in a way that can be maintained and sustained over the long term: that is, resources that would not become dated too quickly and that would maximize return for effort (Bowness, 2017; Crozier, 2018). This faculty need might also be why most larger institutions have adopted open textbook initiatives, rather than open pedagogies, since they represent an incremental change to current business models. However, the sustainability of any open education initiative or strategic policy depends on how we define open, how we facilitate open, and how we pay for, distribute, and work in the open (Downes, 2007; Tilak, 2015).

Impact of Open on How Universities Do Business

According to Davis, Little, and Stewart (2008), an examination of open education must begin with students' needs, learning objectives, and the philosophical position of the institution in relation to the resources available. Next, the design of the course, its technological backbone (where it is hosted), and how it will be supported must also be examined, alongside institutional systems (e.g., registration, advising, quality assurance, etc.) and norms. Coherent frameworks that attempt to describe the dichotomies between what changes for learners and instructors at the microlevel (teaching), the macrolevel (systemic), the mental (cognitive), and the material (resources), as well as quantitative and qualitative experiences, are few and far between (Engström & Middleton, 1996). I could find no singular framework that described all aspects well. Instead, I developed the analysis of the case through a bricolage of frameworks, drawing on activity theory (Engström, 1991; Vygotsky, 1978), the theory of cooperative freedom (Dron & Anderson, 2014; Paulson, 1993), and finally Zawacki-Richter and Anderson's (2014) micro, meso, and macro categorizations of distance education research. These three frameworks or lenses together offer insight into factors that shape the design and development of a strategy for open education.

The scale of the impact on an institution can be described based on Zawacki-Richter and Anderson (2014). A micro intervention is considered to affect only a given faculty member and his or her students in a specific teaching event. A meso intervention affects the institution systemically, such as by putting pressure on management, organization, and technology beyond a singular course. A macro intervention speaks to large-scale democratization of education and affects values regarding accessibility, ethics, and equity of education.

The qualitative experiences of learners and instructors can be described using the language of freedoms provided by the theory of cooperative freedoms and operationalized initially into a hexagon of freedom by Paulson

(1993). Paulson provides a mechanism to describe the changes to place (where you learn), time (when you learn), pace (how fast or slow you learn), medium (the media used for learning), access (ability to learn regardless of qualifications or obstacles), and content (what you learn). Dron and Anderson's (2014) adaptations of this hexagon created a decagon that added the learner experiences of technology (tools used for learning), method (the approach and pattern of learning), relationship (from whom you learn and how to engage with them), delegation (freedom to choose), and disclosure (freedom to decide what and to whom it is revealed).

Activity theory provides a description of the transactions among people, technology, and learning (Engström, 2009; Nardi, 1998). An activity system by definition is a multifaceted, voiced network of inter-connections (Engström, 1991). In the most recent revision or third generation of activity theory, Engström (2009) summarized the five prin-ciples of change in an activity system as follows: interactive transactions among factors (prime unit of analysis), multivoiced, affected by history of change, existing with structural tensions (contradictions), and periods of reflection and evaluation that instigate new evaluation. This theory sets the stage for the beginning of the conceptual analysis, and I start with a review of the past.

The (In)Complete History of Open Education at CBU

In the context of my position as teaching and learning chair in Open, Online, and Blended Learning at CBU, as well as in my role as academic lead for the Educational Technology programs offered by the Depart-ment of Education for the School of Education and Health, I am regularly engaged formally and informally in conversations about course design, accessibility, and professional development for faculty with regard to the use of technology. As such, I have had opportunities to observe and be part of, if only tangentially, micro-, meso-, and macrolevel decisions on the development of teaching and learning at CBU using educational technology. Understanding the current context of the case starts with a journey into its past and the evolution of the overall educational technol-ogy strategy at the university. I am aware that the following story is not comprehensive and that others might have additional details or examples of practice. To describe the formal methods of this ethnographic examination of service design, I gathered data for this section from public documents and oral recollections of faculty and staff at CBU through informal conversations with me in my position in the university and not as part of a formal research investigation. Therefore, the history that I share here is also an unofficial version recounted with my own biases.

CBU Mission and Values

Cape Breton University is small, with annual enrolment in any given year being generally a bit below 2,500 full-time students. It is also one of the youngest universities in Canada, and, though it frequently appears in last place in alternate years in the *Maclean's* Survey of Universities, faculty members take pride in a few statistics shared in this report. CBU tends to rank in the top 10 when it comes to student-teacher ratios and authentic research opportunities for students. This speaks to the core values and mission of the university. Born from the need to serve the remote island population, CBU (re-)established itself in 2004 as a primarily undergraduate university providing liberal arts education for students who wanted to stay on the island. Although face-to-face programming dominates the university, a few departments dip into online learning, with two of them offering fully online degrees. In both fully online programs, the majority of students are located in Nova Scotia; however, both national enrolment and international enrolment are growing. As the beginning of a round of federal austerity measures affected all institutions of higher education in Canada in 2014, CBU started exploring ways to streamline operations and increase enrolment dollars.

Pre-2014 Technology Use and Adaptation for Education at CBU

In 2014, the CBU campus-wide Department of Distance Education (DE) consisted of one full-time person. The small size of the university meant that very few people on campus were delegated specific online learning tasks. In addition to the lone distance education administrator, a second centralized support was the administrator of the campus LMS, who worked in the Department of Information Technology (IT), which offers general hardware and software installation, maintenance, and troubleshooting support for faculty members and students alike. As on university campuses across Canada, the DE department experienced shifts in centralization and decentralization prior to 2014. Initially, the DE department was a centralized service for the whole university, housed within the Extension Department, which coordinated all of the certificate and diploma programming and shared the Master of Education degree with Memorial University in Newfoundland. All academic units developed materials through the support of the DE department, which therefore had a larger number of employees and resources. In 2009, the Extension Department was replaced by the offering from the Department of Education of a Bachelor of Education program alongside the teacher education programs that had constituted the majority of the certificate and diploma programming at the university. Development and maintenance of online offerings became the responsibility of each academic unit. The DE staff member hired after the change in 2009 was responsible for coordinating and supporting the enrolment of online students. The Department of Education included in the job description of its new manager of teacher education responsibilities for technical support for faculty members and students and online course development for the graduate-level programs offered (the aforementioned certificates, diplomas, and master's program courses). This was the only department in the university based on an online learning position. This was not surprising given that it was also the largest developer of online learning offerings. Outside the Department of Education, the Department of Communities and Connections offered a Bachelor of Arts degree that could be taken largely online, as did a few other departments on campus. In the absence of a central authority or strategy for online learning (beyond the university's adoption of Moodle as the LMS in 2009), departments were free to develop their own strategies for online learning. Up to this point, no department at CBU had offered any open course.

Developments in the Department of Education, 2014–15

In the 2014–15 academic year, enrolment in the Department of Education consisted of 38 on-campus undergraduate students, 15 community-based (blended) undergraduate students, 12 blended graduate certificate students, and 156 fully online students in one of five graduate certificate or master's programs (T. Macdonald, Manager of Teacher Education, personal communication, 2015). This meant that 42% of the students in education were online and "invisible" to the campus community in a university that predominantly promotes face-to-face interaction. The fact that they were invisible in the system factored into the decisions that followed for online learning design. Given that administration determined resource allocation, it was not really aware of or able to account for these students through the usual systems in place (a problem compounded by the nature of enrolment in education programs, which occurs in May rather than the usual September and January intakes). As a result, financial supports did not entirely follow student numbers. The resources to support online learning, having been dismantled prior to 2009, were spread out across the campus and found in unusual places. Naturally, faculty members were responsible for all aspects of the design, implementation, and delivery of online learning. They could turn to the central IT department for technical support and to the teaching and learning centre for online learning pedagogy and practice help, and support for social media and graphic design was provided by the Marketing Department. In 2014, the Department of Education started exploring opportunities to offer graduate education courses with open options. The department did so at the teaching or microlevel of course interventions. The primary aim of opening up graduate courses was based on Dewey's (1916) "learning by doing" pedagogy, asking educational technology students to participate in alternative models of education through authentic experiences and to support the building of a community of practice for distance education students. A secondary aim arose from discussions in departmental meetings: offering open content as a means of increasing both the campus and the community profile of the department. The goal of interventions at this level was not to offer fully open courses but to explore the possibilities of open education in the educational technology program, given our resources and limitations.

The primary resource in the Department of Education was human: our students and all of our faculty members, many with extensive experience in teaching and engaged in exploring technology-enhanced teaching and learning. In terms of financial resources, the budget for interventions was limited, falling within the normal course operating budget. Interventions were thus designed and implemented by faculty members with the aforementioned supports available. They therefore needed to be simple to implement, and that made readily available social media platforms attractive. This led to another critical limitation that needed to be assessed: although CBU itself had no official policy on the use of social media for teaching, Nova Scotia had (and still has) some of the most restrictive policies in Canada in relation to information, data, and privacy protection in the form of the Freedom of Information and Protection of Privacy Act and Personal Information International Disclosure Act (Server Cloud Canada, 2016). To mitigate any potential risk to participants and liability of the university, I adopted an informed consent approach through the use of a social media field trip waiver adapted from the current CBU field trip waiver (Snow, 2017) since all potential users of our content would be adults engaged in learning about online learning. Students were always given the option of non-participation without ramification for grades; however, when they did choose to participate, it was with the full knowledge of the "dangers" of participation in the "wilds" of social media. With that in place, three interventions were designed.

Facilitated Conversation Around a Twitter Hashtag

In one course, students were given an assignment to join Twitter and to tweet once a week using the course hashtag IDTIPS. In preparation for Twitter use, students discussed the advantages of using real or anonymized personas in Twitter as well as the impacts that tweets can have on careers or personal lives. Students who did not feel comfortable using Twitter were given the option of participating in an LMS discussion forum instead. I monitored both the hashtag and the discussion forum to ensure that both groups recognized my presence. There were no set synchronous times for tweeting, giving the students freedom of time, medium, and disclosure (Dron & Anderson, 2014). Students were also asked to respond to at least one tweet a week posted to this hashtag as well as to curate their Twitter feeds by following others in the field. Students chose from whom they would learn and had a degree of autonomy in what they would learn. I seeded the hashtag weekly with concepts from the course. In some cases, I posed specific questions or challenges to students. To encourage participation from those not enrolled in the course, I created small mediating artifacts, for example YouTube videos with requests from others to respond to videos. Alternatively, open journal articles/reading materials were shared.

Finally, simple questions or requests for readers to create and share artifacts of their own were proposed. One such student creation, a diagram of the instructional design process, gained a great deal of traction for the student, being retweeted over 100 times the week after it was initially shared. Rather than being assessed on their participation in the Twitter activity, students were assessed on their personal evaluations/reflections at the end of the 10-week experience.

Using social network analysis tools to evaluate the impact of this intervention, it was found that, though a small cluster of communication developed, it remained focused on the instructor, and many students were actually talking to themselves. The hashtag was successful in attracting attention from instructional designers and other professionals in the field, though it remained student driven. It did have the effect of increasing the notoriety of the instructor and, perhaps by extension, the university. Indeed, the level of communication on Twitter caused a rise in my profile as was evident from an increased number of followers and comments made directly to me by instructional designers whom I met at subsequent conferences along the lines of "Oh, you are the one from Twitter. . . ." Participating students' informal comments to me highlighted that one of the primary opportunities that the hashtag offered was a space for students from previous classes to reconnect with one another (since distance education students had no central organizing space beyond courses within the LMS that ended each term).

Sharing Classroom Products on the Department of Education Facebook Site

The nature of Twitter meant that, as soon as a course was over, the major activity of the hashtag also disappeared. Activity on the hashtag was also isolated to educational technology students. In a discussion stemming from a departmental meeting, faculty decided to try to increase engagement with the public by sharing products of courses through the departmental Facebook page. Within all courses, at both the graduate level and the undergraduate level, students were invited to participate in an open informal learning community on Facebook. Rather than asking students to create their own blogs or digital artifacts on their own sites and sharing them privately with the instructor, this intervention aimed at elevating the status and meaning of their work by promoting it through digital curation on the departmental Facebook site. The initial intention of the site was to promote the department and to share information about educational events with the local community. However, with the adoption of this type of sharing, a stronger bidirectional learning community emerged.

To avoid duplication of effort, one person, the administrative coordinator for the graduate programs, was in charge of posting updates. All faculty members were invited to suggest posting students' products after first obtaining the appropriate permission from any course conducted in the department. Consent was determined by receiving a simple email from students whose work would be shared. To avoid pressuring anyone to share work, it was suggested that students not be asked to share items until the end of the term, though this was left to the discretion of the individual instructor. Students were also asked whether or not they wanted to be identified with the shared work. Their products, such as essays in blog form or teaching resources, would be linked and shared on the Facebook site with commentary about their applicability for teaching.

A short description of the item was then created by the faculty member and passed on to the coordinator. This required a little work outside the normal parameters for teaching; however, requests from instructors were unanimously seen as positive by students, who took great pride in sharing their work. It was determined through social network analysis that this intervention gained far more traction in the local community than our previous efforts at engaging the community in the Department of Education.

There were exponentially more shares and comments appearing in multiple clusters beyond the teacher-centric responses found in the previous Twitter intervention Although the Facebook intervention did not offer students any control over the content of their learning directly, nor was it established as part of the formal learning within a course, it did change the relationship dynamics among the department, students, and the broader community. By supporting students as leaders, far more engagement and discussion emerged on the Facebook site, and classroom teachers working in schools began posting comments and feedback on the site.

Deliberate External Partnerships

The interventions discussed have been asynchronous text- and image-based experiences. Education faculty also wanted to offer students voice-based synchronous opportunities. The format of the third intervention was open but by invitation only. Still working toward the goal of supporting professional lifelong learning and "community around education," students were invited to participate in virtual conferences using webinar software. For example, in April 2016, the Canadian Network for Innovation in Education (CNIE) hosted a virtual conference and solicited participation from faculty members and graduate students across Canada. This became the culminating activity for students in the final year of the graduate diploma in educational technology. Although not mandated, students were encouraged to share their applied research projects in short presentations during the virtual conference. They could submit their projects for presentation through the peer review process or simply attend and view the presentations of their classmates and others.

Students were prepared for this event by prior scaffolding activities held within core prerequisite courses. Students were given opportunities to participate in live webinar events restricted to class members in order to help them become familiar with webinar tools and etiquette. In addition, partnerships were established with the University of Manitoba for closed sharing between students enrolled at each institution during a mini-conference. This gave them the opportunity to do a presentation using unfamiliar virtual presentation software as well as to listen to presentations with an unfamiliar audience. Anecdotal evidence from students indicated that the intimate sessions between universities, though initially somewhat intimidating, were subsequently useful in gaining experience and perspective on technology-related issues. Students who went on to present in the open CNIE conference received valuable feedback from peers on research design and evaluation.

2015–16 and the Rise of MIKM 2701, a Mi'kmaw Studies MOOC

Former CBU president Dr. David Wheeler was one of several university presidents promoting provincial support for tuition-free enrolment for all students in postsecondary open education. As a result, the course entitled MIKM 2701: Learning from the Knowledge Keepers was launched in 2014 and presented face-to-face on campus to 13 credit-registered students, being live-streamed during each of the 13 weeks of the course. The live stream was available to anyone to view as a public broadcast on Bell Media's cable network channel and saved as an archived recording. The videos recorded during this time are still available and hosted by the university through Vimeo, free of charge (https://vimeo.com/album/4376432).

Although the course facilitators and CBU administrators participated in several discussions with xMOOC providers while considering the design and development of MIKM 2701, it was quickly determined that the style of instruction and the business model for resource creation were not suitable in that they were incongruent with the learning experience that facilitators wanted to provide. However, the varied methods of cMOOCs served as exemplars of practice for our efforts in the open.

The design of the course was low-tech, in essence a three-hour conversation once a week that became known as Mi'kmaw Monday. Mi'kmaw knowledge keepers—that is, elder speakers—were invited each week to share what they knew about the various themes of the course. The course was facilitated by two CBU faculty, one of whom was Stephen Augustine, then the dean of Unamaki College. Three types of participation were offered: students could enrol and receive full credit (accounting for

13 face-to-face enrolments), or participants could register to receive a certificate of participation. Alternatively, participants were encouraged to register and come to the face-to-face session or watch it online. To receive a certificate of participation, participants were asked to complete reflective essays on the evening courses and submit them to the course instructors at the end of the course. Interaction in the live sessions was supported in multiple ways.

Face-to-face students could ask questions by coming up to one of two microphones in the room, and distance education students could participate through the concurrent live tweet chat #TALIAQCBU. At the height of the course, the Twitter hashtag trended number one in Canada during the live sessions for multiple weeks. An associated, closed Facebook community was established to support students as well and grew to over 3,000 members. The Facebook community was monitored and facilitated by course instructors, a member of the Marketing Department, and a teaching assistant. The overwhelming public response to the course took the university by surprise. The registration process, via email, caused such heavy traffic on the university network that the email server was flooded and shut down for two days. The management and maintenance of the course became the full-time job not only of the two course facilitators but also of three support staff members located in various departments of the university. The course facilitators were unable to read and respond to all of the direct messages that they received during the course because of the sheer number of people who reached out and wanted to connect directly. Although the course ended in 2016, it has left a lasting legacy. The Facebook group is ongoing, and, though the facilitators rarely engage or post in it, participants regularly share learning and information among themselves. During the subsequent two years, there was discussion on what to do with the videos and whether to reoffer the course using them. To respect the elders and knowledge keepers who shared their experiences, the videos created (three hours in length) would not be edited/remixed without their explicit permission.

Nevertheless, for all its popularity, the course offered proved to be unsustainable. It was incredibly labour intensive, and, despite the number of students opting to take the certificate, it is unlikely that the course covered the cost of its creation. However, cost recovery was not the goal; rather, it was the awareness of Mi'kmaw issues and an opportunity for CBU to engage with the community in open discussion. Again, from available information, there is no direct way to measure or track if the course was successful in increasing access to education. An analysis of themes arising from the participants' reflections indicates that the course was successful in meeting its goals of supporting awareness of Mi'kmaw history and current issues as well as transforming conversations about Mi'kmaw-non-Indigenous relationships (Augustine, Root, Snow, & Doucette, 2017). The course has been highlighted by Tony Bates in his research on "pockets of innovation," which arguably has raised the profile of the university. Despite its success, staff and faculty consulted agreed that it could not be done again that way. The course was highly contextual and is not scalable, part of its success being the dynamic between facilitators and participants. It was determined that what worked in this instance could not be packaged and reused to the same effect. Furthermore, doing so was not the spirit of intent of open education at CBU.

2016–17: The Development of a Sustainable Model

When asked about the next steps for open learning, Tanya Bran-Barrett, the dean of research and teaching and learning stated that "out of knowledge keepers we developed the open digital learning opportunities strategy. We call them Little Open Online Courses or LOOCs, in a 3C model—that is credit, certificate or curiosity" (Bran-Barrett, MacDonald, Sakalauskas, & Baker, 2017). The university wanted a greater impact than the micro-interventions outlined in the first pilot, but the resource-intensive second pilot was not sustainable. The goal of the open strategy was to connect local people with people from around the world while aiming for excellent teaching and learning design. A global approach for the campus needed to be developed that built on the best features of both.

Currently, interested faculty can apply to offer a 3C course. The 3C designation represents a course offered for regular credit, with a certificate similar to that established in MIKM2701, and fully open to the public (the curiosity option). Curious students are encouraged to register, but registration is not required for participation. Therefore, it is impossible for CBU to track the number of participants motivated by curiosity. Dedicated software was adopted to allow registration outside the official campus system that centralizes registration and removes this work from course facilitators. Since there is no single design model for the 3C courses, much of the design is left to course instructors to determine. However, there is a basic template for the certificate of participation and for curious students' participation. All courses are offered in a variation of multimodal learning with synchronous, face-to-face options in many but not all offerings. Credit students participate in the course with the assistance of the learning management system and by attending face-to-face sessions, if they are offered. For some courses, face-to-face sessions are replaced by online synchronous events using web-conferencing software, whereas others are completely asynchronous.

Credit students participate in the manner outlined in the syllabus, as per any regular course offering. However, in addition to the standard LMS engagement, each course has an associated Facebook page. This is the real home for the certificate and curious students, yet students registered for credit can also join the closed Facebook group associated with the course, though it is not a requirement. Courses with a face-to-face component are often live-streamed through Facebook Live directly into the closed group, where certificate and curious students can gain access to the instructor's lecture. By making access optional for credit students and by explaining the risks of participation to curious and certificate students, all participants can make informed choices for participation, thereby allowing the university to meet privacy and protection requirements. Faculty members are counselled on social media and given help in deciding if they want to use such media with their personal identities or have identities created for this purpose. Although Facebook is not ideal software for learning, it was chosen as the platform because of its accessibility and the ease with which students and faculty members can adopt the technology.

To support the streaming lecture, a permanent broadcast space—designated as the 3C room—was created with a small budget of $10,000. An interactive whiteboard was installed as well as a responsive camera system allowing for the same type of streaming as made possible by Bell Media but with far less labour involved. Since the streaming classroom is dedicated, the equipment does not need to be set up and then removed for each lesson, as was the case for MIKM2701, thus saving about five hours of labour per class. A stage was also developed by adding curtains, lights, an interactive whiteboard, and comfortable chairs. Basic cameras installed in the ceiling allow for several camera angles on the stage. Encoding of video and streaming is done with open access software. All videos recorded are archived and organized in an open library.

The decision not to develop a more specific recipe for 3C-structured courses encouraged faculty members to develop courses that aligned with their objectives, thus recognizing that all courses are highly contextual and need different approaches. However, the structure implemented was intended to create a robust support network for faculty members and students. Centralized supports were established for the former not by creating new positions but by reallocating the roles of staff members already on campus. A staff member from the Department of Communications with a strong background in video production and editing was moved to the teaching and learning centre. The lone distance education administrator was associated with the 3C courses as the first point of contact for all curious and certificate students. Her role is to help the students get connected technically and to liaise with them in order to build a relationship between the student and the university. The educational developer in the teaching and learning centre rounded out the team supporting faculty members in the production of course content and the hosting of live events. An undergraduate student (peer) facilitator hired for each course enables dialogue within the Facebook group and participates in all of the live sessions in order to monitor social media and bring questions forward. All peer facilitators are trained prior to starting work on a course.

Through the refinement of the 3C courses initiated in the fall of 2016, the aim of open education at CBU was achieved. It became clear that relationships were at the heart of operations and that open education was a means to connect with students who would not normally attend the university. In most MOOC models, individuals can either disappear or skyrocket to "fame" through social amplification, but in the LOOC or 3C model learning is a relationship-building experience. Anecdotal evidence shared by the distance education coordinator outlines the diversity of learners—be they senior citizens, housebound, local learners, or distant learners—and shows how enthusiastic and thankful curious and certificate students can be given the opportunity to engage in a learning community in this way. Participants often email the distance education coordinator to tell her about their experiences in the course and what the opportunity to participate has meant to them. In the 10 courses offered as C3 courses since January 2017, the registration numbers are still much lower than those for MIKM2701 (only 1,700 registrants in total compared with over 24,000 participants in one term in MIKM2701), but these courses represent the evolution of a strategy that can now support sustained growth over time.

Analysis of How We Got from There to Here

When I examine each initiative as an activity cycle that took place from 2014 to 2016, I see the evolution of the CBU open learning strategy. CBU moved from singular microlevel interventions to a macrolevel strategy based on the learning that emerged from the delivery of each course, though there was no strategically planned learning. What emerged was a change in the university through relationships, as based on conversations with stakeholders or actors in the system. One of the advantages of a small university is its ability to communicate quickly and to share learning from a variety of perspectives. Although not captured in the description of the interventions, the multiple perspectives—from the technical administrators to the teaching faculty and the financial/administrative leaders—informed one another of the success of the varied projects via formal and informal conversations and consultations so as to arrive at the 3C model. Previous studies have identified both altruistic and strategic motives for the adoption of open modalities (Murphy, 2013; Pena, 2009). Arguably, in this case, the motivation was both to serve students and to lower costs, yet there were well-documented tensions among financial restrictions, faculty time, and student engagement (Crozier, 2018; Murphy, 2013; Olcott, 2012).

With regard to financial restrictions, in all interventions presented in this case study consideration of financial support drove the choice of platform. The most expensive design (MIKM 2701) was supported by a partnership with an external provider, but it added another layer of complexity to the administration. It would not have been possible without the focus on and prioritization of a working policy to support the experiment of large-scale opening. The lack of dedicated policy support followed by funding has been indicated as a major limitation for postsecondary strategic development that necessitates cultural and practical shifts in how the institution organizes teaching and learning (Bossu, Brown, & Bull, 2012; Friesen, 2009).

The case offers evidence of a second key theme that emerged from the literature: the time required for faculty members to develop high-quality materials. The strategy that appears to be the most sustainable in all three cases is recording or capturing live open events, be they text (tweets) or voice/video (webinars or live streams), with some post-event support, for example, in the case of video, a high-quality archived product that can be reused. Essentially, the process adopted by the university supported the faculty member in creating a high-quality OER that was highly contextual as opposed to the reuse of OERs such as the Khan Academy resources, highly generalizable but limited in applicability for the same reason (Rao, Hilton, & Harper, 2017). Through supported C3 course development, the university worked toward sustainable policy by incrementally and strategically building the capacities of faculty members, thereby reducing resistance among tenured faculty members to the "extra work" encountered in development (Crozier, 2018).

The third theme relates to student engagement and the type of relationship that the university and faculty members want to build with students. Here we must return to the prime unit of analysis or the interactions of parts of the system. The primary mediating artifact or technology as outlined by Dron and Anderson (2014) selected for open students was social media as a means to engage the public collaboratively. This had a disruptive effect on the rules of engagement in terms of the decagon of freedom in relation to discourse, disclosure, and relationship formation of learning. In 2014–15, students emerged as leaders of learning; they did so as well in 2015–16 in a different way as exemplified by the longevity of the Facebook community. Changing the rules and the mediating artifacts allowed for the evolution of a new division of labour and for the strategic centralization of some of the university's resources to support learning. There was also an overall feeling of greater satisfaction among staff and faculty in engaging in open learning.

Evaluating the system's quantitative measurements of effect size proved to be impossible with the limited data available. Each pilot was conducted separately, over time, without a cohesive strategy. Like many other institutions, CBU does not track online students separately from on-campus students (Bates, 2017). Enrolment and admission services at CBU have little to no recourse in capturing open participants' experiences or even their identities, unless they choose to share such information.

Conclusion

Although portrayed as a deliberative investigation of a sustainable, open course delivery strategy at CBU, the process was far from strategic. It emerged, much like the learning in cMOOCs themselves, from pockets of innovation and sharing throughout the university and by learning from mistakes. The approach to distance education reflects the university's approach to education in general in that the driving forces were embedded in community and relationship building. Not only relationships with professional members of the community but also relationships with one another (e.g., student-student, student-faculty, faculty-staff-administration) comprise one of the central strengths of small universities, an area where they can compete with larger, more resource-rich institutions. It might seem to be counterproductive to talk about open education in this context when open education has become synonymous with MOOCs. However, open education is much more than this; it is also about service to one's community, in our case to the people of Cape Breton Island. Of course, increasing recruitment and promoting one's institution are considered in the dialogue; open education is not, nor can it be, an entirely selfish act in a university of this size, but determining the scale of open education offerings is an ongoing process and an evolution, from very small to very large to something in between.

References

Augustine, S., Root, E., Snow, K., & Doucette, M. (2017, July 27). *Working towards reconciliation in Mi'kma'ki through a co-learning journey*. Toronto, ON: World Indigenous Peoples Conference on Education (WIPCE).

Bates, T. (2017). *Tracking online and distance education in Canadian universities and colleges: 2017*. Vancouver, BC: The National Survey of Online and Distance Education in Canadian Post-Secondary Education.

Bossu, C., Brown, M., & Bull, D. (2012). Do open educational resources represent additional challenges or advantages to the current climate of change in the Australian higher education sector? In M. Brown, M. Hartnett, & T. Stewart (Eds.), *Future challenges, sustainable futures. In Proceedings Ascilite 2012: Future Challenges–Sustainable Futures* (pp. 124–132). Wellington, New Zealand. Massey University.

Bowness, S. (2017, April 4). The open educational resources movement is redefining the concept of online textbooks. *University Affairs*. Retrieved from https://www.universityaffairs.ca/features/feature-article/open-educational-resources-movement-redefining-concept-online-textbooks/

Bran-Barrett, T., MacDonald, T., Sakalauskas, H., & Baker, L. (2017, November). *Multi-access learning: Cape Breton University's open online learning initiative*. Paper presented at the Fostering Cross-Institutional Collaboration with Technology Enabled Learning Conference, Sydney, NS.

Camilleri, A., & Ehlers, U-D. (2011). *Mainstream open educational practices: Recommendation for policy*. Retrieved from https://www.researchgate.net/publication/260423291_Mainstreaming_Open_Educational_Practice?enrichId=rgreq-0afb251dd71060d8e02f19f3053992d6-XXX&enrichSource=Y292ZXJQYWdlOzI2MDQyMzI5MTtBUzozOTc4NzQoOTI5MTk4MDhAMTQ3MTg3MjA3OTk4OA%3D%3D&el=1_x_2&_esc=publicationCoverPdf

Campus Alberta. (2015). *Alberta OER: About*. Retrieved from http://albertaoer.com/about-us

Carey, T., Davis, A., Ferraras, S., & Porter, D. (2015). Using open educational practices to support institutional strategic excellence in teaching, learning & scholarship. *Open Praxis. (7)*2. Retrieved from https://openpraxis.org/index.php/OpenPraxis/article/view/201

Clarà, M., & Barberà, E. (2013). Three problems with the connectivist conception of learning. *Journal of Computer Assisted Learning, 30*(3), 197–206. Retrieved from https://onlinelibrary.wiley.com/doi/abs/10.1111/jcal.12040

Daniel, J. (2012). Making sense of MOOCs: Musings in a maze of myth, paradox, and possibility. *Journal of Interactive Media in Education, 3*, part. 18. Retrieved from https://jime.open.ac.uk/articles/10.5334/2012-18/

Davis, A., Little, P., & Stewart, B. (2008). Developing an infrastructure for online learning. In T. Anderson (Ed.), *The theory and practice of online learning* (2nd ed., pp. 91–118). Edmonton, AB: Athabasca University Press.

Dewey, J. (1916). *Democracy and education.* New York, US: Macmillan

Dhanarajan, G., & Abeywardena, I.S. (2013). Higher education and open educational resources in Asia: An overview. In G. Dhanarajan & D. Porter (Eds.). *Perspectives on open and distance learning: Open Educational Resources: An Asian perspective.* Vancouver: Commonwealth of Learning.

Downes, S. (2007). In Ives, C., & Pringle, M. (2013). Moving to open educational resources at Athabasca University: A case study. *International Review of Research in Open and Distributed Learning, 14*(2), 2–13.

Dron, J., & Anderson, T. (2014). *Teaching crowds: Learning and social media.* Edmonton, AB: Athabasca University Press.

eCampusOntario. (2016). *Open content initiative.* Retrieved from https://learnonline.ecampusontario.ca/Content/open-content-funding

Engström, Y. (1991). Activity theory and individual and social transformation. *Multidisciplinary Newsletter for Activity Theory, 7/8*: 14–15.

Engström, Y. (2009). Expansive learning: Toward an activity-theoretical reconceptualization. In K. Illeris (Ed.), *Contemporary theories of learning: Learning theorists . . . in their own words* (pp. 53–73). New York, NY: Routledge.

Engström, Y., & Middleton, D. (1996). *Cognition and communication at work.* Cambridge, UK: Cambridge University Press.

Fraser, S., & Deane, E. (1997). Why open learning? *Australian Universities' Review, 40*(1), 25–31.

Friesen, N. (2009). Open educational resources: New possibilities for change and sustainability. *The International Review of Research in Open and Distance Learning, 10*(5). Retrieved from http://www.irrodl.org/index.php/irrodl/article/view/664/1388

Hylen, J., van Damme, D., Mulder, F., D'Antoni, S. (2012). *Open Educational Resources: Analysis of Reponses to the OECD Country Questionnaire.* Open Education Working Papers No 76. OECD Publishing. http://dx.doi.org/10.1787/5k99orjhvtlv-en

Jones, C. (2016). *Networked learning: An educational paradigm for the age of digital networks.* Cham, Switzerland: Springer International.

McGreal, R., Anderson, T., & Conrad, D. (2015). Open educational resources. *International Review of Research in Open and Distributed Learning, 16*(5), 161–175.

McGreal, R., Miao, F., & Mishra, S. (2016). Open educational resources: Policy, costs, and transformation. In F. Miao, S. Mishra, & R. McGreal (Eds.), *Open educational resources: Policy, costs, and transformation* (pp. 1–12). Burnaby, CA: UNESCO.

Nardi, B. (1998). Activity theory and its use within human-computer interaction. *The Journal of the Learning Sciences, 7*(2), 257–261. doi10.1207/s15327809jls0702_6

Olcott, D., Jr. (2012). OER perspectives: Emerging issues for universities. *Distance Education, 33*(2), 283–290.

Pena, H. (2009). *Higher education: The success and challenges in open education resources (OER)*. E-Prints in Library and Information Science (E-LIS). Retrieved from http://eprints.rclis.org/13743/1/pena.pdf

Rao, A., Hilton, J., & Harper, S. (2017). Khan Academy videos in Chinese: A case study of OER revision. *International Review of Research in Open and Distance Learning, 18*(5), 305–312.

Server Cloud Canada. (2016, August 30). *Nova Scotia's privacy laws & the Canadian cloud*. Retrieved from https://www.servercloudcanada.com/2016/08/nova-scotias-privacy-laws-the-canadian-cloud/

Siemens, G. (2015). The role of MOOCs in the future of education. In C. Bonk, M. Lee, T. Reeves, and T. Reynolds (Eds.), *MOOCS and open education around the world* (p. *xiii*). New York, NY: Routledge.

Snow, K. (2017). Social media field trips: Using disruptive technologies without disrupting the system. *Journal of Educational Multimedia and Hypermedia, 26*(2), 193–209.

Tilak, J. B. G. (2015). Global trends in funding higher education. *International Higher Education, 42*. Retrieved from: https://doi.org/10.6017/ihe.2006.42.7882

Vygotsky, L. (1978). Interaction between learning and development. In M. Gauvain & M. Cole (Eds.), *Readings on the development of children* (pp. 34–40). New York, NY: Scientific American Books.

Zawacki-Richter, O., & Anderson, T. (Eds.). (2014). *Online distance education: Towards a research agenda*. Edmonton, AB: Athabasca University Press.

What Really Works in a Blended Learning Graduate Program?
A Case Study of a Faculty of Education

Maurice Taylor, Shehzad Ghani, and Michael Fairbrother

As Zawacki-Richter and Anderson (2014) asserted, online distance education is a comprehensive, many-sided, and multifunctional process. In their seminal work, the authors "developed a validated framework of research topics that help organize the field and identify research gaps" (p. 2). Each of these frames of reference calls for a different theoretical justification and research method. This chapter falls within the microlevel research stream for understanding teaching and learning in distance education and empirically explores the lived experiences of students and professors in a blended learning graduate program.

According to Owston (2013), it now appears that blended learning has the potential to transform higher education. This pedagogical approach is viewed as an opportunity to redesign how courses are developed, scheduled, and delivered in both undergraduate and graduate programs. As Garrison (2016) pointed out, at the heart of blended learning redesign are the goals of engaging students in critical discourse and reflection. In a similar vein, Campbell and Schwier (2014) suggested that a more modern constructivist instructional design is needed for online education where individuals and groups co-create new knowledge. They also maintained that learners play a much more active role in a constructivist environment. A blended learning pedagogy could also offer the same kinds of student engagement features.

Building on the research in this microlevel frame of reference and from the perspective of open university systems, Conrad (2014) proposed that learning is a social activity immersed in different social contexts that result in different understandings. Moreover, interaction and communication among members who collaborate in a learning community are at the core of the learning process. However, Conrad posed a challenge by questioning how we can accommodate current learning needs and preferences using new media and online course design.

In an effort to unravel part of this question, our study sought to understand better which practices really work for graduate students and professors teaching in a blended learning format. With empirical evidence of how best to combine text and voice in blended learning still in its infancy, it also attempted to explore some initial insights into the balance between text and voice in a Faculty of Education graduate blended learning program. For the purpose of this study, the term "blended learning" was defined as the "attempt to match the affordances of information and communication technologies with the immediacy of face-to-face education" (Anderson & Zawacki-Richter, 2014, p. 490). The chapter begins with a focused literature review on adult learner characteristics and interaction and communication in learning communities. This review is followed by a brief description of the conceptual context used in the study and the research questions that guided the investigation.

Literature Review

This literature review considers two connected viewpoints for understanding teaching and learning in the microlevel research stream using new media and online course design. With the growing population of adult students now more present in graduate higher education, it is important to address how educational programs can accommodate the learning needs and preferences of such students (Taylor, Vaughan, Ghani,

Atas, & Fairbrother, 2018). In addition, since communication and inter-action in blended learning courses are at the heart of active learning and student engagement (Garrison, 2016), it is also essential to recognize the types of communication strategies and interaction tools that students in higher education use to connect with their peers and professors.

Adult Learner Characteristics

Much of the research on the characteristics and preferences of adult learners is drawn from Knowles's andragogical model of adult learning (Cercone, 2008; Phillips, Baltzer, Filoon, & Whitley, 2017; Stevens, 2014). Steeped within the social context of how best to meet the needs of this growing population, the ever-expanding literature on adult learning, adult development, and characteristics of adult learners is interrelated yet focuses on various factors that influence how these mature students can be best supported in higher education.

Rabourn, Shoup, and BrckaLorenz (2015), using data from 146,072 students who participated in the 2013 and 2014 National Survey of Student Engagement (NSSE), compared traditional college students and adult learners. They found that adult learners are more likely to take all of their classes online, to begin their initial education at another institution, and to be more academically engaged than traditional college-aged peers. They also have positive perceptions of teaching practices and interactions with others but find their campus services to be less supportive. Furthermore, the researchers found that these diverse adult learners tend to pursue flex-ible educational offerings, are drawn to different types of institutions, and have specific and sometimes immediate goals in mind. However, general-izing these findings to a Canadian population should be done with caution. According to a recent report by the Canadian Digital Learning Research Association (2019), distance education, online courses, and blended learn-ing are more firmly established in the United States than in Canada.

In addition, Phillips et al. (2017) investigated the perspectives of adult learners on the characteristics of effective instructors. Using a mixed methods research design, they surveyed 132 learners from an adult liberal arts undergraduate program in the northeastern United Kingdom. Some of the key findings indicated that adult students benefited from instructors who had knowledge of and respect for mature learners, demonstrated applied knowledge in the fields in which they taught, were flexible, and understood the demands unique to this population of learners. Participants reported that instructors were ineffective when they dismissed their life experiences, lacked interest in their prior knowledge and real-world constraints, and possessed arrogant teaching mannerisms. These findings suggest the importance for faculty members to find connections, model respect, and clearly communicate with adult learners in ways different from those that they might use when teaching a class of traditional college-aged students.

Another important contribution to the literature was the synthesis report by Osam, Bergman, and Cumberland (2017) on the barriers faced by adult learners in higher education. This review used the framework of Ekstrom (1972), which categorized barriers to adult learning as institutional, situational, and dispositional (Osam et al., 2017, p. 55). Findings indicated that the barriers that adult learners continue to face have not changed in over 30 years. The authors also described the inadequacies within higher education institutions offering online learning to address the current needs of adult learners compared with those of traditional college-aged students. This was particularly evident in situational barriers such as financial burdens as well as in how services in higher education addressed dispositional barriers to learning exemplified by fear of failure and academic insecurity.

A three-year longitudinal study conducted by Stevens (2014) compared and contrasted the perceptions, attitudes, and preferences of adult learners in higher education representing six geographic regions in the United States. In this study, 173 participants were surveyed on a range of questions about the adult learning experience. Follow-up telephone interviews were conducted with 86 of the participants to deepen the data from the initial survey results. Key findings suggest that the majority of adult learners work full time, view family and work activities as major obstacles to their academic pursuits, and want to pursue higher education as full-time students. The majority of the participants favourably viewed the use of technology and the flexibility of online and blended learning. Although these adult learners found study groups helpful, they were not supportive of mandatory group projects. Important in the results were motivational factors such as increased earning potential, self-satisfaction from increased educational prowess and completion of a degree, and being examples to their children. Moreover, flexible scheduling of academic courses through online and blended learning formats positively affected their motivation.

In sum, a number of important ideas are conveyed in this abbreviated literature on the characteristics of adult learners and their experiences in higher education. Foremost, the preferences of adult learners need to be understood and supported better through the infrastructures in higher education. The barriers to learning faced by adults can be understood by acknowledging their social roles and understanding that their social contexts are very different from those of traditional college-aged students. Further research is needed on how to address these issues, and the new medium of blended learning might offer some promise for better integrating graduate adult learners into higher education. What seems to be missing in this literature is exactly how graduate students experience a blended learning program.

Communication and Interaction in Blended Learning Courses

Twenty-five years ago, Mason (1994) observed that interaction was the basic component of the new age of education and central to the progress and success of student learning. More recently, scholars of blended learning have emphasized the need to broaden the concepts of communication and interaction as new formats of learning continue to evolve. For example, using an action research and case-based methodology, Vaughan (2014) investigated blended learning design features and supportive assessment activities that increase levels of student engagement through collaborative learning applications. Both quantitative and qualitative methods were used to collect data from 273 students and eight instructors in one Canadian university. Information was collected in seven first-year blended learning courses over the two-year program. Initially, professors were interviewed and then requested to complete an online survey. Students were also requested to complete a different online survey. A select group of students were then invited to participate in focus group discussions in order to investigate the impacts of collaborative learning applications such as blogs, wikis, and clickers on student learning and engagement. The main results indicated that professors have a general inclination to use the tools at hand to improve student communication and interaction. This was also evident in students' tendency to associate a high value with using collaborative learning applications to complete a range of assessment activities.

Similarly, Wang (2010) examined students' online and offline interactions in two Taiwanese colleges to gauge the extent of collaborative learning among students. Content analysis of students' weekly blogs and journals and instructors' observation notes was used to reveal the students' collaborative communicative characteristics. One of the key findings was that students demonstrated successful collaborative learning in an asynchronous networked environment. As well, it was found that the implementation of information and communication technology (ICT) tools in a blended learning environment encouraged social interaction among students and increased their level of engagement. However, the implementation of ICT tools did not automatically help to facilitate students in their use of active learning strategies. From a teaching and learning lens, could it be that faculty members still have some difficulty identifying appropriate training and practice using ICT tools?

Furthering the literature on communication and interaction, Tayebinik and Puteh (2012) investigated students' perceptions of community when integrating face-to-face classes into fully online courses. They interviewed 48 undergraduate students at a Middle Eastern university using an open-ended interview schedule. The results from the study suggest that the participants' high level of satisfaction with the blended learning format was related to how they viewed the meaning of community. For example, common themes were high perceptions of a sense of community, more effective student-instructor interactions, positive views of blended courses, and increases in student-student interactions.

In a similar vein, Babb, Stewart, and Johnson (2010) explored students' perceptions of constructing communication in blended learning environments by using the seven principles of good practice in undergraduate education identified by Chickering and Gamson (1987). Online survey data were collected from 75 undergraduate students enrolled in blended courses at a large university in Texas. The results indicated that the principles of active learning, student-student interaction, professor feedback, and communication of high expectations for students actually determined students' perceptions of performance and satisfaction. It is interesting to note that, even though students who had positive outlooks on their performance by discussing course material online with their peers, they were much more selective when it came to interacting with their professors. These students seemed to benefit from online communication with their professors only when it was related specifically to course expectations and feedback.

In sum and based on the cited literature, students who take blended learning courses seem to use a variety of communication strategies and interaction tools to connect with their peers and instructors. However, the disadvantage of using a blended learning pedagogy is that students are required to be on campus and have to acquire ever-changing ICT skills that can present a steep learning curve. It is also apparent that the target population of such empirical investigations is drawn from traditional college-aged undergraduate students. Therefore, it is imperative, especially in the microlevel research stream for understanding teaching and learning, that studies explore the lived experiences and practices of graduate students and professors who have adopted a blended learning pedagogy and their need to develop communication and interaction.

Conceptual Context

As Zawacki-Richter and Anderson (2014) suggested, research topics at the microlevel of teaching and learning in distance education need to be empirically explored, critically analyzed, and theoretically interpreted. They also advocated that such research questions should be posed within a theoretical or conceptual framework. Given the exploratory nature of the investigation, the conceptual context for this study is Garrison, Anderson, and Archer's (2000) Community of Inquiry (CoI) framework for online and blended learning communication. This model has been the focus of extensive research and validation for over a decade (Garrison, 2009). The premise of the framework is that higher education is both collaborative and individually constructed. This premise is considered useful because it brings together three converging concepts: cognitive presence, social presence, and teaching presence. Cognitive presence is taken to mean the extent to which students in a community of inquiry can construct meaning through sustained communication. Social presence is how the students identify with the community as a whole in which they can trustingly communicate with each other and therefore develop interpersonal connections. And teaching presence, multidimensional and performed by the instructor, consists of design, facilitation, and instruction (Akyol & Garrison, 2008; Garrison, 2009).

Although the framework does focus on the educational experience created by instructors and students, it is limited in distinguishing among different methods of teaching and learning in online and blended learning environments. In particular, it also does not centre on the types of text and voice as teaching methods. Despite these limitations, the framework can still help us to answer questions related to the microlevel research stream for understanding teaching and learning. Three research questions guided the study. (1) What are graduate students' experiences in a blended learning program? (2) What are professors' experiences in a graduate blended learning program? (3) What variations of voice and text are used by the graduate students and professors who teach in a blended learning program?

Methodology

In the following section, a brief description of the research design and instrumentation, we discuss the site location and participants. We also provide an overview of the complete data analysis.

Research Design and Instrumentation

A qualitative approach was used as the research design for this study. "Qualitative researchers are interested in understanding the meaning people have constructed, that is, how people make sense of their world and the experiences they have in the world" (Merriam, 2009, p. 13). As noted by Creswell (2013), qualitative researchers tend to use approaches and methods such as grounded theory, ethnography, case studies, interviews, focus groups, observations, narrative analysis, and discourse analysis to seek in-depth subjective and multiple perspectives as a means of exploring a problem in depth. In this research, a case study method was employed using semi-structured interviews, document and artifact analyses, and researchers' field notes. They served as multiple data collection sources for the study and helped to triangulate the findings.

Qualitative data were obtained from semi-structured interviews with students and instructors in a Faculty of Education in a medium-sized Canadian university in eastern Ontario. The interview schedules were developed based on the international literature on blended learning and the CoI research, and they were pilot-tested with both professors and students in the faculty. Interview schedules for students and instructors consisted of three demographic questions and nine open-ended questions. Overall, each semi-structured, face-to-face interview lasted between 45 and 60 minutes. A second data source incorporated documents and artifacts. The documents were related to blended learning courses such as institutional policies and regulations, course syllabuses, evaluation surveys, and assessment tools. Artifacts included students' projects, assignments, and weekly reports. A third data source comprised researchers' field notes, which provided insights into the interviews and enabled investigators to consolidate the findings and to establish the validity of the data obtained during the study.

Site Location and Participants

When the Strategic Mandate Agreements submitted by Ontario universities to the provincial Ministry of Training, Colleges and Universities in 2012 were examined, it became apparent that postsecondary institutions in the province needed to embrace new methodologies, such as the large-scale adoption of blended learning courses. This change was precipitated by a need to move away from the traditional lecture-based pedagogy and an increase in the availability of new technological teaching tools. To fulfill this blended learning commitment, the university chosen for this study committed resources from the Office of the Vice-President, Academic, to have at least 20% of all course offerings in a blended learning format by 2020. The rationale for choosing the Faculty of Education as the site location was based on reports from an intra-university working committee indicating that this faculty had taken a leadership role in establishing both online and blended learning within the institution.

The participants of the study were 27 key informants from the Faculty of Education, including 18 students and 9 professors. The student participants had taken at least two graduate courses offered in a blended learning format. As well, the professors had at least one year of teaching experience in a blended learning format in the faculty.

Data Analysis

To determine patterns in the qualitative data sources, the research team used the constant comparative technique (Merriam, 2009). In preparing the raw interview data, pseudonyms were assigned to each key informant to protect confidentiality and identity. Analysis of the interview data and field notes involved five steps:

1. exploring the data by reading through the responses;
2. coding the data;
3. using codes to develop themes by aggregating similar codes;
4. connecting and interrelating themes; and
5. constructing the narrative.

First, participants' responses to interview questions were converted into transcripts. Next, in order to develop themes, researchers read through the transcribed data several times and then consolidated these themes and created the narrative. In addition to the analysis of qualitative data obtained from interviews and field notes, an analysis of the documents and artifacts was conducted using a Likert-type criteria grid with indicators associated with social, cognitive, and teaching presence.

As a final step in the data analysis, the narrative themes drawn from the three data sources for graduate students were examined using an analytical chart (see Appendix A) depicting the six key principles of the andragogical model of adult learning (Knowles, Holton, & Swanson, 2011). These principles include the learner's self-concept, experience, readiness to learn, problem-centred orientation, internal motivation, and need to know. Since Merriam and Bierema (2014) discussed these six principles in detail, we present a short statement of them here. The learner's self-concept is related to the importance of having a voice in what and how one learns. An adult's accumulated life experience is a rich resource for learning and integral to her or his identity. Readiness to learn is connected to the social roles and developmental tasks of adulthood that create a need for learning. Adults are motivated to learn to deal with an issue or problem of immediate concern and have a desire for immediate application. Internal motivation is related to self-actualization of the adult learner and puts the individual at the centre of the learning transaction. Adults want to know why they need to learn something and how what they learn will be applied to their immediate situations.

This tool was created to help identify possible matches between the andragogical model of adult learning and the text-based communications and verbal interactions evident in the emergent themes and key informant quotations from the data sources. As well, in the same manner as professors' narratives, a modification of the Blended Learning Course Quality Rubric was employed to identify possible matches between text-based communications and verbal interactions evident in the emergent themes. This rubric was developed by Teaching and Learning Support Services at the university where the data were collected. The tool was developed based on best practices in course design, and it was intended to help guide instructors in the development of quality blended learning courses. The rubric consisted of four main criteria: course design, learner supports and resources, use of technology, and course organization and content presentation. Each of the main criteria was accompanied by several descriptors to be used in a checklist format by an instructor (see Appendix B).

Findings

We present the results of the data analysis path under three headings. Each section corresponds to one of the three research questions and includes (1) the lived experiences of graduate students; (2) the experiences of professors teaching in a graduate blended learning program; and (3) the variations of voice and text used in a blended learning program by students and professors.

The Lived Experiences of Graduate Students

Central to the learning needs of graduate students in blended learning courses was the importance of developing trust with peers and the instructor at the outset. Social interaction exercises conducted during the face-to-face sessions before going online were instrumental in establishing a level of comfort with disclosure of academic and personal content. As Shelia reported, "when the professor uses meaningful ice breakers and trust-building exercises, you get a sense of who you are going to be working with."

During the introductory face-to-face session, it also seemed to be important for students to know which small group they would be participating in during the online components. This need also raised the issue of sequencing face-to-face and online sessions. Most students preferred at least two or three face-to-face sessions before beginning online group work. Mohammed put it this way: "I like to have enough class time interaction with the professor and try to figure out what the course is all about." There was also a tendency not to feel satisfied with one face-to-face and then one online sequencing throughout the course or with large blocks of online learning. What seemed to be more engaging for the students was a continued sequence of either face-to-face or online sessions together. Another interesting aspect of the theme was how the climate of mutual respect among peers during the face-to-face sessions acted as a motivator for learning new content. Zhang, an international student who had taught in a Chinese university, believed that the small group format for assignments made her feel more comfortable. Peers interested in the Chinese educational system came to respect the cultural differences in learning.

Acquiring critical thinking skills, one of the graduate program learning outcomes, was identified as a key area for most students, especially when working through online learning modules. They preferred problem-posing scenarios, searching for alternative solutions to case studies and unpacking the weekly readings with each other in their small groups. Sandy thought that knowing the basic principles of critical thinking first and then having time to practise them in class and online increased her metacognitive skills.

Critical thinking skills are viewed as an indicator of cognitive presence in the CoI and were acknowledged as an important area of expertise in the work-related student projects gathered during data collection (Garrison, Anderson, & Archer, 2000). Graduate students believed that critical thinking was an important part of their professional and academic lives. Alice, a part-time student employed in a hospital, described it this way: "As a practising RN and a nurse educator, critical thinking is an essential skill for me to master and model for my students."

All graduate students thought that being part of a community of practice was important. Some mentioned that the professor sets the tone for how that community develops and collaborates by real-time interaction in class and weekly online communications. For example, Michelle reported that the personalized discussion questions posed after the guest speaker presented during a face-to-face session made her more aware of the community resources now within her reach.

However, students who had taken a full online course were dissatisfied with the amount of feedback received from the professor when they were working online. Jason said that "I felt like the instructor wasn't really there when we did our postings, and we would go off on these meaningless tangents." Another common theme related to the community of practice was active student engagement in learning. Many students recognized the importance of continuity between classroom and online learning. Alia put it succinctly: "If I can't figure out where we are going when I'm online, I lose motivation very quickly. I like how the prof explained the flow of the course in our first face-to-face sessions." Another graduate student had a similar remark: "I need to know the backgrounds of my group and how the course fits together before I can start challenging student opinions."

Another pattern that emerged from the students' artifacts was related to knowledge building. Working through a community of practice within blended courses enabled students to increase their levels of interaction among peers and the instructor and to gain new perspectives on the course content in the face-to-face and online discussions. Chris put it this way: "During classroom discussions, or in my online community of inquiry group, each member offered an original perspective which provided me with a full range of responses to consider in forming my own thoughts and increasing my knowledge base."

Challenges of blended learning comprised another theme in the data from the graduate students. Poor instructional design, poor navigation, technical difficulties in uploading documents in online sessions, and not enough time to get to know peers were the most cited factors associated with learning dissatisfaction. Marcia, a thesis student, suggested that "professors should be trained on how to teach in a blended learning format before they actually instruct. I had a prof who changed the online assignment mid-stream in the course, and it completely confused everyone." Also a challenge for more mature graduate students was the steep learning curve using Blackboard Learn, the university's learning management system (LMS). Abdul, an international student who had arrived on campus a few days after the course had started, went on to say that

> I had never taken an online or blended learning course before, and I was overwhelmed with trying to learn the technological aspects like logging in, let alone the course content, which was outside of my field of practice. I struggled a lot over the course and felt that I never really made a connection with my classmates.

This idea was also supported by the researchers' field notes. For example, some students in the age range of 45–55 described the intense learning curve in trying to master the new LMS, far different from basic computer use. This lack of ease in navigating Blackboard Learn acted as an impediment and affected weekly online progress at times.

Experiences of Professors Teaching in a Graduate Blended Learning Program

One key theme that emerged from the data for professors was related to motivation. Many respondents reported that the current increase in the size of a graduate class was a main motivator in trying out a blended learning pedagogy. Another motivating factor was related to trying out different ways of organizing the course content and communicating with students. As one respondent, Jennifer, explained, "I wanted to move away from blogging and wikis for a change, so I tried having the students develop a small group action research project during our in-class sessions, and then I supported them as they continued their work online."

There was also a recognition that all graduate students are now equipped with the technical skills to move easily through online learning using a range of tools available in an LMS like Blackboard Learn. Since graduate students seemed to be more comfortable with using technological tools, there is a sense that professors see this comfort as readiness to embark on a blended learning pedagogy. As one professor, Mary, mentioned, "I was interested in trying out a new method of blended learning and was curious to compare it with my more traditional classroom teaching style." Gerald, a professor who had three years of blended learning teaching experience, believed that it was important to do some design training on learning objectives and structuring small group work in learning modules. He also thought that it was important to talk with colleagues who had only taught online courses because context in blended learning is crucial.

Another theme that emerged was the impact of blended learning. The vast majority of professors interviewed declared that they observed a higher quality in assignments coupled with more student engagement. For example, one professor described how Skyping in a guest speaker during an in-class session and then having an open plenary discussion increased student participation. Some professors had also tried different sequences in designing both classroom and online formats and used blogs to fill in knowledge gaps between sessions. Mark, another seasoned blended learning professor, said that "I use the face-to-face sessions to pick up on any unresolved questions from the online learning sessions, and I've noticed a better quality of weekly work." Another professor, Joanne, who had recently developed and completed her first blended learning course, believed that the reflective journey and personal experiences shared with peers using both formats seemed to be richer. She added that "I have moved away from [the] research type of assignments and more into reflection and professional growth type of assignments."

Exploring a blended learning pedagogy also emerged as an important theme from the data sources. Professors who had several years of experience teaching in this format claimed that a well-defined course structure and continuity between in-class and online learning were important design features that influenced student progress. Having students participate in small group discussions while in class and then carrying those stimulating discussions online seemed to work for some of the respondents. Linda, a professor teaching her third blended learning course, pointed out that "the learning objectives for each session need to correspond to the learning strategies that you choose, and this is dependent on the core concepts of that session." Adam, a professor new to the faculty, also mentioned that "my choice for some of the technological tools used for the online sessions was research based." Another respondent brought out an important point about the range of student ability with technology and claimed that "I try to keep in mind that some students like technical experimentation while learning online, and others don't. I spend a lot of time navigating with the whole group while we are together at the beginning." Some professors also thought that conducting interviews with former graduate students as a means of determining needs and approaches when redesigning a blended learning course was an important preparatory step in defining the pedagogy. Frank, a seasoned professor, put it this way:

> I knew about 10 months in advance that I would be teaching a new blended learning course, so while I was teaching that same course in a full face-to-face format I interviewed several students to find out what aspects of the content should become learning modules and which content should remain as in-class sessions. I also got a clear sense of how to balance individual and group work in both formats. For me, the lesson I took away from those interviews is that the course content actually drives how you make decisions about sequencing the in-class and online learning sessions.

Also related to the theme of blended learning pedagogy were the important features of the well-structured course outline and the needs assessment conducted at the beginning of the course. These features helped to create and define this community of inquiry in both face-to-face and online sessions. In particular, the important information collected from the needs assessment questionnaires helped to create exercises that developed trust among student group members and provided momentum in establishing this new form of pedagogy.

Creating a faculty culture was another key theme. All professors indicated that having an incentive such as course design support from the university's blended learning initiative was an important factor in their decision to move forward in creating a new blended course. Paul reported that "I can now hire a TA who has the technological expertise to help me design and deliver the course. He already knows that posting too many course documents can become boring for the students." Another respondent claimed that this university-wide initiative was becoming more visible and that a four-part certificate course on designing blended learning offered by the Centre for University Teaching (CUT) provided the necessary skills and knowledge to feel confident in undertaking course development. As part of the blended learning initiative in this university, a needs assessment was conducted by CUT among faculty members that prompted the development of this certificate course. Martha explained that "taking that course helped to identify the misconceptions around blended learning and provided a lot of demonstrations and hands-on tips."

Also related to faculty support was the idea of in-house champions. All professors indicated the importance of the informal faculty support group in existence for over three years. This group of professors gathered at the end of each semester to share their experiences, challenges, and stories. Brian, a former member of this informal group, realized that he could call on a faculty champion at a moment's notice whenever he bumped into a snag such as getting the flipped classroom formula just right.

Variations of Voice and Text Used in a Blended Learning Program by Students and Professors

Within the three themes related to graduate students—developing trust, acquiring critical thinking skills, and establishing a community of practice—were variations in both textual communications and verbal interactions. These variations were used to support many of the principles inherent in Knowles's andragogical model of adult learning. In developing the learner's self-concept, verbal interactions were used by both the instructor and peers to increase social interactions during the in-class sessions, and textual communications through online trust-building exercises continued this psychological climate of respect and collaboration. A readiness to learn was enhanced when text-based assignments focused on work-related content and verbal instructions were given by the instructor on how to use and navigate the LMS.

Different voice and text communications were also used to create a problem-centred orientation for the students. For example, during the class sessions, small group discussions that centred on the weekly readings provided an opportunity for students to try out new ways of questioning and to practise their critical thinking skills. This type of skill acquisition was also practised during online sessions. As well, text-based case studies that were part of the online module helped students to search for alternative solutions to current educational problems as they worked together in their CoI groups. Students were motivated when the instructor explained the continuity between the face-to-face sessions and the online sessions each time the class met on campus. They also enjoyed learning from each other during the in-class oral presentations. In addition, knowledge building was improved through online textual communications since they gave students more time to reflect and respond to each other in their discussion forums.

Within the three themes from the data from professors—motivation, impact of blended learning, and exploring a blended learning pedagogy—was also a wide variation in voice and text combinations used by professors. This was evident across the four main criteria of the modified Blended Learning Course Quality Rubric: course design, learner support and resources, use of technology, and course organization and content presentation. Textual communications such as the course syllabus were used during the first face-to-face session to introduce the new blended learning course objectives, and they were posted on the LMS for careful review. Learning activities as part of the course design incorporated both voice and text. For example, Skyping in a guest speaker for a face-to-face session seemed to increase student engagement, especially when discussion among classmates took place. In one instance, the professor used small groups in class to create an action research project and then followed each group online as they continued through the steps of the project. For the criteria of learner support and resources, there was an indication that the text-based communications among the small online groups related to the online module provided higher-quality submissions. One professor found that students were comfortable giving him verbal feedback in class on how to improve a part of an online module. As well, some professors mentioned that their students felt more comfortable giving face-to-face feedback to them when some aspect of the online content did not work.

In the purposeful integration of technology, it seemed that there was a balance between voice and text communications. For instance, in-class interactions between the instructor and students were more important in addressing unresolved questions and issues raised in the online discussion forums. In addition, students were eager to attend a final face-to-face session in the course in which each small group member would share his or her reflection on the journey through the online modules. The use of blogs between face-to-face sessions helped to develop course continuity for some students, and the text-based personal growth assignments gave more time for individuals to think through their positions. In terms of course organization and content presentation, there was an indication that posting too many course documents online could demotivate some students. It also seemed to be important for the instructor to spend time in class at the beginning of the course to navigate the blended learning course content and to illustrate how the technological tools would be used.

Discussion

Situated within the microlevel of the teaching and learning framework for distance education espoused by Zawacki-Richter and Anderson (2014), and guided by the theoretical orientation of the Community of Inquiry, this study attempted to understand better what really works in a graduate blended learning program. Overall, the results indicate that mature adult learners enrolled in a graduate blended learning program have specific learning preferences as an outgrowth of this new pedagogy and that professors who use the approach reach toward meeting the needs of this student population. It also seems to be clear from the findings that learning is a social activity for both the graduate students and the professors as indicated by their lived experiences. Both key informants co-create knowledge as individuals and in groups. What seems to be highlighted is the importance of the social roles of the graduate student. This context is closely connected to their social responsibilities as worker, parent, and community advocate. This context appears to be different from that of the traditional undergraduate student. In addition, results seem to indicate that certain voice interactions and text communications can be identified by both the graduate students and the professors who participated in the investigation.

Since there is a dearth of empirical evidence in this area, the following section contains a discussion of three arguments related to this topic: (1) interactions and communications and the search for balance between voice and text; (2) a tool for professors to improve the quality of blended learning; and (3) how focusing on characteristics of adult learners will help to improve blended learning for graduate students.

Interactions and Communications: The Balance Between Voice and Text

As Zawacki-Richter and Anderson (2014) contended, professors' and students' perpetual conception and maintenance of interactive circles and community of practice are instrumental in sustaining the development and success of any form of online learning. In this particular study of practices in a blended learning program, we saw the importance of interaction and communication circles through voice and text as students and professors collaborated to form a learning community both in class and online.

Based on the analytical charts and the raw data, some type of balance between voice and text does exist. For example, graduate students used problem-posing scenarios and unpacking of weekly readings in their small groups as verbal interactions to sharpen their critical thinking skills. As well, they practised these foundational skills through online textual communications, which afforded them additional time for deep reflections and then written communications with their interactive CoIs. The importance of developing these skills is in line with Garrison's (2016) assertion that redesigning a blended learning course should have the objective of stimulating students to use critical discourse and reflection. Furthermore, professors employed reflective journey assignments as an assessment technique using voice in small group face-to-face sessions and then carried forward these engaging conversations online through text communications.

As well, one of the major motivating factors for graduate student progress was continuity between face-to-face and online sessions through voice and text. Both the verbal interactions and the textual communications helped the students to feel connected with the "ebb and flow" of the course and to sustain their communities of practice. One consequence of this balance between voice and text was that it enhanced the important aspect of building trust among all members of the group, including students and professors. Vaughan (2014) alluded to this, mentioning that both students and professors recognize the significance of tools of interaction in blended learning for developing trust. In addition, professors emphasized the role of blogs and wikis as textual communications and verbal interactions during the face-to-face sessions in order to resolve student queries that they developed during the online sessions. As mentioned in the literature review, Wang (2010) also found that blogs and journals—types of information and tools of communication in a blended learning environment—can inspire social interaction among students and increase active engagement in the learning process.

Tayebinik and Puteh (2012) made an important point when they stated that overall satisfaction with blended learning improves as collaboration among members in the community of practice and interaction among peers increase. This collaboration can take on various forms. What we found in this study is some early evidence that balancing voice interactions in the face-to-face sessions with text communications during the online sessions can help graduate students to develop trust, acquire critical thinking skills, and build sustainable communities of practice.

A Tool for Professors to Improve the Quality of Blended Learning

One of the theoretical justifications for using the CoI framework for this study was that, over the years, it has guided the idea that "information and communication technology provide[s] the opportunity to create communities of learners that support engagement and collaboration" (Vaughan, Cleveland-Innes, & Garrison, 2013, p. 3). A strength of the framework is the interplay among teaching, cognitive presence, and social presence that can provide a road map for understanding the complex dynamics in a blended learning environment. And, as was the case in this study, nesting the research questions within this framework did allow an understanding of some of those blended learning dynamics as experienced by graduate students and professors. Although the framework does highlight the importance of selecting content, setting climate, and supporting discourse, it is difficult for professors to use these indicators as guides for evaluating their own practices when teaching in a blended learning environment, especially with more mature adult graduate learners. As Ross and Collier (2016) declared, there is now a need for the evaluation of learning design and teaching practice as emerging technologies and digital education are transforming postsecondary institutions. Furthering this argument, Conrad (2014) noted the increasing use of voice, video, social media, and other immersive technologies as important tools of engagement for blended and online learning. At the same time, Conrad challenged those working in online education to do a better job of accommodating the current preferences and needs of learners in this new medium.

To meet this challenge, the two analytical charts used in the data analysis for determining variations of voice and text used by graduate students and professors who teach in a blended learning program can be used as a starting point for instructor self-evaluation. Appendix A, the text and voice analytical chart using the andragogical model of adult learning, can help instructors to create unique learning experiences for adult learners in a blended learning environment. For the purposes of this study, the columns in the analytical chart of themes and quotations were used in the data analysis. For example, using the learner's self-concept, the first andragogical principle in the model, the matching theme of developing trust and the quotations from two student key informants were identified by the research team. They then identified the textual communications and verbal interactions from the theme and quotations. However, using this chart without these two columns, the instructor might simply record the types and frequencies of textual communications and verbal interactions associated with each of the six adult learning principles. This tool could be used in either designing a blended learning course or after delivering such a course to check for the balance between text and voice in both the face-to-face sessions and the online sessions.

Additionally, Appendix B, the user-friendly voice and text analytical chart using a modification of the Blended Learning Course Quality Rubric, could be used in a similar fashion when teaching mature graduate students. As previously mentioned, this rubric was developed based on best practices in course design, and it is intended to help guide instructors in the development of quality blended learning courses. In this study, once again the columns in the analytical chart of themes and quotations were used in the data analysis. For example, using course design, the first criterion in the Blended Learning Course Quality Rubric, the matching theme of exploring pedagogy and the quotations from the two professors were identified by the research team. They then identified the textual communications and verbal interactions. Using this chart without these two columns, the instructor could again record the types and frequencies of textual communications and verbal interactions across the four main course criteria and indicators when planning or delivering face-to-face and online sessions. Taken together, these charts could act as a self-evaluation tool for instructors to improve the quality of their blended learning designs. Identifying the different modes of communication that they use in digital learning and the efficacies of speech and text might be a mechanism to support mature graduate students in their development of critical and reflective thinking.

Improving Blended Learning for Adult Graduate Students

Although Garrison (2016) posited that blended learning can transform higher education by revisiting and redesigning the way that courses are developed, it is evident that work still needs to be done. Tensions persist over the purpose of blended learning and whether or not it is an administrative measure designed to handle an increasingly large number of students on campus and to lower the costs of operations while attempting to preserve the quality of instruction and student experience. Research indicates that, by not meeting the unique learning characteristics of mature students, many barriers will continue to impede their educational opportunities (Osam et al., 2017; Phillips et al., 2017; Rabourn et al., 2015).

Blended learning is an approach in higher education that shows some promise and benefit to mature learners even though mastering some of the technological communication tools might actually impede the ongoing dialogue with professors and peers. As described earlier, Campbell and Schwier (2014) and Conrad (2014) have suggested that courses designed to provide social and cognitive activities by integrating students' real-life experiences are effective in motivating learners.

What seems to emerge from the findings is that good-quality blended learning design can address adult learners' characteristics and reduce institutional barriers to higher education. For example, developing trust, acquiring critical thinking skills, and being part of a community of practice are essential elements in blended graduate education. These findings resonate with the work of Merriam and Bierema (2014), who identified the positive aspects essential for improving adult learners' academic experiences. As well, the results suggest that, through both textual communications and verbal interactions, professors have flexibility in how they integrate the real-life experiences of graduate students in course content. Therefore, an effective blended learning pedagogy seems to lend itself to a course design that involves the fusion of face-to-face and online learning activities for individuals and groups. This could be the case for institutions that have adopted and funded blended learning initiatives at large. Yet essential for implementing a university-wide blended learning strategy is a faculty culture developed through technological and pedagogical support services as well as by recognizing in-house champions (Taylor, Atas, & Ghani, 2017).

As the demographics change in institutions of higher education with more opportunities for adult learners to increase their academic and work-related knowledge, the barriers that they face remain a concern (Stevens, 2014). However, getting a glimpse of how graduate students and professors actually experience blended learning can provide some insights into tackling such barriers. At the core of this awareness is the fact that adult learners have unique self-concepts, experiences, motivations, and problem-centred orientations.

Conclusion

Although this study was conducted in a particular faculty of a medium-sized Canadian university that has adopted blended learning, the results are not generalizable. Nevertheless, the case does raise some interesting additional questions for further inquiry, such as how graduate students can become more involved in course design for blended learning initiatives so as to meet their unique educational needs and how professors can become more aware of the learning needs of mature students. Additional research is needed on the applicability of the self-evaluation tool for professors in their search for quality blended learning design. These questions will inform future work on the quest for the finest course offerings in blended and online learning.

Appendix A: Text and Voice Analytical Chart using the Andragogical Model of Adult Learning

Andragogical Model of Adult Learning	Theme	Quote	Text-based communication	Verbal Interactions (Voice)
1. Learners Self-concept Psychological elements of respect, trust, collaboration				
2. Experience Connecting life experience with developmental tasks				
3. Readiness to Learn Use of instructional techniques – real life applications				
4. Problem-centred Orientation Immediate problem-solving; social roles				
5. Internal Motivation Self actualizing, learner centered, intrinsically motivated				
6. Need to Know How to apply it; real or simulated tasks				

Appendix B: Text and Voice Analytical Chart using a modification of the Blended Learning Course Quality Rubric

Blended Learning Course Quality Rubric	Theme	Quote	Text-based communication	Verbal Interactions (Voice)
1. Course Design				
Learning Outcomes				
Learning Activities				
Assessment Activities				
2. Learner Support & Resources				
Course Basics				
Communication & Interactions				
Student Feedback				
Instructor Feedback				
3. Use of Technology				
Purposeful Integration of Technology				
Ease of Use				
4. Course Organization & Content Presentation				
Course Orientation				
Course Navigation & Content Presentation				
Appearance & Design				

References

Akyol, Z., & Garrison, D. R. (2008). Assessing metacognition in an online community of inquiry. *Internet and Higher Education, 14*(3), 183–190.

Anderson, T., & Zawacki-Richter, O. (2014). Towards a research agenda. In O. Zawacki-Richter & T. Anderson (Eds.), *Online distance education: Towards a research agenda* (pp. 485–492). Edmonton, AB: Athabasca University Press.

Babb, S., Stewart, C., & Johnson, R. (2010). Constructing communication in blended learning environments: Students' perceptions of good practice in hybrid courses. *Journal of Online Learning and Teaching, 6*(4), 735–753.

Campbell, K., & Schwier, R. (2014). Major movements in instructional designs. In O. Zawacki-Richter & T. Anderson (Eds.), *Online distance education: Towards a research agenda* (pp. 345–380). Edmonton, AB: Athabasca University Press.

Canadian Digital Learning Research Association. (2019). *Tracking online and distance education in Canadian universities and colleges: 2018 public report.* ECampus Ontario.

Cercone, K. (2008). Characteristics of adult learners with implications for online learning design. *ACCE Journal, 16*(2), 137–159.

Chickering, A. W., & Gamson, Z. F. (1987). Seven principles for good practice in undergraduate education. *American Association for Higher Education (AAHE) Bulletin, 39*(7), 3–7.

Conrad, K. (2014). Interactions and communication in online communities: Towards an engaged and flexible future. In O. Zawacki-Richter & T. Anderson (Eds.), *Online distance education: Towards a research agenda* (pp. 381–402). Edmonton, AB: Athabasca University Press.

Creswell, J. W. (2013). *Qualitative inquiry and research design: Choosing among five approaches.* Los Angeles, CA: Sage.

Ekstrom, R. (1972). *Barriers to women's participation in postsecondary education: A review of the literature.* Washington, DC: National Center for Educational Statistics.

Garrison, D. R. (2009). Communities of inquiry in online learning. *Encyclopedia of Distance Learning, Vol.2,* pp.352–355.

Garrison, R. (2016). *Thinking collaboratively: Learning in a community of inquiry.* New York, NY: Routledge.

Garrison, R., Anderson, T., & Archer, W. (2000). Critical thinking, cognitive presence and computer conferencing in distance education. *American Journal of Distance Education, 15*(1), 7–23.

Knowles, M., Holton, E., & Swanson, R. (2011). *The adult learner. (7th Edition).* Amsterdam: Elsevier.

Mason, R. (1994). *Using communications in open and flexible learning*. London, UK: Kogan Page.

Merriam, S. (2009). *Qualitative research: A guide to design and implementation*. San Francisco, CA: Jossey-Bass.

Merriam, S., & Bierema, L. (2014). *Adult learning: Linking theory and practice*. San Francisco, CA: Jossey-Bass.

Osam, E. K., Bergman, M., & Cumberland, D. M. (2017). An integrative literature review on the barriers impacting adult learners' return to college. *Adult Learning, 28*(2), 54–60.

Owston, R. (2013). Blended learning policy and implementation. *The Internet and Higher Education, 18*, 1–3.

Phillips, L. A., Baltzer, C., Filoon, L., & Whitley, C. (2017). Adult student preferences: Instructor characteristics conducive to successful teaching. *Journal of Adult and Continuing Education, 23*(1), 49–60.

Rabourn, K. E., Shoup, R., & BrckaLorenz, A. (2015). Barriers in returning to learning: Engagement and support of adult learners. *Paper presented at the Annual Forum of the Association for Institutional Research*. Denver, CO. (pp.1-32).

Ross, J., & Collier, A. (2016). Complexity, mess, and not yetness: Teaching with emerging technologies. In G. Veletsianos (Ed.), *Emergence and innovation in digital learning* (pp. 17–34). Edmonton, AB: Athabasca University Press.

Stevens, J. (2014). Perceptions, attitudes, and preferences of adult learners in higher education: A national survey. *Journal of Learning in Higher Education, 10*(2), 65–78.

Tayebinik, M., & Puteh, M. (2012). Sense of community: How important is this quality in blended courses. *Proceeding of the International Conference on Education and Management Innovation,* Singapore.

Taylor, M., Atas, S., & Ghani, S. (2017). Exploring the experiences of students and professors in a blended learning graduate program: A case study of a faculty of education. *International Journal of Mobile and Blended Learning, 9*(1), 1–15.

Taylor, M., Vaughan, N., Ghani, S., Atas, S., & Fairbrother, M. (2018). Looking back and looking forward: A glimpse of blended learning in higher education from 2007–2017. *International Journal of Adult Vocational Education and Technology, 9*(1), 1–14.

Vaughan, N. (2014). Student engagement and blended learning: Making the assessment connection. *Education Sciences, 4*(4), 247–264.

Vaughan, N., Cleveland-Innes, M., & Garrison, D. R. (2013). *Teaching in blended learning environments: Creating and sustaining communities of inquiry*. Edmonton, AB: Athabasca University Press.

Wang, M. (2010). Online collaboration and offline interaction between students using asynchronous tools in blended learning. *Australasian Journal of Educational Technology, 26*(6), 830–846.

Zawacki-Richter, O., & Anderson, T. (Eds.). (2014). *Online distance education: Towards a research agenda.* Edmonton, AB: Athabasca University Press.

Embodiment and Engagement in an Online Doctoral Research Methodology Course

A Virtual Ethnographic Study

Gale Parchoma, Marlon Simmons, Michele Jacobsen, Dorothea Nelson, and Shaily Bhola

To inform continual improvement in doctoral research course design, the research team drew upon insights from practice and aggregate findings from internal surveys of student and alumni engagement in previous years' offerings of an advanced research methodology course at one research-intensive Canadian university. Since multiple sections of this doctoral research course were offered each year at the research site, with 16–20 enrolments per section, and since this course was foundational in introducing doctoral-level learners to advanced research methods, we decided that it was critical to understand deeply the nature of learners' online interactions and engagements using insights from Zawacki-Richter and Anderson (2014) as part of our redesign process. Students engage in the course online through two learning management systems (LMS): Desire 2 Learn (D2L) and Adobe Connect. In previous sections of this course, student interactions had taken place primarily via asynchronous communications facilitated through weekly text-based online discussions and group projects. Synchronous discussions had typically taken place during a series of three to four Adobe Connect two-hour audio sessions, dispersed across one term.

In this chapter, we report findings from the first year of a two-year study of purposefully designed and sequenced cycles of (1) weekly instructor-designed, formal, asynchronous text-based interactions; (2) periodic instructor-designed, formal, voice-based Adobe Connect sessions; and (3) less formal, student-led, voice-based Adobe Connect coffee sessions in one online doctoral research methodology course. The goals of this study were (1) to examine critically our own design and teaching practices in this doctoral course; (2) to engage with, extend, and problematize dimensions on which student engagement has been described, measured, and reported in the broader peer-reviewed literature; and (3) to seek ethnographic traces of diverse forms of student engagement, including student reports of perceived embodiment, within our data sets.

Literature Review

The first section of this literature review examines conceptualizations of student engagement. The second section posits an extension to the literature on conceptualizations of embodiment to include the potential for embodied student experiences of engagement in online courses. The third section considers interdependencies among conditions for learning, the social-material complexities of learning environments, and engagement. We conclude the review with an examination of liminal spaces that can either inspire or disrupt student engagement.

Student Engagement

French philosopher Maurice Merleau-Ponty (1964) defined engagement as "our presence when things, truths, and values are constituted" that "summons us to the tasks of knowledge and action" (p. 25). This is well aligned with the definition of student engagement as "the interaction between the time, effort and other relevant resources invested by both students and their institutions intended to optimize the student experience and enhance the learning outcomes" (Trowler, 2010, p. 3). Both definitions require that those involved in learning and teaching be actively present and focused on achieving shared goals.

It has been argued that student engagement can be enriched by active educational practices involving collaborative tasks and problem-based forms of learning (Boyer Commission, 1998; Carini, Kuh, & Klein, 2006; Kuh, 2001, 2009; Nomme & Birol, 2014; NSSE, 2015; Reid 2012). Reid (2012) contended that the National Survey of Student Engagement (NSSE) is designed to estimate the amount of time and effort that students put into educational endeavours. NSSE reports have indicated correlations between student engagement practices and active and collaborative learning (Kuh, 2009). Canadian institutions of higher education use NSSE results to understand student engagement better (NSSE, 2015). However, Reid (2012) cautioned that NSSE methods are limited since they cumulatively report students' experiences over a whole year rather than within a course.

Our study examined student engagement and learning in two instances of an individual inquiry-based doctoral research methodology course. Inquiry-based pedagogy comprises "practices that promote student learning through guided and, increasingly, independent investigation of complex questions, problems, and issues, often for which there is no single answer" (Lee, 2003–04, p. 2). In the research site's Doctorate of Education program, students are supported in becoming practitioner-scholars who link research to professional practice as a key component of their learning. Therefore, students' development of working knowledge—coming to see the role of research in understanding and eventually improving "the actual working practices of experienced practitioners in their field" (Sgouropoulou, Koutoumanos, Goodyear, & Skordalakis, 2000, p. 111)—is a central goal.

Where asynchronous, text-based communications have been, for more than a decade, the primary online learning environment of higher education (Bell, 2015; Garrison, 2011; McConnell, 2006), Sgouropoulou et al. (2000) argued that, when learners are practitioners developing research expertise "in real-world working contexts, this kind of [text-based] technology [alone] proves to be insufficient" (p. 111). In response, Jones,

Asensio, and Goodyear (2011) identified three priority areas for networked learning research and practice:

> (1) the use of asynchronous communications technologies to support collaborative learning among geographically and/or temporally distributed groups of students; (2) the use of synchronous video communications to allow remote access to live lectures and demonstrations; and (3) approaches which mix the use of Web resources with asynchronous or synchronous interpersonal communication. (p. 24)

The third focus aligns well with Dixson's (2010) argument that there can be a connection between the use of multiple communication channels and higher student engagement and a correlation between student-student and student-instructor communication and higher student engagement. More recently, Bell's (2015) findings have indicated that learners' written text in asynchronous online forums, though reflective, is primarily the product of individual thought rather than collaborative interaction. Voice, however, as communicated through synchronous spaces, can facilitate an immediacy that contributes to the development of social presence and trust and support the collaborative construction of knowledge.

Taking Jones et al.'s (2011), Dixson's (2010), and Bell's (2015) findings into consideration, we adapted the existing course design. It was important to augment the existing design, which included

1. weekly text-based asynchronous communications;

2. periodic (three to four per term), more formal, instructor-designed and led, synchronous Adobe Connect sessions in which learners were given opportunities to reflect and build upon their weekly asynchronous, text-based D2L postings in response to course readings, to query their progress in meeting course requirements, and to receive guidance from the course instructor; and

3. interspersed, less formal coffee sessions in which students were simply invited to join an Adobe Connect session and check in with their instructor and their peers in order to lead conversations on

what they were thinking about (Bell, 2015), where their inquiries were taking them (Lee, 2003–04), and any challenges that they were encountering.

By including various opportunities for students to engage across the modes of more and less formal channels for communication and interaction (Dixson, 2010; Jones et al., 2011), it was our goal to provide multiple enriched ways to engage actively in educational practices involving collaborative tasks and problem-based forms of learning (Boyer Commission, 1998; Carini et al., 2006; Kuh 2001, 2009; Nomme & Birol, 2014; Reid 2012).

Embodiment

Although the notion of embodiment might initially seem to be out of place in a discussion of designing online learning, Winn (2003) has forwarded an argument that learning is situated in complex interactions among our minds, our bodies, and our physical and/or digital environments. Within this complex set of relations, our minds need environmental feedback transmitted via our bodily senses and constructed by our bodily actions in order to make sense of ever-changing environmental conditions. Winn argues that our physical bodies "serve to externalize the activities of our physical brains in order to connect cognitive activity" to physical and digital environments, and he refers to "this physical dimension of cognition" as embodiment (p. 7). Although his argument is sufficiently current to be of use in an interest in virtual/online environments, it is rooted in earlier inquiries into interdependencies among mind, body, and environment for the purposes of understanding experiences in relation to learning. For example, in his work on the embodied nature of human perceptions and cognitions, Merleau-Ponty (1964) argued that without his "'lived body' [he would] cease to consciously experience the world" (p. 239). Because the processes of learning require conscious attention to experiences situated within an environment, it follows that conscious experiences of being in and interacting with an environment cannot be separated into differing cognitive and physical dimensions of learning because these dimensions co-constitute each other.

Max van Manen (1997) interrogated the concept of embodiment with the aim of identifying co-constituting dimensions that can be examined to understand the complexities of experiences. His work resulted in a four-dimensional framework, which we have translated into embodied dimensions of online learning experiences: (1) corporeality: experiences of what learners are physically doing as they learn; (2) spatiality: experiences of where learners are physically situated when they are learning; (3) temporality: experiences of time as learners are involved in learning; and (4) relationality: experiences of learners' interactions with others (including their instructor, peers, learning resources, and mediating technologies that connect learners within an online learning environment).

Because the technologically mediated nature of online learning influences corporeality, spatiality, temporality, and relationality, it is worth considering online teaching and learning environments as partially designable and partially emergent. Learning experiences emerge through reciprocal interplays between human and material (Sørensen, 2009) elements of the networks that connect them. Thoughtful designs for learning can play a key role in constructing and stabilizing these connections by considering the embodied dimensions of online learning experiences.

Embodied Engagement as Embeddedness

Winn (2003) linked his explication of embodied learning to the concept of embeddedness, an "interdependence between cognition and environment" (p. 7) that leads back to our discussion of student engagement. Trowler's (2010) definition of student engagement as interactions among the time, effort, and relevant resources directed toward optimizing students' experiences and enhancing learning outcomes can be linked to Winn's (2003) concept of embeddedness, in which "the embodiment of cognition in physical action and the embeddedness of cognition" within interactions across physical and digital environments "are closely connected" (p. 7). Stolz (2015) extended this argument by indicating that engagement as a way of becoming embedded in a teaching and learning context is not only cognitive but also emotional, practical, and aesthetical. By reflectively and reflexively considering the complexities of conditions that influence active student engagement, and the embodied dimensions through which online learners experience learning, we can come to a deeper understanding of the socio-material contexts in which our professional practices are situated.

Liminality

A key factor in understanding varied levels of student engagement, varied capacities to become embodied and embedded in a learning experience, is the encounter with a liminal space. The term "liminality" has been explored widely in the context of a transitional space that connects the previous state of a learner's understanding with the new and transformed state. This in-between space is often "uncomfortable or troublesome" (Wood, 2012, p. 200) for the learner and involves a transformation in her or his "ontology or subjectivity" (Land, Rattray, & Vivian, 2014, p. 200). Meyer and Land (2005) have expressed liminality as a liquid space that transforms and is transformed by the learner when he or she travels across it. The learner can experience a sense of being suspended in this space (Meyer & Land, 2005), oscillating between the previous understanding and the new perspective (Orsini-Jones, 2006). Land, Meyer, and Baillie (2010) have discussed the journey through a liminal space as comprising the pre-liminal, liminal, and post-liminal spaces. In the pre-liminal space, learners encounter troublesome knowledge, and when they eventually pass through the liminal space they are transformed and hold a changed perspective in the post-liminal space. However, experiencing liminality is not as simple, linear, and compartmentalized as suggested by this categorization. Walker (2013) argues that "too much uncertainty in this liminal state and the learner will not be able to progress beyond a surface understanding. Not enough uncertainty and the learner will not make the required transformation" (p. 250). The liminal process is recursive; it subjects the learner to back and forth movements between prior conceptions and emergent ideas (Land et al., 2010).

The participants in our study were successful, experienced, professional practitioners, many of whom work in leadership roles in their home institutions and are in the beginning stages of becoming practitioner-scholars;

therefore, linking research to professional practice is a key component of their doctoral learning experiences. A critical part of this learning process is letting go of the assuredness of current professional expertise in order to adopt an openness to unexpected research findings. Therefore, this liminal learning space can be fraught with ontological and epistemological challenges for students as they encounter troublesome knowledge, which can disrupt engagement/embeddedness.

Our Study

Our study is situated in the redesign of a Doctorate of Education online course. The course is considered foundational for introducing doctoral-level learners to advanced research methodologies. Our over-arching research question was how can purposefully designed cycles of less formal, synchronous, auditory discussions, and more formal, asynchronous, textual discussions, support enhanced student engagement and learning? We also explored how less formal, synchronous, auditory communications can support collaborative student development of working research knowledge and how more formal, asynchronous, textual communications can support a student's development of personal research knowledge.

Participants

Four of 13 doctoral students in the 2015 fall semester offering of our redesigned doctoral methodology course agreed to participate in the study. Three participants were female, and one was male.

Methodology

Drawing from the traditional field of ethnographic research, virtual ethnography seeks to "explore the making of boundaries and the making of connections, especially between the 'virtual' and the 'real'" (Hine, 2004, p. 26.). Historically, ethnography attempted to "gain an understanding of the symbolic meanings attached to the patterns of social interactions of individuals within a particular group" (Cole & Knowles, 2001, p. 17). It involves "systematic investigation through a process of extensive and extensive participant observation, participation, and interviewing within a designated cultural group" (p. 17).

Hine (2004), in her summary of online research methods, noted that "virtual ethnography is, ultimately, an adaptive ethnography which sets out to suit itself to the conditions in which it finds itself" (p. 2). Hine (2000) offered 10 principles necessary for virtual ethnography, which has guided our study. We can understand through ethnography the various ways in which the Internet can be socially meaningful, insofar as the Internet can be understood as both culture and cultural artifact in which iterative and interconnected interactions can be positioned as virtual and embodied. Challenges for virtual ethnography involve not only identifying these sites of interaction but also making sense of how they come into being through contiguity. In doing so, we are invited to think about how the making and remaking of space through mediated interaction are significant for an ethnographic approach in virtual realms. Virtual space ought not to be thought of as an existing reality filled with disembodied emptiness. Rather, and as Hine (2000) stated,

> it has rich and complex connections with the context in which it is used. . . . It also depends on technologies which are used and understood differently in different contexts, and which have to be acquired, learnt, interpreted and incorporated into context. (p. 25)

Social interactions as shaped through a miscellany of media contexts are well woven within heterogeneous flows of virtual interaction. Hine (2000) reminds us that, in terms of virtual spaces, an ethnographic approach seeks to make intelligible place as community and to make recognizable that which constitutes culture. Hence, virtual ethnography involves traversing fixed boundaries between and locations of subjects, at the same time delineating enactments of connectedness between the "'virtual' and the 'real'" (p. 26). Delineation is not without its limits. Ethnographic entities within cyberspace can be configured and reconfigured, purposed and repurposed, by way of researcher reflexivity. "Practically, it is limited by the embodied ethnographer's constraints in time, space and ingenuity" (p. 26).

Unlike traditional forms of ethnography, in which the researcher travels to the field, virtual ethnography maps and unmaps field connectivity within a governing network. Through these fields, the material of the virtual and that of the real have different boundaries as constituted by fluid, folding regional spaces. As a process, virtual ethnography involves recursive rather than fixed, stable, totalizing practices. Always already incomplete, virtual ethnography concerns context specificity as contingent on research questions instead of "truth" systems steeped in objectivity.

Critically reflecting on the ebb and flow of assemblages within interactive networks as well as grasping how the researchers developed a shared understanding of these assemblages under investigation are integral to virtual ethnography. Being submerged and continually engaged in the virtual allows the researcher to coordinate ethnography through teaching and dialoguing with students in virtual places as organized and inscribed through various synchronous and asynchronous arrangements. One can therefore get a sense of how social relations become meaningful in online settings that can enhance student learning.

Data Collection and Analysis

Traditionally, data collection for ethnographic researchers involves interviews, focus group discussions, participant observations, and archival and document analyses. Ethnography involves being present in the social field and being situated in the lived experiences of other cultures to understand the broader political landscapes. Our virtual ethnographic approach drew from and built on these traditional ethnographic methods. We broadened the scope of our instrumentation to include visual and written data as circumscribed by synchronous and asynchronous modalities. Specifically, our data collection involved five sources: (1) online interviews; (2) focus group discussions and archival data (asynchronous components of D2L): (3) transcripts from formal Adobe Connect sessions; (4) informal virtual coffee sessions); and (5) self-reflexive oral narratives.

We gained ethical approval from the university through an internal ethics review board. Participants were invited by a third-party recruiter. Data were anonymized by a third-party transcriber. To safeguard confidentiality and anonymity, pseudonyms were used for all participants. Our preliminary findings on data collected in the first year involved two rounds of individual and collaborative coding with continuous discussion. The first round of coding was descriptive, and through self-reflexivity we developed a shared understanding of the phenomena under investigation. That is, how are patterns of relations performed within the socio-material assemblage of an online graduate course?

We used the following guiding interview questions.

1. Provide a brief description of your experiences participating in the Adobe Connect teaching and learning sessions. How were they structured? What kind of impressions did you take away from them?

2. Provide a one-minute description of your experiences participating in Virtual Open Office Hour sessions. In what ways did you find Virtual Open Office Hours helpful with your individual or collaborative learning?

3. Can you say a bit about your experiences with the Virtual Coffee Session discussions in relation to the scheduled Adobe Connect teaching sessions? Did you find any difference in those two settings?

4. Did you see any differences in the ideas you shared in your posts on the Desire2Learn discussions, the written posts, and your verbal participation in the Adobe Connect sessions?

5. To what extent did you find the sequencing of the Adobe Connect sessions and the Desire2Learn discussions helpful for your learning?

6. Did you find that there were any differences in the kinds of ideas that you shared in voice through Adobe Connect sessions and the kinds of ideas you shared in your written posts on Desire2Learn in the threads?

In our second round of coding, we established analytical codes by way of alignment with the difference from and/or the extension of the reviewed literature. Through repeated corroboration of the coders across data sets, we were able to distill and formulate three themes that provide insights into what happened, how that happened, and why it did.

Preliminary Findings

The intention of our course redesign was to provide distinct but linked spaces for various kinds of interactions among learners, the instructor, and learning resources. The course outline, assessment rubrics, required and recommended readings, and weekly text-based discussion threads were housed in our D2L learning management system. Links to the periodic, more formal, instructor-designed and -led, two-hour Adobe Connect teaching sessions and interspersed, less formal, student-led, one-hour Adobe Connect coffee sessions were also accessed through D2L. We had anticipated that student-participants would distinguish among the different purposes of these modes of communication. However, their reports of their experiences engaging in the course via text and voice across the modes of communication varied.

Experiences of Designed Purposes of Text- and Voice-Based Interactions

We expected student-participants would primarily perceive weekly text-based discussion D2L forums as spaces for posting reflections on readings and posting draft work for peers' and the instructor's feedback. Although the students consistently engaged in these activities, a substantial number of postings also included reflections on Adobe Connect auditory discussions. For example, Stella posted the following comment in the discussion during the second week:

> I enjoyed getting connected with all of you during our first on-line session last week. I appreciated listening to the discussion and learning more about the concepts around methods and methodology for our research. After reflecting on your posts, the readings, and the conversation during our first Connect session, I am already shifting some of my thinking and uncovering new understandings that will guide my future research.

Many of the postings also included methodological position taking followed by queries about potential implications for specific choices. An example from each participant follows.

Stella: I do not believe that there is a universal truth that exists, although I do believe in the concept of an overriding universal morality. Or at least that such a concept should exist. . . . I think that duo-ethnography is something that I should explore.

Amy: I echo [a peer's] sentiments when it comes to wondering how complicated it will be to be a pragmatic researcher. I, too, think that it is so early in the course, and I have a lot to learn. I am cautiously taking it all in. . . . I think when we talked in the summer my caution had to do with this week's topic. Believing that you were more positivist inclined, I was questioning whether you would be able to sustain research that seemed to be at odds with that.

Zack: To me, this week's readings have asked us to consider not merely positions and/or paradigms, and/or the positives and negatives of one position or paradigm over the other, of if there are even positives or negatives at all; rather, these readings have illuminated the "dilemma" of being researchers who have chosen to research ourselves: that is, humankind. . . . As such, these readings have brought to the fore the following persistent topic/dilemma: that one is "required," as a subject, to reflect on and eventually project one's subjectivity, which is explicated through our alignments with certain ontological, epistemological, axiological, and methodological stances, one of which may be one's choosing to disregard and not align with any of these, which is a stance in and of itself.

Mary: Do we not, as researchers, have to become aware of, what I will package as, "biases" and then remove those biases, ourselves, our "distinction," and any others that do not ensure the research findings can stand on their own, and gather those that do?

We perceived that the primary purposes of the more formal, two-hour, auditory, Adobe Connect synchronous sessions were for the instructor to lead discussions of key concepts and to respond to learners' requests for clarifications of expectations for assessed work. However, these sessions became dominated by further advice seeking on assignments in relation to implications for specific methodological choices. For example, Zack expressed a concern that, in choosing a specific methodology, he would first have to "lay out the philosophy of [his intended research] questions" and then decide on "an overarching question on top of that." He then asked for the instructor's advice on how to work through that process.

The less formal, one-hour, Adobe Connect coffee sessions were intended to be unstructured spaces for learners to lead and engage in social and scholarly dialogues. However, student-participants reported perceiving few, if any, differences between the more formal and the less formal auditory sessions. Three of four participants reported not being especially aware of which type of auditory session they were participating in in a particular week. Rather, they were more focused on just "attending" a weekly class (Amy) in order to check in with their peers and the instructor and to "keep up the momentum that everyone" sought (Stella). In the focus group interview, the interviewer was asked to clarify the difference between the more formal teaching sessions and the less formal coffee sessions, and the explanation was understood clearly only when the delineation between one- and two-hour sessions was made. During her interview, Amy reflected on the focus group and said that she "was maybe the one who didn't really see a huge difference between the two." She went on to explain that the "norm" for her was to attend "weekly classes" and that on a given day she "actually wasn't even usually aware of when" she was "attending a one- or two-hour class."

Tracing through the evidence of what happened during the first year of our study, we did not find that student-participants experienced the more formal text-based D2L discussions and audio-based Adobe Connect teaching sessions as different from the less formal Adobe Connect coffee sessions (as we thought they would be). Rather, our three designed teaching and learning spaces became overlapped and entangled and influenced participants' experiences of all three modes of communication that we set out to research as well as the roles of recordings of both more and less formal Adobe Connect sessions.

Experiences of Engagement of Learning Through Text and Voice

Although our D2L data indicate that the student-participants were highly engaged in the weekly text-based postings, their focus group and individual interview accounts of what and why they posted varied across cognitive, emotional, and practical considerations. Cognitively, they were concerned with posting refined ideas and defending the ontological and epistemological positions that underpinned their methodological choices and requesting feedback from their peers and providing feedback to them. For example, Zack reported that, when he posted content on D2L, he wanted to be confident that he was supporting a position that he had taken in an Adobe Connect voice-based session. He wanted to take the "time to filter through the books" to ensure that what he wanted to say was "just right" because he did not want to cite an author "out of context." He wanted to write "exactly what he wanted to say" without "misconstruing it," make it "nice and clear," cite the author to whom he was referring, and "even provide the page number." He also wanted to hear what his peers were "thinking" in relation to his postings and the readings because

> you're reading famed scholars who have thought about this well.
> I wanted to hear about "Joe" and "Jane" who were in this course
> with me, who were at the same level as me, and have never thought
> about it to that level. That's how we are all going to get there, right?

Amy provided a similar account of her experiences of posting in the text-based discussions. She said that before she felt comfortable contributing she wanted time to "deliberate" and that her "strength" was "writing." However, she did not "necessarily like the back and forth on the D2L discussion boards" because sometimes people "have very different views," and "it sometimes feels like you will always have people that want to have the last word." Mary noted that she was "very methodical" in her preparations for posting to D2L. She "typically printed" others' postings, read them carefully before she chose the ones that she would "respond to," and then went back to readings to be sure that she was referring to "exactly the notion" being discussed. Stella suggested that, for people who are "very reflective and like to take their time and really need to ruminate and think about" what they want to say, "the D2L discussion board[s]—if people respond to them—would be [the most] useful [part of] the entire process."

Emotional considerations also played a role in their text-based posts and contributions to audio discussions. Stella reported her sense of the importance of interpersonal relationships, in terms of both the entire class becoming "one community" and her belonging to a sub-community of four class members who maintained closer bonds through "Sunday night Skype meetings" in which they "continued conversations" and discussed their weekly class "experiences." Amy expressed her impression that, because the content of the course was challenging, she and her classmates were reluctant to speak in the Adobe Connect sessions, especially in the beginning, because "people were afraid." Similarly, in the early D2L discussions, there was "just a lot of uncertainty with people—with all of us, I guess—understanding the terminology or understanding the theories involved." Mary noted that, in order to feel confident that she was ready to contribute during the Adobe Connect sessions, she would do "a little bit of pre-read outside of the assigned readings" so that she was "prepared to offer a little bit more contribution." She added that over time she thought that the class came to "love the conversations" held in the Adobe Connect teaching sessions so much that they would take the lead away from the instructor to deal directly with topics that were "pressing for people."

In comparison, in preparation for the coffee sessions, Mary appreciated having an opportunity to reflect on "key writers that were going to be discussed" and have "some questions ready." She thought that this was why later on in the term, in the "less structured" coffee sessions, "everyone had lots to talk about." Zack noted that "the first coffee session was a little rough because everyone was new to each other" and therefore reluctant to speak, but once they felt free enough to ask classmates how they were doing anxieties started to dissipate. He added that perhaps "because they were called coffee sessions they had a bit more of a fun sound to them," and over time he and his classmates were not as concerned that less well-thought-out comments would have "bad outcomes," so they were less anxious about saying "something stupid" or "I don't agree."

Reports of practical considerations that influenced engagement focused on functionalities of the technologies and sensitivity to effective use of time. Zack noted how many times he and his classmates encountered problems "with the technology," and "that's quite frustrating," but he remarked that it was a shared problem, "a shared clumsiness, and you got to feel good amongst each other because of it." Amy noted that she did not "mind the Adobe Connect sessions" when they were "working." She liked that they were synchronous because she felt that she was "in [and part of] a class."

All participants reported frustration with the amount of time in the Adobe Connect sessions that a subset of peers took to query the instructor about grading. Each of the participants reported that the assessment rubrics were sufficiently detailed, and repeatedly listening to a subset of peers wanting direct instruction on how to get top grades left them "tuning out" because they experienced these times as "distracting" and "dead."

Mary recounted having to learn how not to lose time by accidentally deleting text written on the D2L discussion board. She noticed that, if she typed a post directly into D2L, she "would sometimes lose two or more paragraphs" and that "other people had the same problem." "Sometimes you can lose the whole thing." So she and others chose to write in Word and then copy and paste the text into D2L. By making the shift from writing directly into a discussion board to writing with a word processor, Mary found that she wrote in a more formal and detailed way, "almost like a paper."

One component that we did not directly consider in our research questions was the audio recordings of both formal and informal Adobe Connect sessions. However, in individual interviews, two participants spoke about the importance of the recordings. Mary noted how much she valued the Adobe Connect sessions, but because of competing time commitments she had to "miss a couple," which "interrupted" her learning, so later she would "go back and review the recordings" to catch up. Amy used the recordings for a different purpose. In the course that she took in the term after she had completed our course, she would go "back to listen to last term's recordings" because, "after having gone through the class and understanding the material more," she wanted "to go through" them to find the "focused" parts where she had asked questions and received responses from her instructor to check if her "understanding" of what she had heard "had changed."

Experiences of Embodiment of Text and Voice

In our analysis of the dimensions of embodiment, we found traces of participants' experiences that included (1) corporeality: experiences of what participants are physically doing when they are learning; (2) spatiality: experiences of where they are physically situated when they are learning; (3) temporality: experiences of time when they are involved in learning; and (4) relationality: experiences of their interactions with others (including their instructor, peers, learning resources, and mediating technologies that connect them within an online learning environment). We found these traces across participants' reflections on D2L text-based postings, more and less formal audio Adobe Connect sessions, and Adobe Connect recordings. For example, Mary's account of losing text carefully composed directly into D2L discussion spaces, and her linking of that loss at least partially to "using a touchy, 'magic' mouse," provided a physical explanation of her decision to compose text using a word processor, with which Mary found that she wrote more formal and specific types of posts.

Zack described "the freedom" that he found in D2L discussions to link readings that he found "outside the required readings" in the course syllabus and sometimes readings that he had encountered in previous courses to respond to peers' posts. He reported his spatial and temporal experiences of "freedom" as providing openings to "go off on tangents," which he found "very important" for his learning. In comparing his experiences in Adobe Connect teaching sessions with his experiences in coffee sessions, Zack thought that the teaching sessions had "a more planned-out trajectory" from which he and his peers did not want to "divert." His sensitivity to a more formally organized learning space encompassed assumptions about how learners were expected to engage. However, Mary reported that sometimes during the Adobe Connect teaching sessions class members did divert conversations to deal directly with different topics more "pressing" for them.

Stella noted "the course would not have been as successful for anyone, definitely not for me, if we did not have a regular space weekly where we would be able to speak to each other in real time." She preferred the Adobe Connect teaching sessions because she found that they allowed time for the instructor to create opportunities to "dig a little deeper into content." She valued "most of all" having "conversations and dialogue" about "the concepts" that she and her peers "were talking about" in relation to their "own research," their "own work," and their "own experiences."

Amy, like her peers, worked hard to balance the demands of work, life, and study. She soon came to recognize her "multitasking" limitations during the Adobe Connect sessions. She reported that it took her "a long time to get used to listening and watching the chat posts," and though she had planned to do so she did not "take notes." She later followed up on topics raised in Adobe Connect discussions via D2L textual reflections on what she had heard. Like Amy, Mary was concerned about the ability to focus her attention during synchronous auditory sessions, so ahead of each session she prepared "sticky notes" with "questions" and references to "readings" so that she would feel more confident that she could speak to what she was thinking in real time.

Within the evidence of engagement and embodiment in our findings were different traces of participants' concerns about relationality with their peers, their instructor, and their learning resources and how mediating technologies influenced embodiment in and engagement with learning.

Liminal Experiences

As the course progressed, participants continued to refine their methodological choices and rationales for their research. They also continued to oscillate between liminal tensions of assuredness and uncertainty. Participants reported varied experiences of uncertainty about key concepts involved in methodological decision making. In a first week D2L discussion post, Stella told a peer that she looked "forward to somewhat uncomfortable exchanges" as they discussed their current positions on making methodological decisions. Amy expressed a desire for the clarity that comes from the ontological stance that allows one to believe in an objective, single reality. I long for the perceived simplicity of being a positivist, yet I cannot deny that my world is socially constructed, as I am constantly questioning my positionality. . . . Even with my superficial understanding, I feel an immediate affinity for such theories as Feminist Standpoint Theory and Critical Race Theory that, in themselves, denote a lack of a universal experience.

Amy wondered whether she was being "cowardly sitting on the fence if [she did] not go far enough down the continuum to define [herself] as a pragmatic researcher but stop[ped] short at situationalist."

During the first week, Stella reported being "challenged by the idea of participatory research" in relation to her "work in this doctoral program." Given her current understanding of "participatory research" as involving research participants "from the first moment of the research," she could not conceptualize how that would be possible "given the requirement that we have a fully developed research proposal for candidacy and ethics review before we can begin to contact those who will be involved in our research." By the third week, Stella had new concerns:

As I have read each of the articles/chapters so far in this course, I have identified with some aspects of each approach described. Just when I think I have located myself, I come across something about the approach that just doesn't fit. I wonder if I can be a mixture of approaches, although so far I seem to be drawn to those that are (mostly) commensurate. I am somewhat fearful of candidacy as my head is spinning with all of the information presented thus far, and I do not know how I will sort out all epistemological approaches in order to defend the approach I (or rather my research question) choose.

Although his posts in the first and second weeks expressed assurance that Zack understood methodological decision making, by the third week he began expressing uncertainty:

What catalyzed this thought was my (today's) post-coffee-session reflection on last week's discussion regarding the Siegel article. I found it unsettling that I felt genuinely nervous (rare for me) to state my opinion. And, I would contend, that some of you felt the same way—like it was "risky" to say this or that. But . . . why? We are all intelligent adults, putting in a lot of hard work, studying complex and diverse issues, so, why should I feel worried?

Discussion of the Findings

Having drawn upon Bell's (2015) propositions that learners' written text in asynchronous online forums, though reflective, is primarily the product of individual thought rather than collaborative interaction and that synchronous voice facilitates an immediacy that contributes to the development of social presence and trust, and supports the collaborative construction of knowledge, we expected to find more distinct differences in how the participants interacted across modes of communication. Rather, we found that the asynchronous textual discussions, and the more and less formal synchronous audio sessions, interacted, overlapped, and entangled socio-material spaces (Sørensen, 2009). Relations performed in text and voice included frequent social interactions across modes of communication, including interactions directed toward building trust and community and interactions directed toward constructing individual and collaborative knowledge. Individual participants' preferences for and comfort levels with communicating via text or voice appeared to be more influential in the emergence of patterns of relations and unpredictable based on the mode of communication. Patterns of communication became inter-referential (Chastine, Zhu, & Preston, 2006) as participants read textual posts and/or listened to audio recordings or, in one case, established a Skype back channel in order to reflect on previous communications and prepare for future text- and audio-based discussions.

Our findings support Dixson's (2010) premises that there can be connections among the use of multiple communication channels, student-student and student-instructor communications, and student engagement. We found evidence of frequent, reflective, and reflexive student-student and student-instructor communications across different modes and of Stolz's (2015) cognitive, emotional, and practical dimensions of student engagement. Cognitive engagement in both asynchronous and synchronous communications left traces of participants' conceptual development and refinement, methodological decision making, and ontological/epistemological positioning and repositioning. Traces of emotional engagement were found in expressions of welcoming peers into discussions, desire for and formation of a course-based learning community, as well as at least one sub-community, and accounts of moments of assurance and anxiety. Traces of practical engagement focused on reports of technological disruptions and the resulting positive and negative impacts on engagement and on finding ways to make effective use of time.

Embodiment was identified by locating evidence of complex interactions among participants' minds and bodies with physical and digital environments (Winn, 2003). We found evidence of each of van Manen's (1997) four co-constituting dimensions of embodiment. The reports of learner-participants on what they were doing physically as they learned included the artifacts with which they were working—sticky notes, a "touchy" mouse, books, printed and digital discussion posts, audio recordings, and so on—and how working with these artifacts supported or hindered their engagement and learning. The reports on where participants were physically situated when they were learning included being in home offices and public workplaces and being logged on to D2L, Adobe Connect, university library databases, and so on. Accounts of temporal experiences of learning included references to balancing work, life, and study and often to previous courses. Relational interactions including with the instructor, peers, learning resources, and mediating technologies were identified across data sets and marked by the desire to be perceived as a competent member of a learning community. Across dimensions, the participants encountered and worked with challenging concepts and thought processes and periodically found themselves alone and/or together in liminal spaces (Meyer & Land, 2005).

Conclusion

Our analysis indicated that participants had various levels of awareness of the purposes of our designed and sequenced cycles of formal, asynchronous, text-based interactions; formal, synchronous, voice-based sessions; and less formal, student-led, voice-based coffee sessions in an online doctoral research methodology course. Yet it was evident that participants engaged deeply with each other, with the course instructor, and with learning resources across channels of communication. Evidence of cognitive, emotional, and practical dimensions (Stolz, 2015) of student engagement highlights the emergence of interacting, overlapping, and entangling socio-material spaces (Sørensen, 2009). Unlike Bell's (2015) findings, we found that preferences for communicating via voice and/or text strongly influenced when, where, and how participants engaged in the course. Modes of communication did not privilege or preclude where learners engaged in social and/or scholarly interactions. Patterns of communication became inter-referential (Chastine et al., 2006), and both individual and collaborative knowledge-building activities were distributed across textual and auditory media. Even though learners were engaged in an online course, there were influential corporeal, spatial, temporal, and relational dimensions (van Manen, 1997) of embodied learning (Winn, 2003) that both distracted from and contributed to sustained cognitive, emotional, and practical engagement (Stolz, 2015).

One implication for design is that mature learners can benefit from the inclusion of multiple modes of communication to support sustained but diverse ways of experiencing engagement in an online doctoral course on advanced research methodologies. The informal coffee sessions served to extend participant interaction and engagement within and beyond the more formally designed discussion forums and synchronous teaching sessions. Although our findings suggest that enhanced instructional guidance on the purpose and intent of different modes of communication can increase students' awareness, it was also evident that this varied awareness did not appear to detract from how students engaged with each other, the instructor, and the learning resources across different channels of communication. How and why participants engage across auditory and textual media will vary and are less predictable than previous research has indicated (Bell, 2015; Jones et al., 2011), which warrants ongoing evaluation and research.

References

Bell, A. (2015). *The place of "voice" in collaborative online learning: Postgraduate educator practitioners' experiences.* (Unpublished doctoral dissertation). Lancaster University, Lancaster, UK.

Boyer Commission. (1998). *Reinventing undergraduate education: A blueprint for America's research universities.* Stony Brook, NY: Carnegie Foundation.

Carini, R. M., Kuh, G. D., & Klein, S. P. (2006). Student engagement and student learning: Testing the linkages. *Research in Higher Education, 47*(1), 1–32. doi:10.1007/s11162-005-8150-9

Chastine, J. W., Zhu, Y., & Preston, J. A. (2006, November 17 - November 20). A framework for inter-referential awareness in collaborative environments. Paper presented at the International Conference on Collaborative Computing: Networking Applications and Worksharing. Atlanta, GA, USA.

Cole, A. L., & Knowles, J. G. (2001). *Lives in context: The art of life history research.* Walnut Creek, CA: AltaMira Press.

Dixson, M. D. (2010). Creating effective student engagement in online courses: What do students find engaging? *Journal of the Scholarship of Teaching and Learning, 10*(2), 1–13.

Hine, C. (2000). The virtual objects of ethnography. In C. Hine (Ed.), *Virtual ethnography* (pp. 42–67). London, UK: SAGE. doi:10.4135/9780857020277.n3

Hine, C. (2004, July 1). *Virtual ethnography revisited.* Paper summary prepared for session on Online Research Methods, Research Methods Festival, Oxford. Retrieved from http://www.restore.ac.uk/orm/background/exploringorms/rmf_hine_outline.pdf

Jones, C., Asensio, M., & Goodyear, P. (2011). Networked learning in higher education: Practitioners' perspectives. *Research in Learning Technology, 8*(2), 18–28. doi:10.1080/0968776000080203

Kuh, G. D. (2001). Assessing what really matters to student learning: Inside the national survey of student engagement. *Change, 33*(3), 10–17. doi:10.1080/00091380109601795

Kuh, G. D. (2009). The national survey of student engagement: Conceptual and empirical foundations. *New Directions for Institutional Research, 141*, 5–20. doi:10.1002/ir.283

Land, R., Meyer, J. H. F., & Baillie, C. (2010). Editors' preface: Threshold concepts and transformational learning. In R. Land, J. H. F. Meyer, & C. Baillie (Eds.), *Threshold concepts and transformational learning* (pp. ix–xlii). Rotterdam, The Netherlands: Sense Publishers.

Land, R., Rattray, J., & Vivian, P. (2014). Learning in the liminal space: A semiotic approach to threshold concepts. *Higher Education, 67*(2), 199–217. doi:10.1007/s10734-013-9705-x

Lee, V. S. (2003–04). Promoting learning through inquiry. *Essays on Teaching Excellence: Toward the Best in the Academy, 15*(2), 1–6.

McConnell, D. (2006). *E-learning groups and communities.* Milton Keynes, UK: Open University Press.

Merleau-Ponty, M. (1964). The primacy of perception and its philosophical consequences. In J. M. Edie (Ed.), *The primacy of perception and other essays* (J. M. Edie, Trans.) (pp. 12–42). Evanston, IL: Northwestern University Press. (Original work published 1947).

Meyer, J., & Land, R. (2005). Threshold concepts and troublesome knowledge (2): Epistemological considerations and a conceptual framework for teaching and learning. *Higher Education, 49*(3), 373–388. doi:10.1007/s10734-004-6779-5

National Survey of Student Engagement (NSSE). (2015). *Bringing the institution into focus: Annual results 2014.* Retrieved from http://nsse.iub.edu/NSSE_2014_Results/pdf/NSSE_2014_Annual_Results.pdf#page=30

Nomme, K., & Birol, G. (2014). Course redesign: An evidence-based approach. *The Canadian Journal for the Scholarship of Teaching and Learning, 5*(1), 1–26.

Orsini-Jones, M. (2006, August 30–September 1). *Identifying troublesome concepts and helping undergraduates with crossing grammar thresholds via assessed collaborative group work.* Paper presented at Threshold Concepts Within the Disciplines Symposium, University of Strathclyde, Glasgow, Scotland.

Reid, L. F. (2012). Redesigning a large lecture course for student engagement: Process and outcomes. *The Canadian Journal for the Scholarship of Teaching and Learning, 3*(2), 1–37.

Sgouropoulou, C., Koutoumanos, A., Goodyear, P., & Skordalakis, E. (2000). Acquiring working knowledge through asynchronous multimedia conferencing. *Educational Technology & Society, 3*(3), 105–111.

Sørensen, E. (2009). *The materiality of learning: Technology and knowledge in educational practice.* New York, NY: Cambridge University Press.

Stolz, S. A. (2015). Embodied learning. *Educational Philosophy and Theory, 47*(5), 474–487. doi:10.1080/00131857.2013.879694

Trowler, V. (2010). *Student engagement literature review.* York, UK: The Higher Education Academy.

van Manen, M. (1997). *Researching lived experience: Human science for an action sensitive pedagogy* (2nd ed.). London, ON: Althouse Press.

Walker, G. (2013). A cognitive approach to threshold concepts. *Higher Education, 65*(2), 247–263. doi:10.1007/s10734-012-9541-4

Winn, W. (2003). Learning in artificial environments: Embodiment, embeddedness and dynamic adaptation. *Technology, Instruction, Cognition and Learning, 1*. Retrieved from http://www.hitl.washington.edu/people/tfurness/courses/inde543/READINGS-03/WINN/winnpaper2.pdf

Wood, P. (2012). Blogs as liminal space: Student teachers at the threshold. *Technology, Pedagogy and Education, 21*(1), 85–99. doi:10.1080/14759 39X.2012.659885

Zawacki-Richter, O., & Anderson, T. (2014). Introduction: Research areas in online distance education. In O. Zawacki-Richter & T. Anderson (Eds.), *Online distance education: Towards a research agenda* (pp. 1–35). Edmonton, AB: Athabasca University Press.

Conclusion

Leading, Not Following, the Reform in Canadian Higher Education

Jennifer Lock and Michael Power

Charles Darwin is remembered for the many powerful concepts that he introduced to the scientific community, foremost among which was the evolutionary link between adaptation and survival. This book has been about how Canadian institutions of higher education have constantly been adapting to the ever-changing social environment, blending in as it were, negotiating with new stakeholders, new needs, new pressures, and, over the past century, doing so by leveraging educational technology. Intelligently integrating online and blended learning models into course delivery and modulating the use of text and voice in new and creative ways mark a departure from earlier models of distance education as deployed by single-mode, distance education universities. Appropriation and integration of new learning technologies (e.g., online collaborative apps, social media, virtual reality, and artificial intelligence) are redefining how contemporary universities are positioning themselves both locally, in regard to their traditional student populations, and nationally, in regard to their sister institutions. Technology appears to be fostering a sense of *academic pan-Canadianism* that is already a *fait accompli* in terms of research pursuits but only just starting to assume a tangible form in terms of pooling university teaching and potential interinstitutional expertise.

Understanding the potential of integrating current and emerging technologies and assuming the structural limits of their institutions, universities are forging new models of online and blended course delivery that might well herald a new generation of technology-enhanced voice and text components in course design, development, and delivery.

The Changing Landscape

Higher education is challenged in providing greater flexibility in and access to learning for students throughout their lives. This is a catalyst transforming the higher education landscape from traditional face-to-face learning to blended and online learning. Bates (2015) described the "continuum of technology-based learning" (p. 366) that at one end is face-to-face learning with no technology and at the other is "fully online learning with no classroom or on-campus teaching, which is one form of distance education" (p. 365). In between is what Bates refers to as blended learning, which includes various forms (e.g., flipped classrooms, where activities occur during class time and learning of content learning occurs outside of the class time and percentages of learning time both on campus and online). As instructional designers and faculty members continue to design and facilitate learning across Bates's continuum, it provides a rich and innovative learning landscape.

There has been a change in the perception of online learning "in its favor as more learners and educators see it as a viable alternative to some forms of face-to-face learning" (Adams Becker et al., 2017, p. 18). There continues to be a demand for anytime, anywhere learning not bound to being on a campus or in a classroom at regular intervals. Current trends show that more institutions of higher education are increasing their online course offerings (Allen & Seaman, with Poulin & Straut, 2016; Donovan et al.,2019). As noted by Bates (2017), in Canada there is a "strong annual growth rate in online environments and most institutions playing an active role in offering online and hybrid learning" (p. 2). For example, online learning has continued to grow over the past five years, with "approximately 10% per annum in universities and 15% in colleges outside Québec" (p. 17). In Québec, Université Laval leads the way with over

100 programs and 1,000 courses offered online. Furthermore, "blended learning is on the rise at colleges and universities as the number of digital learning platforms and ways to leverage them for educational purposes continues to expand" (Adams Becker et al., 2017, p. 18).

The current demand, along with the evolution of digital communication technologies, is changing where, how, and why students, faculty members, and administrators engage with blended and online learning approaches. In an interview about the future of education, Lock commented, "I think the campus of the future won't be bound by time, physical space or geography. . . . We'll be able to work and study around the world, with anyone around the world, without leaving home" (Berenyl & Moore, 2017, p. 38). With such advances, never before have institutions of higher education been able to reach a larger audience through synchronous and asynchronous communication, paced, non-paced, and through MOOC-based resources collected from the best and brightest minds in the world.

Learning from the Canadian Context

From the work shared by the authors of this book, it is evident that there is an ever-expanding pedagogical landscape within technology-enabled learning environments. This book is a testament to the nature of adaptation occurring in relation to teaching and learning in online and blended environments. In addition, it provides specific examples of the advances of such work as well as the research unearthed through various challenges and tensions influencing the evolution and sustainability of university outreach.

Da Rosa dos Santos (2017), in a study focused on developing online teaching capacities of instructors, described the need for "synergetic relationships between online instructors, academic leaders, and educational developers for the development of online teaching capacity-building processes and practices that create the conditions for meaningful student learning" (p. ii). The concept of a synergetic relationship is paramount in terms of the multiple stakeholders who need to be involved in creating the "blend" in terms of voice and text with the design, development, and facilitation of blended and online graduate education programs. Examples from current research are shown in this pan-Canadian collection of current practices informing the evolution and institutional strategy for blended and online learning.

In the first chapter, Power provided a global overview of how universities have tried to increase their outreach capacities through various technologically enhanced blends of voice and text. As he laid out this generational landscape, he demonstrated not only the changes that have occurred in the technology but also how pedagogical practice has evolved. Faculty members have never been bound by the use of one approach or technology, nor should they be. Rather, they must be able to choose from an array of digital technologies to support their pedagogical goals as they create learning environments for students throughout their lives. Across this overview, the evolution of technological engineering is apparent, but so are its inherent challenges, which affect the nature of voice- and text-based learning within blended and online environments.

In Chapters 2 through 5, the authors examined some of the current work affecting the rigour, success, and sustainability of online and blended learning. Through their research, they shared findings from the perspectives of students, instructors, instructional designers, and administrators. Working from the perspective of an administrator in a university setting, Wilson described the practice of mentoring faculty often reluctant to try new pedagogical approaches and technologies. While encouraging them to be risk takers in their practice, senior leaders also need to take risks in supporting innovation and advocating support for resources devoted to design, development, and delivery of blended and online learning using text- and voice-based approaches. Lock and collaborators reported on the development of an online orientation program for students. This program was developed to support students as they begin their online learning journeys. In their self-study, Costello and colleagues showcased the experiences and reflections of instructional designers who worked with content authors in the purposeful design and effective integration of media and technology in teaching and learning. Furthermore, Kraglund-Gauthier reported on participatory action research involving instructional designers and faculty members in terms of the change in teaching practice and pedagogical thinking. These authors demonstrated how changes are being made in terms of fostering teaching practice and student learning in support of blended and online learning. There is a pedagogical commitment to the teaching and learning experiences within these technology-enabled learning environments.

In Chapters 6 to 9, the authors reported on how faculty members and students are engaging in new ways of teaching and learning using voice- and text-based technologies. Lakhal reported on a study examining current practice using a mixed course delivery system (face-to-face and a web conferencing app for students at a distance) and the benefits and challenges experienced by both students and faculty members. Snow's chapter, on the concept of open, provided insight into the complexities of developing a sustainable institutional strategy for open education where resources are scarce. As institutions of higher education embrace the potential and value of open education, it comes with its own set of challenges. Taylor and colleagues shared findings from a study of current practices of faculty members and students using a blended learning approach. Parchoma and collaborators reported on instructors who design learning in which learners are co-creators of knowledge and learning is represented in text, graphics, and/or video. Access to and use of the technology provide opportunities to learn within a community, yet community members are rarely in the same location. They explore synchronous and asynchronous communication to create interactive and engaging learning environments.

These nine chapters demonstrate the complexity of current work in designing, implementing, and facilitating learning using blended and/or online approaches. This work is not without challenges. Faculty members working in these environments might need to alter and/or refine their theoretical approaches to learning for blended and online contexts. They might need to learn new technologies and take risks in designing innovative practices for voice- and text-based learning environments. They might need to commit more time and resources than they would initially like in developing their confidence and competence in designing and developing courses and facilitating robust learning in blended and online environments.

The authors of this book provide snapshots of current online and blended learning approaches used in eight Canadian universities. The examples shared in the chapters indicate the nature of the research conducted on and informing current practice. Evidence-informed practice is grounding the how and why of this work in relation to instructional design, pedagogical practice, integration of educational technology, and educational development. It is evident from the chapters that various stakeholder groups are working together to increase access to higher education, foster greater flexibility in course and/or program delivery, and enhance quality teaching and learning experiences. As the work of blended and online learning moves forward, it will be critical to maintain robust research agendas and regular reporting to ensure evidence-informed practice and decision making. Parallel is the ongoing inquiry fuelling continual and extended research that will be used to inform practice. We hope that what we have learned through historical and contemporary studies will inform the next steps of the evolution of blended and online learning both in Canada and abroad.

References

Adams Becker, S., Cummins, M., Davis, A., Freeman, A., Hall Giesinger, C., & Ananthanarayanan, V. (2017). *NMC Horizon Report: 2017 Higher Education Edition.* Austin, TX: New Media Consortium. Retrieved from https://www.unmc.edu/elearning/_documents/NMC_HorizonReport_2017.pdf

Allen, I. E., & Seaman, J., with Poulin, R., & Straut, T. T. (2016). *Online report card: Tracking online education in the United States.* Retrieved from http://onlinelearningsurvey.com/reports/onlinereportcard.pdf

Bates, A. W. (2015). *Teaching in a digital age: Guidelines for designing teaching and learning.* Vancouver, BC: Tony Bates Associates.

Bates, T. (Ed.) (2017). *Tracking online and distance education in Canadian universities and colleges: 2017.* National Survey of Online and Distance Education in Canadian Post-Secondary Education. Retrieved from https://onlinelearningsurveycanada.ca/

Berenyi, V., & Moore, J. (2017). What might the future hold for education? The macro view: University education at large. *UCalgary Alumni Magazine, 38.* Retrieved from https://alumni.ucalgary.ca/sites/default/files/2018-08/2017%20Spring-Summer.pdf

da Rosa dos Santos, L. (2017). *The relationship between instructors, academic leaders, and educational developers in the development of online teaching capacity.* (Unpublished doctoral dissertation). University of Calgary, Calgary, AB.

Donovan, T., Bates, T., Seaman J., Mayer D., Martel, E. , ... Poulin, R. (2019). *Tracking online and distance education in Canadian universities and colleges: 2018.* Canadian National Survey of Online and Distance Education. Canadian Digital Learning Research Association. Retrieved from https:// onlinelearningsurveycanada.ca/publications-2018/

Contributors

Alicia Adlington is the Distance Programs Coordinator in the Werklund School of Education, University of Calgary. Alicia has worked in postsecondary education for over 10 years in a number of student engagement roles. Recent successes include developing and delivering sessions to help new graduate students acclimate themselves to the online learning environment.

Shaily Bhola is a PhD student in the Learning Sciences at the Werklund School of Education, University of Calgary. In her research, she focuses on understanding how collaborative argumentation among undergraduate chemistry students can influence their individual meaning making of concepts. She has taught chemistry at the University of Delhi, India, and has been a part of research teams in the United States.

Denise Carew is a Senior Instructional Designer at Memorial University of Newfoundland. While working in a postgraduate technology learning institute, she completed her Master of Education (M.Ed.) in Education and Human Resource Studies, Colorado State University, online offering. Denise specialized in instructional design and performance improvement through the use of training and support. Her interests lie in instructional design and the use of technology for learning in higher education.

Jane Costello is an award-winning Senior Instructional Designer at the Centre for Innovation in Teaching and Learning, Memorial University of Newfoundland. She has a PhD from Lancaster University, UK, in eResearch and Technology Enhanced Learning, and she has a background in educational technology, open educational resources, adult learning, and human performance technology. Jane has published or presented in the areas of networked learning, effective use of social media, mobile learning, and guest speakers. Currently, her focus is on instructional design of online courses, effective integration of emerging technology in learning events, learning resources, and tablet learning.

Daph Crane is a Senior Instructional Design Specialist at the Centre for Innovation in Teaching and Learning, Memorial University of Newfoundland. She has a Master's of Distance Education from Athabasca University. Daph has extensive experience in instructional design, and her research interests are in online assessment and feedback and their impacts on learning.

Michael Fairbrother is a PhD candidate in the Faculty of Education, University of Ottawa. His doctoral dissertation focuses on understanding the influence of teachers' professional learning on classroom instruction with students who have difficulty learning how to read.

Shehzad Ghani is a PhD candidate in the Faculty of Education, University of Ottawa. With a background in Computer Information Systems, his current research interests are digital learning, educational innovation, and formative assessment.

Jane Hanson is a teacher with the Calgary Board of Education. She has been involved with online teaching and learning for over 15 years. She is passionate about online teaching and learning and course development. Jane is currently working with the University of Calgary with online tech support as well as developing and implementing the Online Success Orientation Program.

Michele Jacobsen is a Professor and the Associate Dean, Graduate Programs, at the Werklund School of Education, University of Calgary. Her current research projects include the design and evaluation of participatory learning environments that sponsor knowledge building and intellectual engagement, interdisciplinary approaches to peer mentoring for strong transitions to graduate school, and complex adaptive learning systems in high schools.

Carol Johnson is a Senior Lecturer in Music (Online Learning and Educational Technology in Music) at the University of Melbourne. Her research focuses on online music pedagogy, teaching and learning online, and development of teaching capacity for online faculty.

Wendy Kraglund-Gauthier is an adjunct faculty member with Yorkville University, Fredericton campus, where she teaches courses in the Master of Education in Adult Education and Master of Education in Educational Leadership streams and supervises graduate student research. Wendy is also engaged in supporting faculty members' online pedagogical processes at St. Francis Xavier University. Her own research and writing include effective instructional design and explorations of how adult learning theory and technology can be used in physical and virtual classrooms to promote accessible, collaborative, and safe learning for students of differing ages and abilities.

Sawsen Lakhal is an Associate Professor in the Department of Pedagogy at Université de Sherbrooke, QC, and Director of CRIFPE-Sherbrooke. Her research interests include acceptance and use of technology in education, persistence in online and blended courses and programs, and assessment within competency-based education programs.

Yang (Flora) Liu is a Learning and Instructional Design Specialist in the Faculty of Social Work at the University of Calgary. Her work provides support to online teaching activity and course/module design and development for faculty. Currently, Flora is also a PhD candidate in Learning Sciences. Her research interest is in teacher-designed games.

Jennifer Lock is a Professor and Vice Dean in the Werklund School of Education, University of Calgary. Her area of specialization is in the Learning Sciences. Her current research interests are in e-learning, change and innovation in education, scholarship of teaching and learning in higher education, and experiential learning through making and makerspaces.

Dorothea Nelson is a PhD candidate in Learning Sciences at the Werklund School of Education, University of Calgary. Her research interests include participatory action research, networked learning, the Community of Inquiry framework, third space, transcultural learning, and culturally sensitive course design, particularly the design of a library science program for students within the Organization of Eastern Caribbean States.

Gale Parchoma was an Associate Professor in the Department of Curriculum Studies: Educational Technology and Design, University of Saskatchewan. She was also the National Program Coordinator for Canada's Collaboration for Online Higher Education Research (COHERE), an Adjunct Associate Professor at the University of Calgary, and an associate member of the Centre for Technology Enhanced Learning in the Department of Educational Research at Lancaster University in England. Her research interests were focused on socio-material dimensions of the scholarship of teaching and learning.

Pam Phillips is a Senior Instructional Designer at the Centre for Innovation in Teaching and Learning (CITL), Memorial University of Newfoundland. She is a certified project manager and a per course instructor with the Faculty of Education at Memorial. Pam has extensive experience in instructional design, training and development, project management, and teaching in higher education in the area of educational technology and learning resources. Her research interests are in effective technology integration.

Thomas Michael Power was, now retired, a Full Professor of Educational Technology in the Faculty of Education, Laval University, QC. His research focuses primarily on blended online learning design (BOLD) modelling at dual-mode universities in order to improve learner experience and sustain university outreach.

Marlon Simmons is an Assistant Professor at the Werklund School of Education, University of Calgary. His research interests include culture and leadership and governance of the self in educational settings. Marlon's scholarly work is grounded in the diasporic and communicative network practices of youth. Related to his educational inquiry are the scholarship of teaching and learning and the role of socio-material relations in enhancing student learning.

Kathy Snow is an Assistant Professor of Education and the Teaching and Learning Chair for Open, Online and Blended Learning (2016–19) at Cape Breton University, NS. Before moving to CBU, Kathy worked as an Instructional Designer at the Univesity of Manitoba in Winnipeg. She is the current editor of the *Journal of Professional, Online, and Continuing Education.*

Maurice Taylor is a Full Professor and Chair of University Teaching in the Faculty of Education, University of Ottawa. His research interests are in adult learning and development and blended learning pedagogy.

Jay Wilson is an Associate Professor and Head of the Department of Curriculum Studies at the University of Saskatchewan in Saskatoon. His research centres on innovation in teacher education, experiential learning, and design studio learning environments. He works to support the understanding and growth of pre-service and in-service teachers through his service and scholarship.